To: Stephen,

God Bless + Best wishes,

#No Backing Down Salem

Go Patriots!

To my wife, Krista, who gives me strength. May we together fulfill all of our dreams.

To my daughters, Gianna, Sophia Bella, and Giulietta, whom I love.

To Owa, whom I miss and who will always be my inspiration.

To Dad, Mom, Michael, and Eric, whom I cherish.

To Coach Perrone, whose perseverance and ingenuity helped many, like me, live our dreams.

To each of my teammates, whose individual stories brought me to respect you and provide everlasting friendships.

To my friend, Mike Smerczynski, who guided me through this process.

PRAISE FOR
NO BACKING DOWN

"It is not the size of a man but the size of his heart that matters and it is clear after reading, *No Backing Down* that not only Sean Stellato, but the entire Salem High team has the heart of a champion. Becoming a champion, whether in the ring or on the field, does not happen by accident. It happens by overcoming each and every obstacle that is thrown in front of you. Never has there been a case of a team stepping over, running around, and stomping on more obstacles than the 1994 Witches. True champions."

> - **Evander "Real Deal" Holyfield**
> Four-time boxing World Heavyweight Champion

"I had the unique experience of playing football at Danvers High School where Coach Perrone's sons were my teammates and we competed against their dad's Salem Witches. Sean Stellato certainly captures the enthusiasm associated with playing in the century-old Northeast Conference, and especially against Coach Perrone's high-powered program. *No Backing Down* creatively blends the elevated community emotions triggered by the team's success, teacher's strike and administration's contempt of Perrone. This true story is spiced by Salem's renowned history of unjustified persecution."

> - **Mark Bavaro**
> Two-time Super Bowl champion and Pro Bowler

"Sean Stellato gives a gripping firsthand account of the turmoil that polarized the city of Salem while local officials and politicians unfairly used student athletes as bargaining chips."

> - **Mike Lynch**
> Sports anchor for WCVB TV Boston

"Typically, when you think about Salem, the witch trials come to mind. *No Backing Down* takes you on an extraordinary ride through Salem during a different trial, when the town's high school football team and its coach stuck together through a teacher strike in 1994 with all of the political and psychological implications that came with it. Author Sean Stellato, the quarterback of that team, provides intimate detail from that trying period. He navigates the reader through all the hurdles the group overcame en route to making a Massachusetts State Super Bowl appearance. Ultimately, we see firsthand how life's defining moments can shape individuals. We're also left with another striking reminder of the significance of sports for kids at the high school level. It's about time shared working toward a common goal and the valuable life lessons learned along the way."

- ***Boston Herald***

"Sean Stellato's *No Backing Down* is one of those rare books that you won't be able to put down. It's a thrilling account of the Salem High football team's courage in overcoming the longest of odds, from bruising challenges on-the-field to untimely obstacles off-the-field. It seemed like everything was stacked against this team, yet their determination proved unconquerable. As a legal commentator, I was particularly impressed by Sean Stellato's ability to explain the pivotal and unappreciated role law plays in high school sports. *No Backing Down* is a very enjoyable read."

- **Michael McCann**
  Sports Illustrated

Requests for permission to make copies of any part of the work
should be submitted online at info@mascotbooks.com or mailed to
Mascot Books, 560 Herndon Parkway #120, Herndon, VA 20170.

TEAM VICTORIOUS - Sports Artwork by Premier Pencil Artist,
Nick Johnson / teamvictorious.com

ISBN-13: 9781620867808
CPSIA Code: PRB0714A

Printed in the United States

www.seanstellato.com
www.mascotbooks.com

Sean Stellato

Foreword by Doug Flutie

FOREWORD

On Monday, November 14, 1994, the *Salem News* account of the Salem and Winthrop high school football game played two days prior, titled *Stellato Works Flutie Magic*.

The story reads, "Sean Stellato was thinking about his idol, Doug Flutie in the moments that preceded his electrifying 30-yard strike to Manny De Pena that enabled the Salem Witches to crawl out of the grave and feel reborn in their hold-your-breath 22-21 comeback victory over Winthrop on Saturday."

I have come to learn that there was much more than football that was on the minds of all those involved with that Salem team. Players from diverse backgrounds, and some facing personal tragedies beyond the imagination of Hollywood writers, banded together to follow a legendary coach through obstacles. One of these obstacles was the miracle at Winthrop to teach a historic community about perseverance.

On Halloween, two weeks before the Winthrop game, the Salem teacher's union commenced a strike. The city, flooded with thousands of celebrants, was further log-jammed by the picketing teachers and news media along the road-side. A throng of reporters and cameramen sought to find out if Salem's coaches would be allowed to participate in the New England Game of the Week against undefeated Swampscott.

Out from the page of Salem's dark past, the school administration declared that the coaches would not be allowed to coach while the strike was ongoing. The next day five police cruisers, blaring sirens and flashing blue lights, invaded the team's practice delivering a cease and desist order to Head Coach Ken Perrone. The intimidation by the law enforcement caravan and the prospect of the doom to the coach combined to universally reduce all the players to tears. Simultaneously, the superintendent went on Channel 7 News and equated Perrone with cult leaders Jim Jones and David Koresh. This branding went viral.

With over a hundred years of aggregate teaching and coaching longevity invested in Salem, and knowing the consequences of possible arrest and certain firings—like the falsely accused "witches" of 300 years past—the coaches declared their unconditional loyalty to their team, themselves, and community. After leading the team and beating Swampscott on the last play in front of 12,000 fans and regional TV, the Witches were, unimaginably, tested again with the reality of having to win on the last play of the Winthrop game.

Like Boston College, the Salem team completed its Hail Mary. Like Boston College, the Salem team will be remembered for that achievement. Like Boston College after the Miami game, the Salem team still had more games to play and equal odds to defy. Like Boston College, the Salem team will also always be branded as one that never backed down against any challenge, something more important than football.

- Doug Flutie, 1984 Heisman Trophy Winner

PREFACE
1994 SALEM HIGH FOOTBALL TRIALS

> *"Success is not permanent and failure is not fatal."*
>
> ~ *Mike Ditka*

In 1994, many of my high school football teammates were presented with enormous constraints on their lives, imposed by no one's malevolent intent, but by the luck of the draw. They signed on to that season's athletic voyage, motivated by escapism and hoping for identity.

One teammate departed his apartment each day, passing his mom who was lying on the couch while high on heroin. Another was from a family that was being hunted by a foreign government. A third was being haunted by his brother's bilateral leg amputation, while a fourth endured brutal beatings by his step-father. Unimaginably, a fifth was then raising a son, a toddler at the time, who was ever-present on the sidelines watching his dad gift to him a priceless legacy.

That treatment proved no less inflammatory than that leveled against the innocent in Salem over 300 years earlier during the infamous "Witch Hysteria." The dispersion of the first complaint of witchcraft in "Olde Salem" triggered tests of personal constitutions, the most extreme aspect of which involved the refusal of accused "witches" to confess to sorcery to avoid execution.

300 years later, I saw our community's leaders, the team's coaches, and my teammates undertake actions on the field, in the locker-room, in the media, in the union hall, in court, and in homes similar to those of lore and no less significant. Such conduct, motivated by unyielding resolve, good and bad, compelled me to name this book:

NO BACKING DOWN

Over the years since that season, I became increasingly tormented by the behavior of some of our municipal officials and more awed by the admirable conduct of others, particularly my teammates, coaches, and select community leaders. To research the information necessary to prepare this book, I invested over a thousand hours of: conducting witness interviews, taped and un-taped; watching game and scrimmage films; reading and watching news accounts of the season and associated legal proceedings; reviewing pleadings; and researching local history. I was amazed by the response that I received when performing these tasks, including the former superintendent's refusal to be interviewed.

I was confronted regularly by grown, mature, and accomplished men who exhibited extreme emotional responses—many reduced to tears—recounting their memories of the 1994 season and its aftermath. The lives of so many were profoundly impacted by those events, extraordinarily spiced by the curious interlocking of the evil imagery cast upon our coach in Salem, the crucible of false accusations, with the coaches' and team's fates "hanging' in the balance during Halloween week. Those reactions, signifying how something benign to some, such as a high school football experience, can be life changing for others, and the permanent effect on so many, inspired me to write this book.

I equate my experience with the famed character in *Moby Dick*, Ishmael. Ishmael survived on a floating coffin and withstood the psychologically negative impact of Captain Ahab's breaking of the compass; I like to think that my life was permanently buoyed by playing high school football in Salem, 1994, where history repeated itself with another unwarranted, persecutory environment created by our school superintendent. Our superintendent, acting like the monomaniacal Ahab, shed reason to satiate his dislike for Coach Perrone and compared him to infamous cult leaders.

CHAPTER 1

MEDIA HYPE

"It is the surmounting of difficulties that makes heroes."

~ *Louis Kossuth*

- In 1692, four young girls wrongfully accused a number of people in Salem, Massachusetts, as being witches resulting in the trials, sentences, and deaths of twenty-five: nineteen by hanging, one by pressing, and the balance dying in prison. That episode was dubbed "The Salem Witch Hysteria."

- In 1978, Jim Jones led a cult called the Peoples Temple Agricultural Project in Jonestown, Guyana, in a mass suicide by cyanide poisoning resulting in the death of 909, including Jones himself. That occurrence was dubbed a "Revolutionary Suicide."

- In 1993, David Koresh led a cult called "The Branch Davidians" into an ideological standoff in Waco, Texas, with the ATF, resulting in the deaths of seventy-six men, women, and children, including Koresh. That encounter was dubbed the "Waco Massacre."

In 1994, who could have dreamed that the nefarious imagery generated by those three events would be infused into the lives of the players on the Salem, Massachusetts, high school football team?

"What comes to mind here, when I think about Head Coach Ken Perrone, is cult. Jim Jones, David Koresh at Waco, and the parents and the Salem citizens need to think about that." Those were the words of Salem Superintendent Edward Curtin, in a live interview on November 2, 1994, by John Dennis of Boston's Channel 7 News.

At that time, the unheralded Salem High football team was heading into a showdown with highly-ranked and undefeated Swampscott in a game to decide a likely Massachusetts State Super Bowl participant. Simultaneously, the Salem teachers union had gone on strike protesting a salary proposal that they deemed to be unacceptable. The primary question remained: Would the game be played despite the schools being closed?

Curtin was summarizing the environment occupied by both a teachers strike and the anticipated success of the high school football team, when he gratuitously offered that commentary. The Salem Witch Hysteria of 300 years past was reborn, ironically on Halloween. Instead of witchcraft, Salem became burdened by a public indictment of a community leader being equated with cult leaders, whose membership died under horrific circumstances.

The initial burst was exacerbated by Curtin's additional comments. John Dennis looked hard at the short, condescending, fifty-eight year old martinet of a man. Dennis, an experienced reporter from Channel 7 News, was assigned to ferret out the back story behind rumors circulating around the teachers strike. He descended upon Curtin to ascertain from the Salem School Department's principal policymaker whether or not there would be a game. If so, would it include coaches who were bound from participating in school activities while STRIKING? Further, if the coaches did coach the team, would the act be deemed contemptuous? Would they be subject to any disciplinary action?

Massachusetts was no stranger to this situation. In the previous twenty years, there were municipal teacher's strikes in Brockton, Tewksbury and Belmont. None of the three communities chose to interrupt the extracurricular programs, including football. This was the precedent available to Salem.

Notwithstanding, school being closed due to the strike and a community consensus that the football team should still play their next game, there presented the administration's personal disdain for the teacher-coaches, particularly Coach Perrone. The legal friction was over a teacher-coach being able to strike as a "unionized" teacher in his/her labor dispute over the Collective Bargaining Agreement, but still coach under a second, separate contract for services to the football team independently executed with the Salem School Department. The sides in the community were divided over the legal nicety of a teacher-coach getting "it both ways" or, maintaining important, contractual services to the student-athletes unaffected by the labor dispute.

The legal friction was heated, but paled in contrast to the personal friction embedded in this unfolding drama. Curtin despised Perrone and such was all the more intensified by Perrone accessing the legal argument, justifying his continued presence on both the picket line and the sideline. Perrone came to Salem as its head football coach some twenty years prior. As he had done while previously coaching in Maine, he did not just take over a football program. He took over a community. He linked every aspect of Salem Public School life to the football team. All the elementary schools were organized as the center point for a youth football program. The participants began learning the high school formations, drills, terminology and plays as pre-teenagers. The youngsters were trained to strive to become Salem High School varsity football players. Perrone grew the bands, cheerleaders and booster club into large forces. He made game day a spectacle, dressing over one hundred players from the seniors down to the youth ranks. Elaborate game day programs, apparel, and concessions marked every event. The media seized upon this excitement and the success of the teams that Perrone led. Perrone himself became the object of enormous individual attention in the newspapers. His "Al Pacino" type persona saturated Salem's societal fabric. To many observers, such was a gift to the municipality that greatly impacted the student body.

Others like Curtin were not so convinced. Curtin was a sports lover; he was an extremely intelligent and competent teacher and administrator who, from an academic-oriented discipline, fashioned a different view of Perrone. As one who advanced upward through the ranks of academia, Curtin advocated for a more pure evaluation of the high school experience Salem provided. He questioned the disproportionate value placed upon the "football program" in comparison to the "mission statement" of educating students and developing good citizenship. He knew that the schools provided a refuge for those who desperately needed social services due to the distressed situations of many of Salem's students. Curtin reasoned that Perrone, through the football program's activities, subordinated those objectives. Perrone and those affiliated with his program benefitted from a double standard connecting with behavior: Those on the inside of the programs received free passes for things triggering adverse disciplinary actions to others. The icing on the cake, as it were, was the deluge of positive press Perrone received in spite of these contradictions. With that dynamic as the backdrop, Curtin, staring at the reporter and going deep into himself, gave a response the reporter could never have fathomed.

"We're concerned about young people being manipulated and consequently led astray," he said with conviction.

"So you're equating Coach Perrone's methods on the football field as akin to a cult?" Dennis followed up.

Shaking his finger, Curtin's face settled into an unconscious mask. "Yes. I am."

Dennis picked up the momentum, "Do you think Coach Perrone is fit to coach this high school football team? Should he be coaching any team?"

After a lengthy pause, the superintendent simply gives a razor-sharp, "No. And that's all I have to say on the subject."

Dennis shuffled some papers and left. The superintendent's inflammatory comments spread like wildfire. The next day the story guaranteed Salem national exposure, given the contentious history of false accusations dating back to Salem's Witch Trials. TV reports from the evening news sparked print media to follow suit the next day. *The Boston Herald* headlines read, "Salem coach still at odds." The above-the-fold, front page story in the *Salem News* was headlined, "Salem coach goes on offense after being labeled 'cult figure.'" This was the beginning of media coverage saturated with the day-by-day, incident-by-incident coverage of a community's reconciliation of having a revered icon reduced to the most extreme societal monster.

I woke up on the morning of Thursday, November 3, 1994, with practice on my mind and not knowing that Curtin's remarks were being dissected through wide-spread media frenzy. My parents, two older brothers, and grandma, Owa, sat around the kitchen table. A debate was going on. They saw me come in and went instantly silent.

My father handed me the headlines, uttering, "Big trouble, son."

After reading Curtin's remarks, I gasped.

Owa gave a gentle laugh, and then looked directly into my eyes. "Sean, things are picking up for you. You're taking off. This won't stop you."

I asked her, "How could the 'top guy,' the CEO of a major municipal school department, accuse a legendary football coach of being a cult leader? I mean, that Waco guy led his congregation to death." To make the accusation worse, because those characterizations came from the lips of the superintendent, one with credibility in the community, "people may actually believe him!"

Owa maneuvered closer. Her arms wrapped around me, protecting me from any wandering evil eye out there via her mystical Italian stuff. "Forget about them. History repeats itself," she reminded me as always, adding, "Remember, while Salem's associated with witchcraft, the true meaning of the word Salem, as in Jerusalem, means peace." She made the Sign of the Cross, in that solid "with God" kind of way, saying reverently, "Tomorrow is another day to be beautiful and go forth. Have faith. Right, my boy?"

She had a point; no need to focus on what divides us, but concentrate on what unites us. But, I mused, who would have thought, almost three centuries later, Salem, Massachusetts, is the hub of false accusations destined to divide the community.

My older brother slapped me on the back so hard I almost choked. "Salem's cursed, bro. Get used to it."

I wasn't sure I could.

It was back in the year of 1692, more than 300 years ago, that village townsfolk were falsely accused of practicing witchcraft and hunted down. Nineteen victims were hanged and one man was pressed to death. It was nasty business. So why, I'm wondering, would anyone want to behave this way today? I got upset. I knew a political storm was brewing and I had an eerie feeling my teammates and I were about to be swallowed up by it. If the damning words of teenage girls could cause the harm of yesteryear, the damning words of our superintendent were destined to cause similar harm. I checked the time on the clock. I had to go.

Chapter 2
Walking for Glory
Enter Perrone

> "History, by appraising... [the students] of the past, will enable them to judge of the future."
>
> ~ Thomas Jefferson

I have a vivid memory of my coach from a year earlier in fall 1993, as I was obsessed with the magic of Ken Perrone coming to Salem. I was walking home early evening along the cobbled-stone streets, feeling free in the bracing cold air. The lights of Salem were coming on, the sparkle and shimmer stretching down to its waterfront.

A solitary man wearing a blue blazer with a checkered shirt and tie stops me. "Excuse me, which way to Essex Street, the Hawthorne Hotel?"

I smile, as I stoop to pick up the copy of *The Scarlet Letter* that he's dropped.

His face turns beet red. "Hell," he drawls as I hand it to him, "He's the most iconic citizen in your most historic town. Ya'll can't visit Salem without getting a copy of Hawthorne's book."

I shrug, guess not, and direct him. "Head northeast up Derby Street. It hugs the Salem Common. You can't miss it."

He sprints off in the direction with the same kind of lithe athletic grace Coach Perrone had. They're about the same age but from very different universes, I'm convinced. I pass the Ye Old Sweets shop. The smell of toffee is irresistible, so I backtrack into America's oldest candy shop to spend my last three dollars.

Dinner is waiting for me at home, but I'm not in a hurry. I weave in-and-out of hurried visitors hitting the tourist traps: witch shops, card-readers, spiritual consultants, and proliferation of souvenir Mecca's. Coach Perrone was on my mind. He came to Salem on 4th of July weekend, twenty-two years ago. My father said his arrival was hailed as winning the jackpot. To swap a legendary high school coaching career in Maine for a position as head coach for the Salem Witches, who weren't exactly league champions, had to be a quandary for him while a benefit to us.

In my eyes, I picture him back in 1973, strolling the streets of what would become his hometown, captivated by landmarks and mixed with cool ocean breezes blowing in from the sea. His pre-hiring visit was timed for the spectacular 4th of July celebration which Salem holds every year at Derby Wharf. I picture him first coming here as he sat on the Custom House steps seeing the Maritime National Historic site as fireworks light up the historic Friendship Flag Ship, commissioned in 1797. He strolls over to Pickering Wharf for a cup of its famed clam chowder. No doubt he's well aware of the dark side of Salem's history, but sipping chowder in the twilight, eyes on the South River flowing into Salem Harbor, where to the west, he can just make out Misery Island, the twentieth century resort he'll come to appreciate for its virgin hiking trails.

Not surprisingly, Perrone would measure everything in terms of a football field. He walks the distance up from Salem Harbor, passing the House of Seven Gables located in Derby Street's Historic District. He stops to admire America's oldest wooden mansion, built in 1668 by Captain John Turner, which despite its age, is in immaculate condition. He thinks if the city of Salem pays as much attention to its high school football team as it does to this old house, he will have one hell of a team to coach…if he gets the job, that is. He veers off east in the direction of the Salem Power Plant. This takes him past the Plumber Home for Boys, a place that's been taking in wayward boys since 1855. I smile, knowing at this point how little the coach knew of just how much rebuilding of lives he would do over the next twenty-one years. The Home sits on eighteen ocean-side acres, offering breathtaking views guaranteed to calm any troubled boy, or in this case, the anxious middle-aged coach. He finds his bearings and heads back towards the twinkling lights in the main part of town.

He stops at the Common. It's a well-manicured acre of greenery in the heart of Salem, across the street from the Salem Witch Museum that 250,000 people visit each year but is closed at this hour. Not that Perrone cares, the only witches on his mind are the Salem High School Witches he's hoping to coach. He knows the history of Salem Common well. In the seventeenth century it was used by the military as a shooting range. And in 1914 it made national headlines when it housed the displaced victims of a raging fire that ravaged swathes of acreage and destroyed a thousand buildings in its wake. That aside, it's something else that holds Perrone's heartbeat. To him the Commons has greater significance. To him it is the historic birthplace of one of the oldest high school football rivalry in the United States, dating back to the 1890s when the very first Salem vs. Beverly High football was fought on this ground.

The heritage trail is still buzzing with tourists drifting along its brick sidewalks, dutifully following to the red line meant to keep them on track. Perrone heads onto Essex Street. The Essex Museum is closed, and the Witch Dungeon Theatre, where out-of-towners can't get enough award-winning reenactments of Sarah Good's trial, is dark tonight. He moves on to the MacIntire Historic District. Salty air fills his nostrils, competing with the bouquet of frying fish from late night seafood joints around the pier. He escapes to the Federalist homes near the public library. The Witch House, built in 1642 and one of the oldest dwellings in the country, is drawn to the neighboring Phillips House, once home to a wealthy merchant family. At this time of night, it's all lit up. Staring straight ahead at the landmark structures, he hears the sound of high-heeled shoes clack-clacking up behind him.

Two women stand beside him, eyes fixed on the home. One drinks from a steaming flask. She speaks to the coach in a thick French accent. "I'm French, but I would trade all the architecture of Paris to live in there, no?"

Perrone laughs. "It's not the kind of place a coach would live in," he says half joking.

The East India Square Fountain sits in the heart of town. Shaped like Salem's old harbor with its lower region reminiscent of the shoreline, the fountain symbolizes the connection between the town and the sea. There was a time when sailing ships traveled to and from Salem from the Far East and Europe with cargos that created fortunes, elitism, fueled economies and funded churches, schools, and governments. Stories of seaports interest him. The image of New England's ancient mariners and wealthy patrons parading the boardwalks together, appeals to him, but patronage and funding appeals even more. And he hopes the historic social-democrat ideal of the past is still alive and well and funding flows freely into Salem High.

He moves his eyes out to the sea. Boat lights bob up and down out there in the black water. Collins Cove is to his right, which means Perrone is close to the Hawthorne Hotel, where the idea of a mint tea hits him as just right. The smell of Ziggy's donuts wafted through the air. Tomorrow he plans to visit Winter Island. Built in 1644 on the remnants of Fort Pickering, the forty-five-acre tract was used as a base for the Coast Guard's local search and rescue during World War II. Perrone knew someone who was stationed there.

Afterwards, he plans to spend the rest of his day relaxing under the shade of Salem's exquisite willow trees watching the boats sail around

Beverly Harbor. He wasn't to know at the time, but before too long, he'd be willing to give half his paltry salary to stand beneath those willows once summer practice got underway.

***

It is a humid day, the 6th of July, and a light early morning fog lifts from the pier. Perrone trashes his paper plate with remnants of a fish breakfast. His big interview is in less than an hour. He'd know where he was going. The directions were easy as long as he followed the signs indicating southwest, down Loring Avenue, and passed Salem State College. He'd drive past the neighboring towns of Marblehead and Swampscott. Swampscott would become a name Perrone would never forget. He'd head northwest up Jefferson Avenue to Wilson Road then up to Highland Avenue and follow the signs that lead to the address he hopes to make his home, Salem High. He climbs the steps with grace and with that formidable brand of relentless intensity to the role of the remorseless sports machine that generations of footballers will come to know. Little did he know how the evils of Salem's past would surface. Little did he know that he would be the object of national negative attention. That he, like those accused of witchcraft, would confront the functional equivalent of their Catch-22 of denying witchcraft and dying or confessing and living.

CHAPTER 3

BREAKING GROUND AT BERTRAM FIELD
HEROES

———————————— /// ————————————

> *"As you walk down the fairway of life you must smell the roses, for you only get to play one round"*
>
> ~ *Ben Hogan*

After consuming myself with the fortune of Perrone choosing Salem, I wondered how I would fit in with him. That relationship began to take shape at the 1993 Thanksgiving Game against Salem's arch rival, Beverly High.

There was a cold chill throughout Bertram Field. Still, that didn't stop thousands of fans from bundling up like they were on an expedition to Mount Everest to come out to attend the 92nd Thanksgiving game between the Beverly Panthers and Salem Witches. For almost a century these games attracted thousands of fans, regardless of the team records. Bertram Field, a WPA project from the 1930s, was a stadium with home stands that were an enormous, poured concrete crescent. The crescent and field were mounted atop of one of Salem's highest points, overlooking the city and harbor. The acoustics, especially on a crisp, cold day, were phenomenal. Generations of throngs paraded "up the hill" on Powderhouse Road to attend games. The setup was not just a field, but a perfect athletic alter. Such was the ideal venue for the "all-community" participation cultivated by Perrone.

Salem's freshmen and sophomore football players, who weren't playing in the game, were sensibly dressed in layers to stay warm. They were part of the "show of force" Perrone used to brand his football by suiting up huge numbers for game days. Nonetheless all were mesmerized by the stage they had the fortune to share. Little did they realize they were dressing out of a calculated strategy to intimidate the visiting opponent.

In order to stave off the freezing temperature, some of the players resorted to forming a huddle for body warmth and moving slowly counter-clockwise. I used a trick I've picked up from my Owa. I crammed the hot peppers my Italian grandmother prepared into my cleats to give me some much-needed heat. Although they did not restore their feeling, I felt a sense of pride in my heritage and prayed I could make my family proud. I prepared myself to be the game's hero, the backup quarterback and placekicker. If I was given the chance to kick the winning field goal, I would need to have a warm foot; otherwise, as cold as it is, kicking the ball will feel like kicking a brick wall.

When the final throw of the game sailed over the Salem wide receiver's head, Beverly fans erupted and started the victory celebration as both a Super Bowl appearance and the Northeast Conference Championships were on the line. "Not this year, Perrone. Who's calling the plays, your wife?" A drunken Salem fan yelled out.

I closed my eyes; my interior reaction was intense, but disappointment can sharpen the mind-action speaking louder than words. *Omit nothing,* I told myself, *you need to do this.*

After equipment returns, all 5'6" and 130 pounds of me boldly interrupted the coaches' meeting, which didn't sound like it was going well in the aftermath of defeat. When I finally mustered up the courage to speak, I asked, "Coach Perrone, can you spare me a couple minutes of your time?" He certainly wasn't expecting me and had little time to make up his mind, and as no one knew why I was there, the other coaches politely got up and make a hasty retreat. Coach Perrone made it his business to know about things; he liked to know the value of people.

He sat looking at me, sizing me up.

"Coach," I said, shooting from the gut, "if I'm the starting quarterback next season, you definitely won't be feeling the effects of a Thanksgiving Day loss this time next year!"

He looked at me as if I was on drugs.

"Trust me," I said, rapid fire. "Give me the opportunity, and I can lead this team to the Super Bowl."

After what felt like days, he shook his head in disbelief. "You have never even taken a varsity snap," he quipped.

I caught my breath and was convinced that my pitch went down like a rock in water, so I didn't stick around.

Bertram Field was where it all began. The morning after the game and my Joe Namath blast, I snuck through the chain-linked fence and began to dream. The scoreboard was still lit up, reading "Beverly – 20, Salem – 14." Bertram Field still smelled like popcorn and looked a bit like the arctic. Heavy frost blanketed the field, icicles hung from the press box, and fallen dreams lingered throughout the stadium as the sun slowly rose. I watched the beams of sunlight shine onto the field, forming a gentle test pattern that spread to create the powerful heat needed to thaw the place. *Nature blows me away, the way it provides solutions*, I thought. Shattering disturbance can be turned into peace, brutality into beauty, and I was questioning why and how?

Surely, I convinced myself, it's because determination dominates. This could mean something, but I knew the odds were against me, at least that's what people told me. "Forget it, short skinny kids don't make it in a sport full of giants!"

I might have believed them, except, my Grandma Owa was fond of saying, "Nonsense. God gave you a talent for this, all in blessed time."

I chose to believe her and routinely begged, "Grandma, can't you light another candle; see if you can hurry Him up?" In the meantime I was an undeveloped sophomore forced to live in reality. I convinced myself I would have to get into killer shape, build more muscle, and train longer and harder than humanely possible. If I wanted the starting QB position, I had to earn it. Coach Perrone won't hand me the job just because I had the balls to interrupt his meeting and promise I'd deliver him the championship.

The metal weights in the weighted vest I wore hit my skin, sending sharp pains ricocheting through my torso. Somehow I didn't care. I ran up and down every step from top to bottom of the stadium with a purpose. I was visualizing a trip to the Super Bowl where only one other quarterback, Billy Pinto, had taken Salem twenty years earlier. Sprinting down the stadium steps, I noticed an open copy of yesterday's special edition program that someone had left behind: *100 Years of Salem High School Football*. I stopped running when I saw that the program was opened to a photograph of the 1974 Super Bowl team. I tore through the program to find Pinto's bio and let out a yell, "If he did it, why can't I?" My voice echoed through the stadium. I ripped the team photo page from the program, stuffed it into an empty potato chip bag, and placed it under my vest for safekeeping.

Moments later, a silver-haired man wearing a Salem football jacket emerged from under the stands and asked, "Kid, what are you training for, the Olympics?" I didn't recognize him, but I knew he was a fan. The brim on the cap shielding his eyes hadn't been broken in yet, and the highly polished shiny pins on his football jacket clearly symbolized his support and pride in the program.

I responded, "No, sir, I'm going to be Salem's starting quarterback next season."

He approached, pushing his cap back on his head, breaking into a genuine smile that exposes a space between his front teeth "Tough loss yesterday," he said, extending his hand to introduce himself, "Pep

Cornacchio. Fifty-seven years ago I played on this very field, and I can promise you that wherever you go in this lifetime, you'll never forget your time as a member of the program. God bless you, son, and keep up the good work." And with that, Pep started to walk away, but turned back. "The most exciting Salem High football game I ever saw was played on this very field."

Eyes glued on him, I'm not quite sure if this encounter is real or the product of a tired mind playing tricks on me. I asked, "Who did they play?"

Pep laughed, describing in great detail the hard-fought battle played against Gloucester in which Salem pulled out a win with six seconds left. "I'd best be going," he said, ready to vanish in the distance, before he shot me one final glance. "History, especially in Salem, has a way of repeating itself; stay on your game if you want to see it coming."

Upon returning home, I was so inspired by my encounter with Pep, I couldn't think about anything else. I darted upstairs to the small bedroom I shared with my brothers. I took Pinto's program picture from the potato chip bag and transferred it into a Ziploc bag for safekeeping. Fortunately, I learned early on you don't leave things lying around with two brothers. So to make doubly sure I didn't lose it, I pulled the cot I slept on away from the window and hid the baggie inside the secret hole I made in the far side of my mattress and then crammed it back in position.

"Hurry up, before I eat your dinner," says a voice that turns out to be my middle brother, Eric. "It's leftover turkey."

I was thinking that a plate of Owa's homemade linguini sounded a lot more appetizing.

I quickly ate and quietly slipped out into the backyard. Sitting in the yard tossing the pigskin, gazing up into a constellation of stars blazing in the night sky, I kept thinking about what to do with the 1974 Super Bowl team photo from the program. I came up with the idea to put it in my helmet prior to every game beginning next season for good luck. That way, whenever I needed inspiration, I'd discretely pull the photo out and let it take me back to my chance encounter with Pep.

Suddenly shouts ring out from the deck. "What are you doing out there? You're going to get sick," Grandma Owa declared. "Come in and watch the game with your brothers. And eat, build those muscles."

Later on I headed downstairs for my nightly visit to Owa's room, a habit I never tire of. The ceilings were low, the lights were dim and the stairs had the noisy creaks you'd expect to hear in a dilapidated eighteenth century mansion. I approached quietly. She was deep into her prayer session, hands in supplication, with her black St. Joseph Daily Missal book squeezed between her palms. A widow for thirty-seven years, she was always thankful for "Another blessed day." She had a spiritual side, strong enough to make an atheist want to have faith, and was certainly the foundation of mine.

"Who are you praying for, Owa?"

"Your football coach," she laughed. "I suspect he needs a little help to understand what a dedicated young man you are and to appreciate your commitment to his team. He needs to be able to see your gift. He never could see your brothers' full potential, and I can't allow him to get his third strike."

I grinned at the idea of my old grandma working a baseball analogy into a football discussion. I assured her, "You're not the average grandmother, Owa."

I was about to go and give her some peace and quiet, but before I said my goodnight, she picked up on a touch of uncertainty I was trying to suppress. Her eyes grew big, and I knew something important was coming. "Sean, I've had many disappointments in my life. Losing your grandfather thirty-seven years ago was heartbreaking, but I turned to faith and truly believe we will be reunited in heaven. Work on your relationship with God. He answers prayers." Owa gestured for me to come sit on the sofa with her and eat some nuts.

"Does he really or should I worry?" I asked, not fully convinced.

"Oh, yes," she replied, emphatically. "You are going to be the starting quarterback next season. I believe in you, and you must never stop believing in yourself. Faith can move mountains."

"Goodnight, Owa, I love you," I said, kissing her cheek, and then pulled the blinds for her.

Above the window, a frame hung on the wall. Inside a simple piece of paper had written on it, "The time is now. Worrying is putting faith in fear." Suddenly my curiosity was working again. I asked Owa what it means. She didn't answer, instead she rifled through a drawer and pulled out a dog-eared book and motioned for me to sit down. "I have an old fable I want to read to you. My father read this to me when I was a child."

I made myself comfortable and listened.

"This is a little fable about Mr. Jones who dies and goes to heaven. Peter is waiting at the gates to give Mr. Jones a tour. Amid the splendor of the golden streets, stunning mansions, and the choir of angels that Peter shows him, Mr. Jones notices a strange-looking building he thinks looks like a big warehouse. It has one door and no windows. Mr. Jones asks to see inside, but Peter pauses. 'You really don't want to see what's in there,' he tells the new arrival. When his final tour is over, Mr. Jones is still thinking, so he asks again to see inside the structure. Finally, Peter relents. When the apostle opens the door, Mr. Jones almost pushes him over to enter. It turns out that the big building is stacked with row after row of shelves, floor to ceiling, each shelf filled neatly with white boxes tied in blue ribbons. 'These boxes all have names on them,' Mr. Jones remarks aloud. Then turning to Peter he asks, 'Do I have one?' Peter replies, 'Yes, you do,' and tries to guide Mr. Jones back outside. 'Frankly, if I were you...' Peter tries to explain, but Mr. Jones starts running toward the J aisle to find his box. Peter dashes after him, sighing. He catches up with him just as he opens the box. Peeking inside, Jones takes a pause, and lets out the familiar sigh, one that Peter has heard numerous times before, because, there in Mr.

Jones box are all the blessings that God wanted to give him while he was on earth, blessings that Mr. Jones had never asked for."

I sat motionless with my eyes focused on my grandmother. She closed the book and gave a summation, quoting verse. "Ask, promised Jesus, and it will be given to you, (Matthew 7:7). You do not have, because you do not ask, said James (James 4:2)." She grabbed my hand, holding me with her eyes. "My time is limited, and I want to experience your blessings with you, so make sure you ask for them. Have confidence God will provide whatever you need to live your dream." Her lovely brown eyes were enormous, and her warm hands sent chills through my body. Moisture pooled in my eyes. I put my head down. Sometimes I questioned her ways, thinking maybe faith's just a safety net, but at that moment I was spiritually moved, and in time came to realize my grandmother's fable was a lesson that would help to shape my future.

While I was getting ready for bed, my father stuck his head in to ask, "How was your workout earlier?"

"Cold," I responded. "Real challenging, but very interesting."

He reiterated the word, "Interesting? Got to admit, I've never heard anyone describe a workout as 'interesting.'"

I went into detail about my chance meeting with Pep Cornacchio. "Ever heard of him?"

My dad recognized the name, and it meant something to him. He sat down on my bed beside me. "Pep Cornacchio is Salem football's biggest fan. His heart bleeds Salem's red and black colors. And, God, do I remember the game."

If there was one thing guaranteed to put a fire under my father, it was an opportunity to talk football. "That 1974 game between Gloucester and Salem was the greatest game I ever saw," he said, wistfully remembering. I was listening hard and I wanted to know every infinitesimal detail of play, every inscrutable move on the field. His words spilled out. "I was in the back of the end zone. Salem went on an 88-yard drive with only twelve seconds left on the clock facing a fourth and six, threatening to score the winning touchdown." By then my father was on his feet. He had a big voice and he could use it. He grabbed the football I was holding, transforming it into a microphone which he announced the play-by-play. "With 11,000 fans on their feet, QB Bill Pinto took the snap and dropped back looking for his brother, who was covered by two defenders. No one could break free, so Pinto tossed a blooper to the opposite side of the end zone where Al Larrabee was blanketed by a Gloucester defender. Both men jumped for the ball, and yes, it was Larrabee who got it. Unbelievable, Larrabee had the ball! TOUCHDOWN SALEM! SALEM WINS!"

I was holding my breath and my eyes were as big as the moon. "What an amazing feeling to win a game like that in the final seconds."

He handed the ball back to me and sat back down, calming himself. "Son, you need to train mind, body, and soul for moments like that. They come, but not often, and not without a wicked lot of work. Faith," he mimicked his mother, my grandma.

"What about Doug Flutie, Dad? Was it faith or did he train his mind for that?" I asked, referring to the Hail Mary pass against Miami, a pivotal play for Flutie a decade prior and what surely sealed his Heisman Trophy.

"A combination of both," he answered, well aware that Flutie, at 5'9" was my football hero. My eyes shifted to a copy of *Sports Illustrated* with Flutie on the cover that I kept next to my bed. Doug Flutie never forgot where he came from. The words echoed through him but gave him more drive. "You are too small to play QB." The parks of Natick, as a kid let him live his childhood dreams and develop his craft playing touch football. His dreams got larger and larger. "I think that as soon as someone tells you that you cannot do something, it is motivation. It is always on the back of your mind so you're constantly on edge. Have a little chip on your shoulder and it makes you prepare."

I took the ball and stood up on my cot and it was time to do my impression of Dan Davis the long time BC radio announcer. *Here we go...here's your ballgame, folks, as Flutie takes the snap. He drops straight back...has some time, now scrambles away from one hit...looks...uncorks a deep one to the end zone, Phelan is down there...oh he got it! Did he get it? He got it! Touchdown!! Touchdown!! Touchdown!! Touchdown!! Touchdown Boston College!! He did it!! He did it!! Flutie did it!! He got Phelan in the end zone!! Touchdown!! Oh my goodness...what a play!! Flutie to Gerard Phelan!! 48 yards!! No time on the clock, it's all over!!"*

My father was all smiles, "Believe in yourself." And with that, he grabbed the football from me again and tossed it right back, saying, "Sweet dreams son, I love you."

"Love you too, Dad," I answered, not just out of habit, but because I mean it.

As I lay in bed drifting off to sleep, my mind was racing. The moonlight, sneaking in between the shades that didn't quite cover my bedroom window, hit me in the eyes like stadium lights. I began to visualize it all: being the starting QB, the game-winning Pinto-to-Larrabee touchdown pass, Flutie's heroic Hail Mary, beating Beverly, and living up to my promise to Perrone.

I was mapping it all out in my head and had even started to count down. Before I knew it, the sun was up and I had one less day to prepare for my championship game.

CHAPTER 4
THE PHONE CALL

---///---

> "Victory is not the important item; rather more so, are the lessons in character building that are received on the field."
>
> ~ Bill Broderick

"You punk cracker. Don't ever put your hands on me. Yo, I will kill you. You know where I come from you silver spoon eating mother." In August 1993, an altercation occurred between a Salem QB and an inner city METCO student from Boston that would shipwreck Salem's annual pre-season football training camp program. The Salem team had traditionally made the trip to a Cape Cod camp for one week of training every summer, the object being to isolate the team from any distraction and to develop team chemistry. That year they'd switched camps to one up north in the mountains of New Hampshire, which, as it turned out, was an unfortunate decision. The incident brought forth an edict from the school superintendents' office, issuing: henceforth camp was to be held exclusively on Salem's own school grounds.

More importantly, it didn't sit well with Ed Curtin, the school's superintendent; Perrone was a thorn in his side. A no-nonsense type, he played it straight by the book and was convinced the coach was trying to deliberately cover up the whole fight, and Curtin put Perrone on probation on August 23, 1994, by letter.

Perrone could win football games. He had huge support. Sincere ties between him and the players and fans were one solid unbreakable emotional bond, no matter how many wins or loses he had. He had his detractors. As a young player I was aware that many were jealous of his success and popularity. Others were offended by the volume of publicity he received, and the constant citation of his aggregate win/loss records, which they interpreted as self-promotion. My teammates and I had a sense of this sentiment. Some went on, year after year, opining that his self-promotion showcased his secondary interest for his players and students.

After receiving the probationary letter, Perrone stared at the blackboard in his office. He was taking inventory as depth charts were being written out. Something heavy weighed on his mind. Shaking his head, he muttered to himself, "There's not much talent in this group. On paper we only have one kid who has a prayer of a chance to play college ball." His mind reeled back to how he had to fight like hell to keep this job eight months ago. Under the Education Reform Act of 1993, all hiring and firing of teachers and separately, coaches, was the principal's responsibility. It was four days before the 1993 Thanksgiving Day game that the principal, Karen Baker, asked him to consider a coaching retirement.

At the time, Salem was 8-1 and in contention to win a league championship. Even so, Baker informed him, "You won't get a good evaluation. I don't want to see you embarrassed."

Perrone knew instinctively that this was just another act of harassment. Far from wanting to retire, he let her know it. "What an irrational idea. As long as there are games to be won and energy in my body, the welfare of my team is my priority. I don't plan on going anywhere."

The principal turned her back and walked away. Notwithstanding being on Curtin's "probation" and having Principal Baker's words of

November 1993 in mind, Perrone was still eager to start the 1994 season. He reflected on the program's history.

Football banners hung all over Salem's gymnasium: 1974, 1975, 1986, and 1989. One in particular stood out from the rest, not only because it was larger, but read "Super Bowl 1974." The '74 team was considered the greatest Salem High team ever, although, legendary Salem football coach Bill Broderick might have argued his undefeated 1925, 1931, and 1941 teams would have been worthy of sitting in that category.

It was August 25, a little after seven in the morning. This marked the first day of practice for the 1994 Salem High football team. There was a fresh smell of polish from the school hallways. The newly-painted locker room looked as if the paint was still wet, and the refurbished equipment hung in lockers alongside helmets shining bright red and patiently awaiting their Witch decal.

I stood alone in the gymnasium as my older brother stepped into a coach's meeting. It was on this spot, twelve weeks earlier while tossing the football, I'd had a defining moment in my life.

In the silence of my thoughts, I couldn't escape the negative prediction rolling around in my head when a former Salem coach and teacher had hit me with, "You will never play QB for Salem High."

But then I thrive on situations like this. After tossing thousands of footballs, running hundreds of sprints, and studying endless hours of film, I kept the words with me as fuel for my internal fire. Having to compete for the slot against the two other QBs would be a challenge, but I was as ready as ever.

Shattered dreams from the 1993 season were far less painful. The Witches were eight points away from the Super Bowl. Perrone knew his team lacked the ability to win the big game, and he sure as hell was emphasizing that point to our 1994 squad. He was tough, but underneath, we understood he knew the world of football inside out and appreciated how essential it was to maintain and motivate his team with the same commitment that marked his previous successes. Perrone made sure we knew every elegant win and every singular loss, the how and the why, going back to his 1973 rookie season, that resulted in a major upset win of 14-6 over Beverly on Thanksgiving Day. He emphasized the win, how he felt the experience would give his team confidence for the up-and-coming 1974 season and how the experience would pay off in dividends. That same year 1973, Perrone managed to put the Witches back onto a winning track with a 5-4-1 record; the 1974 season Salem would run the table in the Northeastern Conference going 10-0. It was the first undefeated season since the former Holy Cross star and Salem coach, Walt Sheridan, and his 1959 team traveled south to the Orange Bowl in Florida, only to be beaten by Miami Edison 46-6, and would become one of Perrone's three undefeated seasons as a football coach. Salem lost in the 1974 Super Bowl game in overtime. A late fumble cost the Witches in a 21-20 heartbreaker vs. Andover, the top-ranked team in the state. Perrone's 1975 team might go down as the most talented group of football players ever assembled at Salem. They lost a nail-biter 15-14 to Saugus to finish the year 9-1 and share the Northeastern Conference Championship with Saugus. By then Salem was ranked third in the state out of 52 teams but, unfortunately, '75 was just another year without a state title.

The following season was a rebuilding year, but that didn't stop Perrone. He reloaded with stronger bullets, and by 1977 the Witches were 8-2, falling just 5 points shy of making the Super Bowl. The next several seasons, Salem was plagued with injuries, finishing slightly above .500, but in 1979 they pulled off a major win, beating archrival Beverly 21-20; a game Perrone emphasizes as being "one of the most exciting wins" he'd ever been involved with.

The 1982 team was one of the stingiest defenses to wear the SHS uniform, posting a league leading six shutouts. Led by a punishing linebacker, Harvard-bound John Keenan, they finished off Beverly 15 to 6 and ended the season 8-2. The following season the team ranked

#1 in offense and defense in the conference, until a heartbreaking 14-12 loss to Winthrop put an end to any Super Bowl dreams. Winthrop eventually won the Super Bowl behind All-American and future Miami running back, Troy Staffia. In another '80s classic Thanksgiving battle, Salem beat Beverly for the tenth time in twelve years, 8 to 6. Over the next two seasons the Witches would finish with winning records and the 1986 team was awarded the Northeastern Conference Championship crown after going 7-2-1.

Multiple milestones were reached during the 1987 season: Perrone won his 100th game at Salem and his 200th career victory with a win over a tough Danvers team. Trailing 24-7 in the fourth quarter, Perrone's boys pulled out a miraculous win. In 1989, the team finished the decade on a positive note going 9-1, with its only loss, a 14-7 defensive struggle, coming against a scrappy Lynn English team that would eventually go to the Super Bowl. For the first time in the program's history, due to freezing temperatures and blizzard conditions, the Thanksgiving Day game was postponed until the following day. The extra bonus day would help the Witches brew up a spell-binding win over Beverly, 20-8, to earn a share of the Conference Championship.

***

During his tenure at Salem, Perrone had only two losing seasons, 1988 and 1990.

One of the reasons why Perrone was successful was because he would allow his assistants the space and freedom to work within the system. In fact, Perrone's loyal core of assistants had stood beside him from his rookie 1973 season. One was Coach Tim Marcoulier, a former football player at John Baptist under Perrone's tutelage, who had gone on to coach with the maestro in Maine, and never hesitated to head down to the North Shore right behind him.

Being among the state's coaching elite, at the age of fifty-two, Perrone lacked the one key ingredient used in the sports world as the measuring stick of success: a Massachusetts state title. That notwithstanding, his creative mind never ceased designing plays and offensive formations guaranteed to give opposing defensive coordinators gray hair before their time. Renowned for meticulous organization, he was a master of preparation and a stickler in the philosophy of "Practice makes perfect." Each new season was a challenge he was prepared for. He had seen it all before.

At the start of every season he put together a new lineup out to prove something, but generally lacking the cohesive rhythmic mechanics needed to win the big game. His job was to make it happen. He'd kick off with, "Ready, let's go," and the phrase from thereon in, "Run it again. Run it again. Run it again," became a mantra that to this day, still plays in my head. Like a fine Italian chef, he would start from scratch, developing his own recipe for an offensive scheme that would work. He'd keep what worked and scrap what did not. The "stack-I" was the base offense, but he used twelve to fourteen other formations. Some weeks he would run five formations, then the following week use something completely different. A master tactician, whether it was two-platooning linemen, short counts, motions, or the unbalanced line, Perrone's offense had more misdirection than a David Copperfield show. His teams scored points and made opponents dig into the depths of their souls to find ways to shut down his offense. Despite the Northeastern Conference having the most parity in the state, remarkably, the program was at the top of the conference year in and year out.

The 1994 team was about as inexperienced as any of his past teams, but with Perrone at the helm, one thing was for sure: They would show up to battle on every Saturday. The players started to fill the gym around 8:30 a.m. The upperclassmen walked in with swagger while the younger kids looked paranoid as if being watched by the law. It was obvious who trained during the off-season. Captain Mark Higley walked in wearing a cut-off shirt with his arms jacked. Senior LB Phil Downes followed, rapping "Juicy" by Biggie Smalls with his Sony

Walkman on his hip. A light-skinned brother from Lynn, hands down the most vocal and athletic on the team, Downes was crossed colored out rocking his Nikes, looking twenty-five with his physique and jerry-curled hair. Underclassmen Elvin Rodriguez and Edwin Canelo strutted in with an entire Latino posse behind them. Jamon Mccellon's dreads were flowing out of his visor as he walked in by himself. Projected as a backup defensive back, Mccellon was ready and eager to fight for a starting job. Manuel De Pena sat quietly outside the gym on the field house steps. Firmly he held the book *Celestine Prophecy*. His wide-rimmed glasses examined each page as he slowly comprehended the message of the book. A minute before the football meeting was about to start, he stood and stretched his long 6'2" frame. He slowly entered the gym. I jogged back in the building with the ball in my hands. A.J. Grimes, who I had been trying to break in the ball with, came sprinting in behind me with a "finally, the day is here" expression on his face.

The coaches stood in the back, observing each player's movements. They knew each player inside and out, making name tags on helmets obsolete. Coach Marcoulier, the defensive coordinator and craziest coach on the staff—who resembled Mike Tyson in his prime—walked through the lineup using a military intimidate your opponent technique, staring down the team. Marcoulier doesn't bite off ears like "Iron Mike," but he will eat live worms during practice, letting them slither whole down his throat to get the kids fired up. Players feared him, yet every single member of the team showed him respect. He'd lived overseas and all over the U.S., which gave him the ability to interact with a broader sensibility than a lot of the team was used to. His tour in Vietnam and exit from the military was fortuitously timed; as Perrone was being hired in Salem, he received an invitation to join the Witch City sporting community simultaneously. Regardless of how many years passed, military was still in Marcoulier's blood. He was proud to have served his country and injected his military discipline into the Salem Witch defenses year in and year out, keeping the Witches in games for all four quarters. He had only played two years of football, but managed to turn himself into a coach of X's and O's, inspiring his defensive unit to follow his passion.

Seventy boys dressed in shorts and t-shirts sat on the gym floor, collectively holding their breath. Perrone's brown eyes gazed over his players. I couldn't help thinking, with his jet black hair, tan complexion and tough guy stance, that he looked more like the kind of guy my dad cautioned me to steer clear of than a football coach.

"Tradition, pride, family, and hard work" were the first words out of his mouth as he addressed the 1994 team. The charismatic words spread through the room like stardust, reducing the high school football players into something akin to a room full of five-year-olds on Christmas morning. The excitement was palpable. Every player wearing a Witches helmet, whether an eight or eighteen-year-old, was important to Perrone. Over the past twenty-one years, his success was directly attributable to the consistency derived from the high school program's feeder system that ensured all teams in Salem would run the same system. From the athlete who was attending his first team meeting to team captain Seth Whitten, Perrone made it feel like an honor to put on the uniform and treated every player with the same respect.

Sweat trickled down the gigantic face of Willie Jones who, at 6'3" and 315 pounds, was already a full-grown man at seventeen-years- old. He had now come a long way since transferring to Salem as a freshman. Gone, but not forgotten, was Henry Street in Passaic, New Jersey. "I used to see crack bottles under the stairway in the building where he lived. Women got raped in that building. It was a real tough Black-Hispanic neighborhood," Jones would say. "Streets were bad. You'd walk to school in the morning passed homeless people drinkin' on the corner. Fightin' was always goin' on." It wasn't until Jones relocated to New England that he realized the scope of the hell back in Passaic. That dump of a town instilled the toughness he brought with him to the

Witch City. Summer school had enabled him to stay on the academic path and football helped him to become goal-oriented, while Perrone's interest in him gave him the faith to want to do something special with his life.

Perrone held his hands up, going on to say, "You train year round for ten games. We've been playing football here since 1890. The tradition is rich and respected. Keep it up. We are only as strong as our weakest link. Some of you guys have dreamed about this day for a long time. Enjoy the journey and work hard. Be honorable and respect your teachers, coaches, parents, females, and this city."

He swiveled towards the team captain, pointing his finger. "Higs, what's the goal for the season?"

Higs spat out, "Beat Beverly, baby."

Perrone elaborated on his point. "We are underdogs and everyone knows it. If that isn't humiliating enough, we're picked to finish below .500 in the conference."

I knew we were better than that.

"Whitten, what's the goal for the season?"

"Coach, to win the Super Bowl," he shrieked.

Whitten's words were what Perrone wanted to hear, but football is more than a game. It is sheer focus, grit, and steel. He wasn't sure the stop-at-nothing killer team spirit was quite there, but it was what he hoped to instill in this group. Holding up a game jersey, he exclaimed, "Wear this with pride."

With seventeen of the team's twenty-two starters gone, the Witches had big shoes to fill. The 1993 team was one of the finest two-way teams in his era, leading the conference in scoring while also yielding the fewest points. Addressing the media, Perrone said what everyone familiar with the program was thinking, "Salem's biggest concern heading into camp is at quarterback." For the first time since 1988, the Witches headed into the season not knowing who their signal-caller would be with three candidates vying to be "the man." All three had seen time last season during some lopsided wins, but none had distinguished himself as the heir-apparent to QB Tom Giardi, another to matriculate at Harvard.

Salem's arsenal was far from being loaded, but it had the makeup of a tough, diverse group. With the senior class of fifteen returning veterans being the smallest numbers during Perrone's tenure, the underclassmen would need to provide the depth. The team was made up of a bunch of transplants. Ranging from Baton Rouge, Louisiana, where senior captain Joe Freeman had his roots; to New Jersey where Carlos Leopoldo, a 6'3", 250-pound defensive end, had migrated from; across the Hudson River to Manhattan, the childhood home of speedy running back Jamal Mercado; to wide receiver Manny De Pena, born in Santo Domingo, Dominican Republic; they came with their families in search of a better life.

Coach Perrone took them as he found them, welcoming all with open arms. Parents had put their trust in the Salem school system to develop their children, to give them the education and skills they never had, and Coach Perrone would assist them in keeping their kids off the streets. The team was ready to play with heart and pride, characteristics Perrone had been instilling in his players for over thirty-seven years. Getting the kids in the right position would be another story, but Perrone's innate ability to play chess positioning with his players was a trait that had made him a premier coach. He got the maximum out of his players. Winning games was important, but developing life skills in his players was where the real championships were won. He was the consummate molder of men.

THE UNION MEETING–MOOSE HALL

Perrone sat in his office watching practice film as it was the heart of double sessions. A stack of mail was dropped off by one of his assistants. Pausing the VHS tape, he sat back in his chair. Perrone's concerns went beyond the lines of a football field. Opening up a letter from the Salem teachers' union, he was about to do the Kareem Abdul-Jabbar hook shot with it into the trash, but skimmed across the words "MANDATORY MEETING" in bold. Sighing, Perrone got a football thought and flipped the paper over. He scribbled down a new play. He then considered the impact of a strike on coaching. He wanted to make his point very clear, referencing any possible teachers strike discussion.

Later that evening, walking into the Moose Hall he stopped in the bathroom. He was perspiring from the humidity. He splashed some cold water on his face, entered the hall, and sat in the back away from the smoking crowd of teachers. He sipped on a glass of water which cooled him off. The panel discussions got underway. He voluntarily walked up to the microphone and reached into his pocket as he prepared some points to discuss. Changing his mind, he decided to speak from his heart and tucked the paper into his jacket. He examined the crowd and saw many familiar faces. All came from different backgrounds and were in this room because they were passionate about what they do. With a deep voice he emphasized that he was 100 percent in support of the vision of the union. "We are clearly underpaid; the Peabody game is two weeks away. If we go on strike before the season starts, I will not coach. But once we get into our season, if a strike occurs I will stay with my team and coach."

Small talk spread through the room. "He showed his hand. Curtin will crucify him," a teacher stated, "I hope that statement does not leave these walls."

Perrone thanked the crowd and exited through the side door. He had a sense of relief that he was able to get that off his chest. It was well past 10 PM and he made his way back to the school's field house to do some more evaluating.

***

In North Salem, Curtin's phone rang. Slowly walking to grab it, he heard on the other line, "Hello. Mr. Curtin, please!"

"Speaking. Who is this?" Curtin snapped back.

After a silence the ice was broken by, "You should know that Perrone announced he will cross the picket line and coach if a strike occurs during the season." The anonymous caller immediately hung up.

Curtin grinded down on his teeth making a sneer and placed the phone back down on the hook. His white whale had surfaced. What Curtin, like Ahab, did not realize was that *Moby Dick* had bit off Ahab's leg because Ahab had started the fight.

Ahab initiated the encounter on a mission to kill *Moby Dick*.

CHAPTER 5
LIVE THE DREAM BITTERSWEET

> *"Control your own destiny or someone else will."*
> *~ Jack Welch,*
> *Former GE CEO, Salem High Class of 1953*

It is widely believed that the major appeal of music is its ability to take us to a place and time we know and love. To this day, whenever I hear the familiar click-clack of cleats on concrete, it takes me back to the scorching humid heat, the feeling of morning dew soaking into my practice pants, clipboards hitting helmets, whistles blowing loud, and players' bodies still fresh as the morning sunrise but wary of the long toilsome two-a-days that awaited.

Salem's practice field is tucked away behind the school, adjacent to a paved sidewalk that led up the steep hill. The field has a trail worn into the grass that is the chosen route of players who opt for the grass over pavement in an effort to save their cleats. Occasionally, however, a player would stick to the sidewalk and I'd hear the sweet music of the cleat click-clacking on the hot top. The field remained lined year-round and was pristine at that time of year. As the season progressed, it would take the pounding of countless practices to wear it down like the two-a-day practice sessions we were about to begin. The fence encircling the field made us feel like we were on an island, free from outside influence. And while we dream of what was ahead of us, for most, the script had already been written: adversity in the classroom, on the gridiron, and in the game of life. Even so, on the field, life was beautiful: fresh air, the camaraderie, the expectations, the belonging. It was like being part of some secret territorial underground that had its own culture. Here on this isolated plot of land is where we would embrace our coach, the man who would chart out the future. Here our team set aside individual egos, transition from urban to suburban life, from classmate to teammate, from friend to family. Players describe it as exhilarant, that sense of awe that makes leaving the game so painful for so many.

The shrill sound of the coach's whistle was like the morning school bell and signified that it was time to get to work. "Bring it up, boys," Perrone yelled, still smiling because so far nothing had occurred to piss him off. We were going to be a challenge and, as a challenge brought the best out in him, it suited him fine.

Over the years, Perrone had watched a lot of us develop from young boys into young men. For the newcomers, he dispensed with the practical implications and introduced his supporting cast of coaches.

Coach Marcoulier still sported a military-style haircut, perhaps to stay cool or look intimidating. His standard appearance included coach's bike shorts, ill-fitting shirt, and arms crossed like a bouncer at a local dive. He stood behind Perrone with his glasses on. His calves looked like Popeye's forearms. Not surprisingly, he handled the defense and would do so again in what would be his twenty-second season.

Next stood Coach Wilbur, a bow-legged man with jerry curled hair. Wilbur was entering his twentieth season, and would again take charge of the wide-outs and defensive ends. He was a PE teacher, but at another school. I admired Wilbur, had looked up to him and believed in his coaching style. He was a detail-oriented coach who worked hard and never stopped expanding his knowledge of the game, attending conferences, clinics, and camps to make himself a more complete football coach.

Coach Baldassarri was a guidance counselor at the high school. He was in charge of the offensive linemen. New to Perrone's staff, Baldassarri was not new to the game, having coached the Witches from 1972 to 1976, and now was back to where he felt was home.

Coach McKenna also coached back in the 1974 and 1975 seasons, but like Baldassarri, this was his first year back. McKenna would run the defensive backs even though he was not under contract with the school system.

Coach Elsaesser was in his fifth season. He had been the Culinary Arts Instructor at the Salem's Colonist Restaurant, as well as an assistant with the freshman team. Jokes about "cooking is for girls" were out of bounds and would earn the occasional jokester an extra lap or some more intense form of corporal punishment.

Coach Mike Stellato, my brother at home but not on the field, was entering his fifth season at Salem High. Mike, I mean Coach Stellato, taught at St. Joseph's, a private school in Salem. Like McKenna, Coach Stellato was not under contract with the teacher's union. Although he was the youngest coach on the staff, Stellato had already put in ten years of coaching in the city. Perrone, undoubtedly, was breeding him to be a head coach someday, perhaps the coach who'd take the reins from Perrone when he decided to step aside.

Looking at Perrone's talented staff assembled on the field was impressive, but there was no doubt in anyone's mind about whose team this would be. Perrone intended to draw out the best in each of us. His philosophy was that everyone on the field had something to contribute to the team, otherwise they wouldn't be there. "The question is not how much ability you have, but what you make of the ability God has bestowed upon you," Perrone preached to the team. I perked up, feeling inspired by what was being said. I wondered if Perrone was talking directly to me. Did he somehow know that every night before bed, my inspirational read was "Make the most of the ability God has given you"? Either way, I was plugged in. "Some of you are faster, bigger, stronger, and smarter. The strong traits you all possess will be exposed and the weaknesses will be developed. If every kid and coach on this team puts forth the best of their ability every time on every play, there will be equal parity among all of us. Gentlemen, that is how a team is created. And remember, the real world, like your opponents on the field, will always try to beat you down and keep you down," he said in a harsh voice. "Respect yourself, respect your coaches, and respect your team. That's what will fortify you."

Perrone definitely subscribed to the "break them down/build them up" philosophy of coaching. We were about to experience what it felt like to have our bodies and minds broken down by the master, and little did I know that surviving Perrone's practices would make playing games feel like a walk in the park. He was old-school, and I suspected that at the conclusion of the first two-a-day, I'd be certain I had reached the gates of hell. I wasn't wrong.

Perrone was a brilliant tactician. His practices were more meticulously orchestrated than the Boston Pops. Salem kids were inherently tough, so he didn't need to spend all week beating up players with hitting drills. Practices were long and grueling. Coach Wilbur swore to us that he had never, in his twenty years as an assistant coach, seen a single wind sprint. "Salem's teams were in tremendous condition because Coach Perrone runs plays around the field up tempo for forty-five minutes without a break. He preserves bodies by limiting practice to two days a week with no pads and takes film study very seriously. He's way ahead of his time on prepping a football team," Wilbur was convincing us.

On the field, despite the absence of wind sprints, practices were intense. Off the field, having declined early retirement, Perrone was under the administration's microscope and occasionally felt pressured to turn the practice motor down a notch or two. He had to weigh that against the some heavy evaluations he faced due to the pariah status he feared he was earning in administrative circles. Then again, with two passing scrimmages, two full scrimmages and the Jamboree, Perrone felt confident he'd be able to find his starting QB, fill seventeen starting positions, and surmount his other concerns.

BISHOP FENWICK SCRIMMAGE

The first scrimmage, against Bishop Fenwick, was on Wednesday morning September 1, 1994. Unlike Salem's pristine field, Bishop Fenwick's football field wasn't well-preserved. The field was located behind the school, as if it had been an afterthought and the grass was burnt and dry. This was a passing scrimmage, the first- ever football combat involving the Witches and the Fenwick Crusaders. With the QB scenario becoming lethally intense, the Crusaders scrimmage was to be the first game-situation evaluations. Perrone instructed the coaching staff to meet at midfield. "Coach them up. Emphasize a good experience is to work on skills. Let's be all positive with these kids."

I was slated as the starter which at this point was, I suspected, rather meaningless, and rotated with Pat Ryan and Sean Sullivan, both of whom coveted the meaningless title I possessed. My stomach was churning from nervous energy. I addressed the offense in our first huddle. Taking a deep breath I remembered what Coach Stellato had told me one night, "Treat games like they were pick-up games at recess." Following my brother's instruction, I visualized recess, remembering how much fun I had slinging the ball around, imagining I was playing in the Super Bowl. It was like a magic pill; the technique worked. I could feel the uncontrolled nervousness subsiding, being replaced with an odd mixture of calm and excitement. Henceforth, I promised myself, I will never again walk onto a field without first convincing myself I'm on a playground at recess, about to play a pick-up football game.

The first play from scrimmage was a Jet Left Sprint Out Pass. This play called for speedy wide out De Pena to stretch the field, allowing me to see the field. He ran a flawless route and when I released the ball, I knew it was dead on. As he had countless times before, De Pena hauled in the pass and took it to the end zone for a 60-yard TD pass. I felt like I was at the top of the ladder it had taken years to build and one rung closer to the clouds that hovered above the field. With that TD pass, the dreamer officially began his ascent. I finished the day going 13 for 20 with the lone TD strike. As a team, the Witches outplayed and outscored Bishop Fenwick. More important to Perrone, he got to witness 91 offensive and defensive plays, every one of which would be scrutinized.

LOWELL SCRIMMAGE

The second scrimmage, a full-contact contest against Lowell, was held on Saturday, September 3, 1994. Perrone huddled his staff in the end zone, "I want intensity from everyone. Quick whistles, we don't need any more players dinged up. The QB situation is our main focus, and I want evaluations in my mailbox first thing in the morning." Despite my performance in the Bishop Fenwick scrimmage, QB Sullivan got the nod as "starter." I tried to convince myself that it really didn't matter who started a scrimmage, but that nagging little voice we all hear in our heads from time to time kept talking me out of it. I remind myself that I broke the ice first with a TD pass just a couple of days ago, and before long, I will get my chance against Lowell. I made the most of my opportunity by linking up with wide out A.J. Grimes for a 42-yard TD pass.

On the football field Edwin Canelo is fast, but on the streets he's faster. Canelo, a sophomore, always complained about his head throbbing, a combined result of playing defensive end on the scout team where 6'3", 310 pound offensive tackle Willie Jones makes him a tackling dummy, and a touch of sleep deprivation. "Can't sleep on summer nights because my room don't have air. Man, it's like a sauna," he'd whimper. Down in his stance with his eyes watching the ball, you can see Canelo has only one thought on his mind, "Make a play." On the snap, he initiates contact, his hands punching with the force he'd needed at "The Point" for one of his street fights.

From the sideline, I could actually see Canelo's eyes expand wide as he hurdled a cut block, putting him in perfect position to make the tackle. But at that very moment, the running back reversed field, prompting Canelo to yell out, "Oh shoot," like a warning to the other side of the defensive line. Canelo planted and attempted to change directions. It was at that moment that I realized Canelo's yell was not a warning to his teammates but, rather, a warning to himself. With Canelo fully exposed and vulnerable, Lowell's All-State lineman lowered the boom to the swaggering sophomore with a lights-out blow. Canelo told us that he literally saw a flash of light run through his head before the opposing player put him down for the count.

Our trainer tended to Canelo as Perrone moved the scrimmage to a different area. Canelo was tough, he always stayed vocal on this field, but the humbling episode immediately diminished his persona. As he came to, Canelo had a burning pain running through his left shoulder. The blow horn signaled time for a water break, but it felt more like watching a boxer being saved by the bell. Canelo wobbled slowly, making his way over to the water hose. We watched the cold water run down his face, then the back of his neck. Canelo was a dreamer, and football allowed him to dream big. Every rep he took on the scout team, he visualized he was playing for the 'U,' the Miami Hurricanes, but of course, that was a surreal fantasy. "Kids from The Point just didn't often catch those breaks," my father had told me. "Shame, but that's the way it is."

Born in the Dominican Republic, Canelo's family arrived with hopes for a better life, but he was not sure about that. From the first game he saw on TV, he was head-over-heels and dreamed football would be his ticket out of The Point. We couldn't have known then but the big hit he'd just absorbed would foreshadow his future: But that was the future, and Canelo, a tough kid, only lived for the moment.

I was certain he had a concussion. He lifted his head up and started to hallucinate. In his mind, a young Hispanic boy wearing his #5 looked through the fence at him. Smiling, he walked over to give him some encouraging words. The boy looked just like him. Seconds later the boy started to walk away. Canelo pulled himself together, slipped through the fence, and followed him. Silently they walked into the woods and they were back in the Dominican Republic. He saw himself with his older brother and mother being chased. Someone was trying to kill them. "What the heck," Canelo snapped back to the present, telling us he was reliving a murder committed by a member of his mother's family, and in retaliation, the victim's family was hunting for Canelo's mother and children. They went from a life of luxury to living in shacks to and hiding in the woods. "Even though my brother and mother didn't have anything to do with it, we had a hit out on us. We were petrified for our lives," he said with a hint of an accent. "My mom saved us. Somehow, she got us immigrated to the United States. We couldn't go back." He had only gone back once to see his father. The vendetta was still active, "They came to my dad's house and my father had to gun up and hide us."

The Point became their new beginning and it was far from luxury. His mom held down three jobs as a housekeeper, a seafood factory attendant, and a waitress supervisor. With no parent around, supervision became obsolete. Edwin grew up too quickly. It was a well-documented fact that The Point was a major drug-infested area where crime was rampant. "You lived it," he'd say. "Everywhere you looked, drugs, marijuana, and cocaine were being pedaled. I was scared, but you adjust to it. It was the hood for those who grew up there, a real tough place. We did what we needed to do to survive." By age twelve, people were pushing drugs on him. He declined, but the memory would stay with him. He claims the Latin community is a place where everyone was on the grind. "There's no one to give a young Latino advice, but plenty of people to ask him to hold and hide their stash for them," adding that the one thing he did learn was how to hotwire cars at fifteen. "I loved dogs but the landlord would not allow them in the apartment. The only pets we ever had were the herds of cockroaches," he laughs. "'Round 1 in the mornin' when moms got in and flipped the light, it wasn' the bulb that blinded us, it was the roaches scatterin' over the walls." It's hard to imagine, but we all thought that was funny at the time. I always liked Canelo and the stories he would tell. One thing I knew, he treated practice with the same commitment that he would a game. Intensity was the angle he took, which only inspired and pushed the underclassmen starters who watched him to want to become better.

The scrimmage ended 20 to 20. Offensively we looked powerful running for 256 yards on 44 carries, but defensively, we did not show up. Meanwhile, the unsettled QB question was no clearer today than it was at opening practice. Sullivan, Ryan, and I remained neck and neck and it looked like a strong finish would dictate who would be named the starter. It could boil down to the Hoffman Jamboree that Friday night.

Ryan was preparing to keep the Ryan Irish legacy going. From his grandfather in the 1940s who was the team doctor for three decades, the Ryan family had always been synonymous with Salem football. One of fourteen children and the eighth boy to play for Perrone, Pat had his sights set on being Perrone's choice for the QB. During the prior 1983 season, Perrone filled his backfield with Ryans, all four brothers: senior Ed at one halfback position; sophomore Steve at the other, Fred at fullback, and junior Joe at quarterback. They were fierce competitors who often argued amongst themselves in the huddle over who was going to get the ball. Pat, following in the footsteps of brothers, would be the fourth son to play QB for Perrone. The Ryan brothers were tough as nails and outstanding athletes. As competitors, both Pat and I were athletic and very competitive, so what it came down to was heart and determination. If the QB decision was to be decided on skills and not politics, I felt it was my job to win.

Sullivan believed it was his job to lose. Perrone was a stickler for tough running QBs and Sullivan defined those characteristics. He was really the only one who had varsity experience. Perrone remembers watching Sullivan in a JV baseball game a year earlier. "The kid chased down a fly ball and ran face first into the fence. Blood was everywhere but it did not faze him. He was stitched up and right back out there."

Up to date, the statistics of the three QB's were: Sullivan was 11-25-169, Ryan 22-31-188, and I was 19-41-224. It looked like Sullivan had the edge after the Lowell scrimmage. He ran the option well. "That doesn't determine anything," Perrone said. "Nobody's stepped forward to be the number one and nobody's fallen back."

BISHOP FEWICK – SCRIMMAGE #2

On September 7, 1994, Bishop Fenwick traveled to Bertram Field to participate in a second passing scrimmage. Let's just say the only thing Salem High players were smiling about was the post-pizza party put on by the Salem boosters. Perrone enjoyed the feed and interacted with parents and fans, even if he had a hard time digesting how his team had performed.

Our pass-catching was, at best, distasteful and our concentration was awful. The longer Fenwick played, the tougher they became. We were breaking down and the QBs were being sacked. This concerned Perrone. Here we were ten days away from the opening up with the number two team in the state and still no decision on who he wanted to name the starter. The team had its third scrimmage in six days. I was frustrated having all three TD passes dropped and over-throwing balls that stalled drives. "Perrone would focus on the positives and negatives with his staff possibly give the number one guy the start on Friday night in the jamboree," my father intoned, showing an article in the September 8 edition of the *Salem News* that quoted the coach. "I will be comfortable with whomever. It's not such a life and death decision.

No matter who it is, we'd feel good about any of the three."

Staring at the paper before breakfast, I had no appetite. My eyes felt heavy from tossing and turning most of the night. Perrone's quote was ingrained in my mind. I was worried; one day to wait before a starter will be named, but what if it's not me? I know I make the most out of every opportunity, and regardless of any decisions that they make on the position, I would continue to accept my role.

MEETING IN THE SANCTUARY

The following day after school, Coach Perrone called all three QBs into his office which was also the "The Pride Room." Walking there, my eyes zoomed onto a quote that read, "Hard Work creates greatness and does not go unnoticed." A shrine of motivational quotes blanketed Perrone's walls, intended for whoever enters his office to gain a sense of determination to succeed. Pictures of his past teams decorate every remaining inch of wall space. The feeling of oxygen pumping through the air was common, because energy levels increased as soon as anyone entered the room. Everything about the office symbolized Perrone's philosophy in life, it was all so neat and organized and well-kept.

Above his desk the 1970 Top 25 National Ratings stood out: #1 Reagan High School, Texas; #2 Massillon, Ohio; #3 Bishop Amat, LePuento, California; #4 St. Rita's, Chicago, Illinois; then was Perrone's Maine Brewer High team, ranked #5 in the country. In 1970, Texas had a population of 11,198,655 to Maine's 993,722. Reagan High was located in Austin, Texas, which had 398,938 residents and 1,800 at Reagan High. Looking at the city of Brewer, Maine, its total population consisted of 9,300 residents and 1,100 students at Brewer High. The playbook on his desk, as thick as a bible, was split into sections with different formations. Stack I, Power Eye, Jet, Wing T were a handful of the formations that were labeled on his blackboard. The bookshelf was in alphabetical order with books pertaining to coaching philosophies from coaching legends: Bear Bryant, Joe Gibbs, Tom Landry, Vince

Lombardi, John Madden, Bill Parcells, Joe Paterno, and Don Shula. Those were the coaches that he admired and respected for their contributions to the game.

Coach Perrone sat back in his chair with his arms folded. His khaki pants were crisply pressed with his black Witches polo shirt tucked into his pants. Sitting on the couch were prospective QBs Sullivan and Ryan. Perrone signaled for me to sit down. At this point I was relieved to sit as my legs were feeling heavy and palms sweaty. I was carrying such a burden of frustration and tried not to show it. Perrone stood up and addressed us. Touching on multiple areas and elaborating on the statistics from all the scrimmages, he made it clear none of us differentiated ourselves. At this point I found myself edging to the front of the couch, and at the time, was certain the senior Sullivan would be named starter.

He had all three QBs one at a time, approach the blackboard and draw up their favorite play, discuss why we thought so, and what defense would be the best to run it against. When I was called up Perrone tossed me a piece of chalk. Approaching the board I turned around and looked at the others. I wanted their undivided attention. "Coach," I said in a timid soft voice, "My favorite play is Jet left sprint out pass, X skinny post. I like it because the play allows me to see the field and gives Manny the opportunity to work in space. With the defense playing a Cover 1, Press-Man, or Cover 3, the play will be successful. I also like it with motion away, which enables a defender to run with the motion taking a defender out of the box." Pausing, I looked at all three, saying with absolute certainty, "This is the play that will get us to Super Bowl." Perrone let out a deep sigh as if he thought I was dreaming. "Okay, Sullivan you have done a fine job. You will be our defensive QB and call all the coverage's. Ryan, like your seven other brothers, you are a true competitor. Stellato, I have seen leadership in you. You will be a co-starter with Ryan. You'll start tonight in the Jamboree and then rotate every other series with Ryan." Wanting to

Later my dad received a call from the Salem Police. The final culprit was one of the other QB's older sisters. The Stellato family declined pressing charges on any arrests, but did seek full restitution.

A STORM IS BREWING

Tensions that were running rampant through the hallways of school had more to do with the teachers being upset over current salary negotiations, than it did with any teammate competition for starting positions. In 1994 the annual starting salary for a teacher with a bachelor's degree was $23,104. If the teacher held a doctorate, with longevity they'd gross $41,209 per annum. The 1,100 student body at the high school saw themselves with more lofty ambitions. But for the 234 students of the senior class, a reality check would soon be knocking at their door. Just about 30 percent of the student body was considered low income; they had started behind the eight ball, plus with the graduating 1994 class earning the lowest Scholastic Aptitude Test (SAT) scores in 10 years, both state and national average, it would be all the leverage Superintendent Curtin and the school committee would need to deny any requests for raises. SAT scores were also a major concern, especially since Salem's scores were 41 points below the national averages. The math portion of the test was 55 points below the national average according to the September 8, 1994, *Salem News*. The administration felt the issue of declining SAT scores was a problem of the Salem public school system, "not just high school education." They wanted to track students who took the test to see how long they had been in the system, and whether the problem could be a lack of continuity in education. Another concern for the administrators was that only 45 percent of graduating seniors would go on to further their education in a four-year college.

Where did that leave the other 55 percent?

Chapter 6

4th Downes

> *"When you're not practicing, remember that someone somewhere is practicing, and when you meet him he will win."*
>
> ~ *Ed Macauley*

Phil Downes sat in Spanish class drawing designs of #44 coming off the edge and blowing up opposing QBs. "Why do I need to learn Spanish? I'm living large in America. I guess there are some Spanish babes I could seduce with some lines."

Roaring crowds and bone crushing hits lived within the 6'2," 220-pounder. In his mind, school was just a blur. "As long as I can play ball, the colleges will come and find me."

It was a warm September day. Anxiety was in the air as the first game was approaching. Downes waited as patiently as a kid waits for his birthday. "Peabody is going to see the real human missile on the field."

It would be his first organized football game at Salem High after transferring in from neighboring Lynn English. He was grateful for a new beginning. To Downes, the message was clear: The streets and crowds he ran with were all contributing to him heading down the path that led to a degree in Menace to Society. The laws of attraction weighed on his mind. He realized negatives were playing a role in his academics and were attracting elements that would keep an anchor on his back. He wanted to change; he wanted to be more than just labeled as a has-been thug that had a ton of potential. Gratefully his aunt felt the same and took him in to live with her in Salem. The final straw came when she realized how bad it had gotten when she sat in with the principal at Lynn English, going through his transcripts: Pre-Algebra F, History F, Spanish F, Science F, English F, Typing F.

Sitting in awe, his aunt was shocked. She emphasized that this was unacceptable and if she was going to give him a fresh start, he needed to get it done in the classroom. The year before, he became intrigued with how Salem's Jack O'Brien ran the basketball program. Sitting in the stands, amazed by what he saw, he could feel his mind transforming at that very moment: the ability and energy of the team, the leadership and charisma of the coach, and the atmosphere. He wanted to be a part of that and was determined to fix his grades and be somebody. His boys were going down the street of no return and his aunt helped him pull a U-turn. The kid was used to playing with fire, and living on the edge was something he continued to do for the first month at Salem High.

He received a going-away gift from his boys: a stolen car. "I would park it down the street, pop the ignition back in, and drive it to school. That is the education I received from the streets of Lynn."

Coming from Lynn, he had the reputation as a fighter, and the first day of school he was ready to make a statement. Usually the new kid gets picked on or gets his respect quick, and Downes got it right away after approaching one of the toughest kids in the school who backed away from the fight. His new teammates at SHS showed him respect out of the gate, and Perrone felt he would make an instant impact. Then again, respect is something he had to develop on Williams Ave. in Lynn. Walking in a certain area, you would catch a serious beat-down.

He got his respect when it would be initiation night to become part of the "Williams Ave. Dogs." Downes was put into the middle of the basketball court and surrounded by the gang. For three minutes, it was anything goes: two-by-fours, bricks, and plenty of kicks to the head. "They then picked me up and told me I was a Dog." He would spend hours on the basketball court and streets to get away from the madness that lived within the walls of his house. He had ball skills and a mouthpiece which put him in another league. That initiation was easy compared to the drugs, physical, and mental abuse that he often would witness at home.

The living conditions were well below par and he would spend hours in his room. His stepfather put fear in the household, constantly beating Phil's mom. Visits from DSS came as often as the mailman. Haunted by the abuse, he decided to stand up for himself and his mom. With his stepfather being so much bigger, he decided to grab a baseball bat. Backfiring on him, he got caught with a right hook. He hit him so hard, his head broke through the wall and split the sheetrock. Going to school with a blue moon in his eye drew more attention, but was covered up. School was not preached in his household and when he was punished, he would not be allowed to attend. He constantly felt like he was running uphill as he tried to piece together his own foundation, but never knew how to do it the right way. With no role models or structure, he often found himself back where he started. His parents denied him just about every opportunity growing up and refused to let him participate in organized sports. When he got home from school he was trying to call chicks and focus on the course of body anatomy.

Living in Lynn, he grew up fast. His parents would host late-night card games where cocaine being left out was as common as a cold. At fourteen years old, he used to kick it with his boys brown-bagging forty ounces of Private Stock or Green Monster. "We always poured out some for our homies," he recalled. He often reminisced with his boys about life in the hood. One course he received on the streets was an A+

in just saying no to drugs. Seeing his mother abuse drugs deterred him from following in her footsteps, but left him with the need to escape. Alcohol filled this gap. Cocaine and marijuana were around, but that was not for him.

He had received a call at his aunt's house before school started informing him something had happened to his mom. He was immediately driven to her apartment in Lynn. When he arrived, he saw her sitting with paramedics which gave him relief that she was okay. As he started to approach her, cops held him back and told him he had to wait in the hall. At that very moment he sensed she was gone. Distraught, there was only one place he wanted to be and that was back at school. Midway through Spanish class, his teacher approached him. Deep down inside he knew something was wrong.

The teacher brought him outside the room, with a startled look on her face. "Phil, it is your mother. She has passed away."

His mom had overdosed. Moisture started to pool in his eyes. With tears dropping to the floor, he slowly walked down the hall. He returned to school, hoping that if he went on with his day, she would be fine and that maybe a miracle could bring her back to life. It, of course, didn't happen.

He grew up quick, and part of him went with his mother to heaven. She would become his source of inspiration. On his jerseys, he wore a patch next to his heart that said "Mom." Whenever he did something good, he would put his hand on the patch and make a gesture to the sky. He prayed she was looking down and was able to see him. The ironic thing was that she never got to see him play. Downes was as tough as can be, but this blindside hit left him down, but not out.

Before games, Downes would sit on the red benches in the Bertram Field House, listening to Wu-Tang, blocking everything out of his mind. With the glare from the sun shining on the red iron bars that covered the windows, he would create his own insane asylum in his mind with levels of violence flowing through his brain. As sweat trickled down his face, he felt the red and white walls closing in on him. Aggression levels running through him would be controlled right until he walked out of the field house, and once he stepped on the green grass the tears would fall uncontrollably. Not because he was sad, but because he was grateful that God gave him an opportunity to have an extended family with the football team. As he stepped onto the field, the switch was flipped. Football meant everything to him and was an outlet that gave him the freedom to escape from his problems and enter a place that brought complete fulfillment into his life. With his mother having passed on and his father gone like the wind, the gridiron became more than a game. It became his life. "Coach Perrone had a great heart. He cared about the players and the program. I felt he could have done a better job of preparing kids to go beyond his program. But for the little money he made, a lot of hours go with his title. When I lost my mom, Coach had every player attend my mom's funeral and that was very special to me."

He clearly remembered his first day at Salem High. Coach Perrone spotted him walking the halls. Perrone had the ability to make new students feel at home, especially potential football players. He instantly brought Downes to The Pride Room. Downes was amazed by the tradition of the program and the energy of Perrone. At that moment he wanted to be part of Perrone's football family.

With a team of mediocre athletes with very little experience and no depth, Salem was not given much of a chance, nor did they deserve one. They were already winners in their own minds. From offensive lineman Dennis Dulong who weighed 155 pounds to defensive lineman Ryan Daley, they feared no one. These kids did not possess the skills of Floridians or the passion of the Texans, but they did have pride. Throughout it all, one thing was certain. Autumn never sleeps in Massachusetts, and its football tradition and success goes deep into the Bay State. Their own coaches were hoping for a winning record. The two-a-days and Heritage Day Parade in August had come and gone, and the scrimmages were in their rearview mirror. Now came the season, the one hundred and second season.

THE PEABODY TANNERS

Perennial power Peabody lurched hungrily in the horizon. This game marked the seventy-fifth game played between the schools. The Peabody seniors did not have to be reminded about playing the lead role in *Down You Go* for three straight years vs. Salem. We had given Peabody their only blemish on their Super Bowl Championship team the year before, shocking them 13 to 7. The game was non-league and Peabody, number two in the state, was a three-touchdown favorite. Outside of Thanksgiving, this was the biggest rivalry and was good preparation for the Northeastern Conference, which was one of the toughest leagues in the state.

"They will be coming for your heads. Have fun and play with class." Perrone exclaimed, "When you score, no celebrating, Mercado, Rodriguez, and Freeman!" Calling out to his offensive weapons. "Act like you have been there before." With the team making its way out of the locker room, I focused on my left inner forearm. I wrote the words OWA in permanent black marker. My grandmother was on my mind. I thought about the sacrifices she made for her family. I knew how much she wanted to be there watching me.

One of Perrone's concerns was shutting down the best multi-sport athlete in the state, Peabody QB, Steve Lomasney. "He's a coach's dream," Perrone said. Peabody, coming off a convincing 34-8 win over Everett, had first-game jitters out of their system.

With two minutes left in the half, Peabody demonstrated why they were second in the state. Lomasney and his receivers started clicking with a short passing game. A 30-yard draw put the Tanners well into Salem territory. Peabody moved the 58 yards in just over a minute. Rage-filled, Downes let his emotions get the best of him. Grabbing a lineman's face mask and calling him every name in the book resulted in a personal foul with 32 ticks in the half. The next play, a scrambling Lomasney tossed a fade ball and Mccellon was in great position, but Peabody's big tight end got leverage on him to pull it in for six. Fans on the Salem side were irate, thinking both the receiver's feet were out of bounds. The point after try (PAT) was no good. 6-0 Peabody.

Frustration was all over our sidelines. On their next two possessions, Perrone gave the nod to Sullivan to take the QB reins. Sullivan was playing a solid game on the defensive side of the ball, but did not have the same luck on offense. He fumbled on the first series and threw an interception to end the game.

HEY, STIFF

"I'm walking home."

"With your pads on?"

"Ya, man. This is my dream, and this is my life." I walked off, sulking. The feeling of rejection running through me, I kept my uniform and helmet on for the entire 2.6-mile walk. I started to second-guess my decision to not transfer to Bishop Fenwick. It would have been a fresh start with no politics. Perrone promised me and my dad a fair shot right before I was going to transfer. Maybe all the critics were right that this kid would never get a realistic chance to lead the Witches. I slowly walked through the hilly Gallows. Reaching out to God, I prayed for an opportunity. I wanted it for Owa, my parents, my brothers, and myself. Reaching into my soul, I searched for answers. I decided to channel my aggressions into hard work and faith.

Making my way into my neighborhood, Witchcraft Heights, a car slowly stopped and a group of young adults started laughing at me and made the remark, "Hey, stiff, it's not Halloween,"

Sitting in church the next day, listening to the choir, I knew that all things are possible through God. The church bells touched my soul, nourishing my faith. The glory of the Holy Spirit shined within me. With Owa's hand on mine, she channeled any negative thoughts from me and replenished me with conviction. She lifted my spirits up which enabled me to focus and go live my dream.

It was only round one and I had a lot of fire in me. No final bell had rung; I refused to shy away. There would be no backing down. I would treat this week of practice like I was getting ready to play in the Super Bowl.

Curtin smiled ear-to-ear reading the *Salem News* sports page the following Monday in his office located in the Middle School West. Rocking back in his chair, he started laughing after seeing the Salem/Peabody score. "13-0. Looks like this will affect Perrone's cumulative record." Curtin thought of Perrone as a carpetbagger with his big ego, self-absorption, and self-promotion. Curtin as the hometowner was entrenched in the Salem sports crowd.

CHAPTER 7

MR. HUSTLE

> *"The greatest accomplishment is not in never falling, but in rising again after you fall."*
>
> ~ *Vince Lombardi*

The Danvers game marked the first conference game of the season and had major relevance in terms of having aspirations of post-season play. Perrone, in thirty-seven years as a head coach, had never opened the season 0-2. The last time Salem had successive Bertram field losses was 1976.

Mark Bavaro, the biggest name in Danvers history, played in the early 1980s. He went on to play nine years in the NFL, win two Super Bowls, and two Pro Bowl selections. Perrone informed his team several times during the week that Danvers had not beaten them in the past decade. "Boys, think how it would make you feel if we lost ten straight to an opponent." Holding up the newspaper, he declared, "Play with a chip on your shoulder."

"We are the underdogs," shouted Captain Higley. "I don't know about you guys, but I am pissed off."

Danvers was looking to make a statement early in the season that they would not be a stepping stone for the Witches. We did not dwell on the loss to Peabody. Perrone did not panic. He continued preaching about preparation and execution. He kept repeating to us how important it was to stick together and take one game at a time. He had the ability to put a spin on certain situations, kind of a reverse psychology. Prior to taking the field, Perrone would hold up newspaper clippings to stir up the team. He would convey his message in a way that made each player feel that he was speaking directly to them. The majority of the time, his team would wear a bullseye on their backs, but he would motivate in a way that they would make the game special. To him it was really personal as he resided in Danvers and his own children had attended Danvers High. He realized a loss would not sit well, especially when he ate breakfast in Danvers Town Square every Sunday morning.

TALKING TREASON

The storm the night before had left the field slippery. It was the beginning of a possible nor'easter. Not only was the weather not cooperating, but the Salem teachers union proposed a three-year contract with a 22 percent salary increase: 5 percent the first year, 7 percent the second year and 10 percent the third. This created tension among the administration and hit them like a category 5 hurricane.

Several of the administrators sat around the table having breakfast at Red's Sandwich Shop, questioning the teachers' rationale for their unrealistic proposal. Where do they think we are going to get 22 percent? Each administrator took turns stating possible theories, and some even estimated when a strike was going to begin. One member was outraged not only in the demands but the threats the teachers were making. One thing that they could all agree on was that the teachers' request was comical.

In the meantime, the beginning of the Danvers game was benign. I waited patiently and got my turn at QB late in the first quarter. I handed off to Mercado, who used his track skills to outrun the rest of the defense for a 51-yard touchdown. It took five quarters to score, but the ice was broken. The fiesta started in the end zone with a fired-up De Pena hugging Mercado and then the rest of the offensive unit joined the celebration. This very moment became symbolic; we became unified. It was two plays earlier that left the Salem coaches stunned. With a torn-up field, Rodriguez turned the gridiron into his own personal ice rink, spinning like a figure skater on ice and then ducking to avoid another tackle. This is when he was given the name The E-Train by Coach Stellato.

It was apparent he was getting better with each rep. He was hindered by a turned ankle but he had all the makings to become an "every down" back. The toughness and ability was clear. With only 11 yards the game before, it was a long week for him, but now he was ready to become the backbone of the offense.

"Ouch! Me Doble El tobillo, (Ouch my ankle is hurting)!" he said to Canelo in Spanish. Danvers moved the ball 70 yards to Salem's 5-yard line where they faced 4th and goal. Facing a similar scenario as the week before, Danvers called an out and up pass, but Matt 'Big Play' Bouchard, at the last tenth of a second, batted the ball down.

Perrone used a combination of misdirection as Rodriguez, Mercado and Freeman sliced through the defense. We faced 4th and 2 from our own 24-yard line with under a minute remaining. The E-Train took the counter and eluded several defenders as Mercado cut the DB before being brought down at the 12-yard line. With the rain falling, I faked the dive to Mercado who was immediately tackled. De Pena stemmed his corner route inside so he had plenty of area to work. Rolling to my right, I threw a duck to the back corner of the end zone plopping into De Pena's hands for a score. It was a moment that I will never forget. Running to the sideline, I felt like I was dreaming. I tried to act like I had been there before. I had in my preparation; I had in my dreams.

In the locker room at halftime, my brother patted me on the helmet, "Turn that inch into a mile." My confidence was soaring and my flame rekindled.

As for Rodriguez, he was icing his ankle which concerned the coaches. The E-Train wanted to build off his performance from the first half. Perrone and his six assistants were not fazed by a 12-0 lead. They were shocked by how physical Danvers was. Chunks of mud scattered on the locker room floor, uniforms drenched with sweat and rain, and eye black smeared on faces made them much more aware that games are won on the field and not in the newspaper.

The second half was a slosh fest in the mud. After numerous exchanges of possessions, I kicked a field goal from 30 yards making the score 15-0 with 4:36 in third period.

Moments later, Danvers took advantage of penalties, moved deep into our territory, and scored on a 24-yard strike by Matt Munzing to wide receiver Steve Crowe to make it 15-6. Danvers attempted a two-point conversion. Munzing faked the dive and ran the option. With DE Leopaldo coming down the line, he optioned the ball to running back J.M. Flint who was angling for the end zone. Downes lurched like a tiger waiting for his prey in the wild with the mindset that he was participating in the Oklahoma drill in practice, a physical tackling drill that was part of our routine. Downes unleashed a bone-crushing hit. Their two-point conversion failed by inches.

In the fourth, Danvers moved the ball to Salem's 20-yard line. Fans started booing as Sullivan's diving interception, was called back because of a Salem penalty. Munzing hit wide receiver Brian Wilichoski on a slant. Making his way towards the end zone, Sullivan came out of nowhere and popped the ball out inches from the goal line.

FLATLINE

Mr. Hustle, Mark Higley, collided with a Danvers player, sending him airborne. Higley eventually landed on the football in the end zone. A flash of red light went off in his head as he lay with the ball in the end zone, taking him back to a time a year earlier when his brother, Mike, was in ICU and flatlining.

All he could think of was the lack of electrical activity due to a case of spinal meningitis which caused gangrene to set in. Higley walked into his bedroom and wanted to wake his brother up. His brother was still in bed, and he gave him a weird look. His eyes were half open, and fatigue was written all over his face. Mark felt if he did not leave him alone, he was going to catch a beat down. The words "what if" kept running through his head. What if he woke his brother up? What if he questioned why his brother was still in bed? What if? No matter what anyone said, he still wanted the answers; if his brother had been seen six hours earlier, could they have stopped the disease from spreading? Instead, a year out of his brother's life was spent in the hospital resulting in the loss of his legs and four of his fingers. It was only a year ago that he left his brother alone sleeping, not realizing the distress he was in.

Starting in middle school, Mark walked a mile to get to school. He loved the fall season. It was when he altered his route so he could walk across Bertram Field. He could smell football in the cool crisp New England air, and the sound of the crunching leaves brought his mind back once again to the gridiron. Daily, he would walk across the high school football field with the cheering crowd in his mind. An enormous rock stood in the south end zone and it was there he made himself at home and he would eat his breakfast high above the field. During his quiet mornings alone with his thoughts, he would dream about being part of something special on the field. The foundations of his dreams were created at this very moment. He saw two brothers tossing a football and paused, taking a deep breath. He thought back to his childhood in his backyard when his older brother, who had four years on him, taught him how to take a hit. "My brother ran over me ten consecutive times. He completely annihilated me and made me think twice about wanting to play." That is where Higs learned the basic law of physics. His brother taught him as long as you go as hard as you possibly can and hit the person in front of you, that makes the battle equal.

He did not attend parties; it was not for him. Higley kept to himself. His coaches harped on how alcohol was poison and counterproductive. Attention deficit hyperactivity disorder (ADHD) contributed to his low grades and he often wondered if the standards by the coaches could have been set higher for academics. "Coaches told me to hit my opponent as hard as I could and I did. If they told me to get B's, that is the standard. I would have."

He sacrificed every fiber in his body when he crossed the bridge that took him out of a civilian life and into the land of organized violence. "Go hit someone" was his motto. "That is what I love to do. I remember hitting a linebacker so hard that a burning feeling started at the tip of my nose, then flowed out the rest of my face and into my head. My teammates are screaming, then I would get a déjà vu feeling like 'Hey, I have been here before.' Then I would glance to my left and Willie Jones would be asking me, 'What do I do?' on the next play. I barely even knew who he was. Concussions came often, but he played through them."

The referee signaled touchback as Salem fans' hearts came out of their throats. An exuberant Salem defense ran off the field. Salem picked up consecutive first downs. The chains were moving, but was the clock ticking fast enough? On 3rd and 22, Freeman took the toss left and went nowhere. Danvers signaled timeout with 3:07 left forcing Salem to punt.

Coach Marcoulier lived by the motto "Offense wins games, defense wins championships." With the offense struggling in the second half, he put the game on the defense, "Let's go drop the hammer, boys." Apparently those words did not stick. It took one 30-yard completion to move the ball to Salem's 15-yard line. Mercado tweaked a knee and DB Corey Perry, who was out all week battling strep throat, was thrown into the fire in the final 50 seconds. The Danvers coaches found our Achilles heel and exposed Perry as Crowe ran an out-and-up for his second TD of the game. The point after was good, which closed the gap to 15-13.

Walking to the sidelines with their heads down, a frustrated Perrone gave the defense an ear full. I waited patiently on the sideline as the hands team made their way onto the field. We recovered the onside kick and it was game over, escaping and avoiding history as the first team under Perrone to start the season 0-2. On the bus ride back to the high school, the team sang a victory chant. I sat in the back of the bus reflecting on my contribution to the win. My body bruised and battered, I had all the remedies and medication to feel better quickly: a win against a skilled Danvers team.

The Monday *Salem News* sports page stuck out like a sore thumb on Curtin's desk. The headlines read, "Rodriguez, the 'E' train, right on time for Salem" and moving his eyes to the right of the page were the bold letters, "Stellato FG decides it." Curtin shook his head in disgust. "Salem had never started 0-2 in the Ken Perrone Era - this is his 22nd year here – and when it was mentioned Saturday, the Witches' coach said he has not been 0-2 to open a season in 37 years as a head coach," said Perrone.

"Sure, you would know that statistic. I bet he reminded Bill Kipouras it was his 248th win too," a frustrated Curtin revealed. His phone started ringing.

"Mr. Curtin, Mayor Harrington is on line one."

"Ed, I just got the word from the labor negotiator Dan Kulak that the union wants a 22 percent raise," said Harrington.

"Neil, what is this about the teachers looking for 22 percent? This is pretty insufferable." The breathing started to get heavy and tempers were ready to flare. Harrington started yelling, "They are nuts if they think they are going to get 22 percent."

"What if they strike?" Curtin replied. "Any teacher that wants to threaten me and stand in those picket lines will be fired."

At this point Harrington knew he had to make a name for himself and getting off course from the substance of the city teachers and kids would enter into his thought process. "Neil, this is a double–whammy, getting hit with an obnoxious request from the Union compounded with more Perrone self-aggrandizement in the newspaper," Curtin stated. Curtin would have to choke down the union and Perrone at the same time.

Putting the phone down, all Harrington could think of was not living in his father's shadow. Looking at a picture of his dad gave him a sense of relaxation. Kevin Harrington was a legendary Division I basketball player who started at St. Louis University. He rose to the position of senate president and served twenty years in the legislature of Massachusetts. He was responsible for Salem State College being developed and making improvements in public education from kindergarten through public college. He was chairman of the special education committee in the 1960s. This committee reorganized all the public colleges and gave them state college status. Before the reorganization, they were primarily just teacher colleges, and only offered education majors. He went into the private sector and had his own consulting and lobbying firm for several years after that.

Mike Harrington, his father's cousin, was a Harvard graduate and state representative. He was a member of the Massachusetts House of Representatives 6th Essex District (Essex County) during the 1960s and 1970s and is now the owner of the majestic Hawthorne Hotel. Michael's father, Joseph, served in the legislature and also was the mayor of Salem in 1948 and 1949, then became a presiding justice in the Salem District Court. Dr. Nancy Harrington, yet another cousin, was the former long-term President of Salem State College. The Harrington's had a political power base in Essex County, which was essentially concentrated in Salem. As the Kennedy family was to Massachusetts, the Harrington's were to Essex County. Mayor Neil Harrington was just not the mayor of a city of 37,988. The man was a rising star and destined to inherit long-term security in the Salem Mayoral seat until such time as he could run for the state senate and take over his dad's seat. His name was always on the short list of the 6th

Congressional District as congressman. He was the Golden Boy of the Massachusetts Democratic Party. There was no limit to how high and fast this guy could go. Family did so much, and Salem was filled with three generations of Harringtons.

In 1989, at the age of thirty-three, he became the youngest mayor in Salem history. Right out of the gate he walked with swagger in his home city. By using the grant money that was available through the state and local governments, his main priority was to make improvements in the city. He was able to do a lot of infrastructure projects, one being working with the Peabody Essex Museum to do a major expansion in the city.

Curtin was part of a symbolically equivalent group in Salem to the Hoosiers' barbershop pundits in the sense that for multiple decades, the sports achievers of Salem were political activists and public office-holders. Having an outsider like Perrone broke the mold.

CHAPTER 8

E-CONTENDER

"What could be better than walking down the street in any city and knowing you're the heavyweight champion of the world?"

~ *Rocky Marciano*

The last time Lynn Classical beat Salem in Lynn under the lights was 1980. That was called bulletin board material. Salem had beaten Classical ten out of the past twelve meetings. Facing one of the pre-season favorites, the Lynn Classical game would tell Perrone where his team stood. "They have a stable of backs, the best depth at running backs in the league. They've got the intangibles that make a champion, the size and speed that everybody fears. We can't let this team get outside on us" (*Salem News*, September 31, 1994). What Perrone didn't reveal was his opinion on his own backs, particularly The E-Train.

THE E-TRAIN

On the other side of the city down at The Point, a different way of life was what several of the team's players were accustomed to. Standing only over a quarter mile long, it was densely populated with 2,815 residents. The household income was about $20,000 less than the average household income in Salem. Most of the apartment buildings stood closely next to each other with flat rooftops. The sidewalks were cracked from harsh winters and never repaired. Weeds filled yards, and buildings were tagged with graffiti. A courtyard on Prince Street sat vacant, resembling a landfill. Clothes hung on front porches. Robbery, violence, and drug dealings were a common way of life. Broken glass and used syringes sat at the edge of the shoreline at Palmer's Cove.

The Historic Salem Tour Guide trolley stood clear of the bridge on Congress Street that led into The Point. Some fought for respect, others pushed drugs to live. These kids were trained to survive, using football as an opportunity to fly from the nest, similar to what their parents did by leaving the Dominican Republic for the U.S. to give their families more. Most had just raw talent and were blessed with skills to excel. They came from single-parent families and would come home only to fend for themselves while their moms were working two to three jobs to keep a roof over their head. Their fathers were as extinct as dinosaurs, gone and forgotten. One particular player had all the talent in the world and terrorized defenses. His name was Elvin Rodriquez, more popularly known as The E-Train.

The kid looked like he was twenty-two, but was seventeen. His legs were like tree trunks thanks to the miles he walked to and from school. His circumstances were much different from mine. His mom, Maria, immigrated to Salem from the Dominican Republic when he was a baby and spoke very little English. Being hungry was a common thing, and Elvin would often sprinkle Orange Tang on bread to give it some sizzle. He would always make sure that the Orange Tang and bread were sealed tight. This made him comfortable, and there would be no surprises like when he would pour out some not-so-Lucky Charms and cockroaches would sprinkle out. Santa Claus never existed in his mind or at his home. His mom knew one thing and that was to work. She did not have time to wrap presents. There were six of them in that small apartment on Harbor Street.

Summers were almost unbearable with no air conditioner and lack of air filtering he opted to spend many nights out on the streets. He slept with winter hats and sweatshirts throughout the winter because the heat would often go out and the oven would only let out so much heat. He shared a room with his mother, but as he matured, he found himself on the plastic red couch in the living room. This gave him the feeling of staying close to his late brother, whose large portrait hung on the wall.

He thought about him every day; he could still visualize his last breath. "The bus was going too fast as he crossed the street on his bike. He never had a chance." His eyes filled up as he clenched a football. "He was my inspiration." The small picture he inserted under his wristband was starting to fade, but the memories never would. He had no push from a father, no relationship with him either, and often a beat-down or black eye from his older brother. He looked up to his brother and tried to reach out to him for answers, but his brother had his own issues, throwing a desk at a teacher and getting expelled while attending Salem High. He did ten years in jail and Elvin often felt he was following in his brother's footsteps. He needed to get respect at a young age and that is what he did. As much as his late brother was Elvin's inspiration, there existed a motivation keeping The E-Train in school and on the field. He was the proud father of Alvin, a toddler who attended all the games and, to the entertainment of all, constantly imitated his dad by practicing kickoffs.

He punked kids and put fear in people. It all came down to survival. He was arrested twice before the ninth grade. He was facing a two-year sentence for assault. With lack of structure and stability at home, and legal problems, he knew he had to change. Coach Perrone enabled him to develop, especially during his sophomore season. Perrone broke down football for him as organized violence, but at the same time, rode him every rep in practice. Perrone required him to run laps for busted assignments. Perrone focused on the gifts The E-Train possessed and turned him from a confused and nervous sophomore to a gladiator his junior season. The kid was paving the way for other kids from The Point community. Kids looked up to him and now wanted to play football. He was an icon to The Point community. Seeing the light, he realized that going to school and excelling on the field could get you a first-class ticket off the streets. He was always at practice and games, which kept him ever occupied, tired, and off the streets.

Every time he touched the ball, he thought he could score. To him, a "carry" was a street fight he was determined not to lose. He did not look at any of this as adversity, but life lessons that were molding him to be successful in the game of life. That allowed him to set goals and have dreams. In the end, it was bringing him closer to his dream of getting a college scholarship. He couldn't get that dream out of his head.

One thing was for certain, with only two night games on the schedule, Salem would be all jacked up to play at Lynn's Manning Bowl.

We had yet to give up a rushing touchdown in two games and would be put to the test by the Lynn Classical offensive line that averaged 260 pounds. Salem had yet to face anyone with Classical's size on the offensive line.

Perrone sat in his office thinking back to the 1991 game when Salem was undefeated and Classical came in and won 8-7. "What do I say to these kids?" Perrone wondered.

At 4 PM Friday afternoon, September 30, three hours before kickoff, Perrone wrote "Contender" on the board in the locker room. He looked at each player and coach in the room. "We've got a big challenge ahead of us tonight. For the third week in a row, we are picked to lose. We are getting no respect. Like a young up-and-coming prize fighter, you need to go out and earn it. This game will tell us a lot of what type of team we are. Let's send shock waves through the entire Northeastern Conference that we are a serious contender. There will be roadblocks along the way, but a true contender will take those obstacles, crush them into gravel, and walk over them. You boys will pave that road which will make you true contenders in life. In whatever you choose to do, moments like this will shape your destiny. I do not want to be looked at as a welterweight pretender, but as one group of seventy heavyweights that refuse to give up and are tough to beat." At this point, every player in the room was zoned in on Perrone. "This is not just about winning, but about believing in yourselves. That when you look in the mirror you like what you see. Every day when I wake up I realize I am in my own ring and I focus on being the best Christian, husband, father, and coach I can be. Temptation can bite us all in the butt, but what it comes down to is controlling your emotions and being disciplined."

Coming off a dynamic week of practice was in Salem's favor. Perrone always believed the games were won during the week. The coaches left the locker room early so the captains could address the team in private. Higley's eyes were bulging out of his head. Standing on the locker room benches, he screamed out the words, "Seventy deep can't be beat. Nothing to lose, boys!" Holding up a picture of the "Swami" from the newspaper who predicted Salem to lose for the third straight week left the players crazed. Several players took turns shredding it, like a group of wolves attacking their prey.

By game time, Manning Bowl was rocking. Coach Wilbur liked wearing hats. It gave him the feeling of being back on the pitcher's mound during his collegiate days while playing for Ottawa University in Kansas. As he placed his Salem cap back on his head, he addressed his defensive ends. The cap, to him, was like Dorothy putting on her red ruby slippers. However it would not physically bring him back to Kansas, but it would mentally allow him to be back in the game. Watching former New England Patriot and Kansas native QB Steve Grogan lead his high school team to the state final inspired Wilbur to want to coach at the high school level. Wilbur was always focused and prepared. He knew football was about adjustments and related it to a game of chess. "I was a small part of a big machine, the element of surprise always kept us on our feet when Perrone's offense took the field," Wilbur stated.

Salem received the ball first and instantly fell apart. On the very first offense play, I fumbled the exchange from center, but recovered. The next play we were called for being offside. Two running plays went for three yards and we were forced to punt. The E-Train had his under-the-light jitters, fumbling on the next two consecutive series. In spite of all the mishaps, Salem knew they could play with the Rams after a scoreless first quarter.

Lynn Classical picked up momentum in the beginning of the second quarter. James Magner slipped into the flat and zigzagged through the Salem defense, leaving Sullivan and Freeman tackling air. Classical took a 7-0 lead. We desperately needed a break and got it with three minutes left in the half. Torpedoes Dennis Dulong and Ryan Daley kamikazed into the Rams' punt returner, forcing a fumble. The ball rolled to the 42-yard line and Higley recovered it.

The E-Train developed a case of amnesia and quickly forgot about the two fumbles. Operating out of the Double Wing-T for the first time during the game worked to Salem's advantage. The E-Train scored on a 30-yard TD run and I converted the extra point, tying the score at 7-7 with 2:31 in the half.

We forced a punt on the ensuing series. The punt hung up high with the stars and the Manning Bowl lights. A.J. Grimes patiently waited and fielded the punt at Salem's own 24-yard line. He broke up the right sidelines, reversed field, and was finally taken down at the Rams' 21. This set up my 20-yard field goal from the right hash. The kick was good and Salem took the lead 10-7 as time expired to end the first half.

"That is how you battle back from adversity," Perrone told the players at halftime. The turning point came in the third quarter when The E-Train express accelerated for a 48 yard TD, giving the Witches a 16-7 lead and sending the Rams into self-destruction.

Late in the fourth quarter, the Witches were hungry-not just for a win, but for the pizza, which Coach Marcoulier rewarded to the player who had an interception, fumble recovery, or forced a fumble. Freeman stepped in front of a Jeff Waldron pass and returned the interception 30 yards, carrying two defenders into the end zone. Twenty-four seconds later, Downes really wanted to make his presence felt in his hometown. Disguising a blitz, he dropped back into coverage and picked off a Waldron pass and returned it for a 35-yard score. Crossing the 10-yard line, he lifted his right arm to the sky in honor of his late mother. Sullivan paved the way with his interception that set up a 30-yard TD by Ryan.

When the game was over, the score was Salem 37, Lynn Classical, 7. Perrone told the boys they earned the right to be called contenders. "You guys could have collapsed after the first quarter, but you fought your way back in the game and are still in contention to win a championship." He told the boys how proud he was of them.

Rodriguez limped off the bus and into the locker room. Near the end of the third quarter, he took a helmet off his already-tweaked wheel and it swelled up like a balloon. He will always remember playing his first night game. It was not just the 155 yards and two touchdowns, but the feeling of victory. He lay on the bench in the locker room with his ankle wrapped in ice. His eyes closed, he was just grateful for the moment. Meanwhile, the small parking lot at the Moose Hall was overflowing with cars indicating that the Teachers Union was yet again at their headquarters having another meeting. Salem Teachers Union President Wayne Turner rubbed his hand through his mustache as he patiently waited to address the union members. Although it was the beginning of October, the air was still mild and the crowd was eager to listen. Some members of the Salem Teachers union, which represented 508 teachers, paraprofessionals, and chapter 1 staff, voted to give the union's negotiating team authorization to call for a strike vote if no progress was made in negotiations by December 31 when the contract expired. They were ready to begin the strike, but it was not unanimous. A strike vote taken that same day by the union membership failed.

Picking up the *Salem News* early Saturday morning and opening up the sports page, Curtin could not believe his eyes as he read the headlines "Fourth-quarter explosion paces Salem 37-7." Turning the page he had a good chuckle reading another headline, "Win has Witches thinking Super."

"It's only week three. What are they getting excited about?"

CHAPTER 9

MANUEL

―――――――――――――――///―――――――――――――――

> "Coaches who can outline plays on a black board are a dime a dozen. The ones who win get inside their players and motivate."
>
> ~ *Vince Lombardi*

The Swami, who predicted games each week in the *Salem News*, had a bruised ego and would be losing his shirt if Vegas betting had been involved. Picking the Witches to lose the last three weeks opened his eyes. He made it very clear that he was showing his trump card and dying to know whether the Witches got a full house that would send him reeling, or if they were just bluffing. From now on, Salem would be the pick every week. No exceptions.

Pressure is something many football coaches and players need to deal with on a regular basis, whether it was to keep your job as a coach or capitalize on that big play that wins a game. Perrone had accomplished many milestones in his thirty-seven years as a head coach, including posting win number 100 against Marblehead in his first year at Salem twenty-two years ago. He did not like to discuss wins even if he was at 249 going into Saugus. The big thing was it showed longevity.

Saugus knew a thing about records. Theirs was in the opposite direction and they had lost twenty-seven straight games. They hadn't won a game since October 26, 1991. To add to this tornado of a streak, Salem started them off on their run downhill November 2, 1991, with a 39-0 trouncing. Deep down inside, Perrone was petrified that his team started the losing skid for them and could be the one that ended the losing streak as well.

On a beautiful, sunny Saturday afternoon, The E-Train took Salem's third play from scrimmage and was met by a host of Saugus defenders. He was starting to understand physics as he lowered his shoulder, pancaking them, and went 54 yards for a TD. After beating Lynn Classical in that blowout the previous week, they were determined not to make history.

On Saugus' next possession, Leopoldo recovered a fumble at their 24-yard line. With Saugus' band playing the song "Tequila," QB Sullivan signaled The E-Train in motion on 4th and 1. Faking the dive to fullback Ryan Daley, Sullivan went 13 yards for his first varsity TD. My extra point was good making it 14-0.

Our defense forced a three and out. The ball was placed at Saugus' 30-yard line. The sun was reflecting off the gold lettering of the football. I wiped my moist hands on Cronin's towel and licked the tips of my fingers as I approached the line of scrimmage. I was a stickler on detail and kept my fingernails cut short to improve my grip on the ball. De Pena was split wide left. His glasses were fogged up from a combination of trash talking of the Saugus defense and the humidity. He had the swag, intellect, and raw ability to reach new heights.

A Saugus defensive back got into press coverage, jarring the words, "Are you a coon or a spic, De Pena?"

The words ricochet off his thick skin. Despite characteristics De Pena was labeled with, he was indeed much different, especially from the people he hung with. He was an articulate kid who constantly analyzed before reacting. He never realized at first the weight football carried in terms of creating opportunities. But when he stepped on

Bertram Field to play in his first varsity game as a sophomore against Winthrop he was ready, catching his first TD pass. This gave him the feeling he was flying and free. He bought into Perrone's philosophies and in return, he received a male role model. While minding his own business with his boys one night, a real life version of the movie *Higher Learning* was taking place down The Point. Several skinheads slowly made their way to Prince St. One carried a loaded shotgun and pointed it to the sky, firing shots while saying, "Spics, niggas, come out, come out!"

De Pena's crew counted the bullets and once the hand signal was given, which indicated they were out of ammo, the animals released from the cages. "No one was coming onto our turf and disrespecting us," De Pena said.

Growing up in Santo Domingo, the family owned property and was wealthy. His mom, Gertrudis, was thriving as a political journalist following the Dominican Revolutionary Party (PRD) Partido Revolucionario Dominicano. She was working closely with President Antonnio Guzman Fernandez, politicians, and well-known musicians. She belonged to the opposing political party and would rally against the government.

Dominican politics were much more aggressive and violent than the United States. The verbal and physical threats came often. When Manuel was back in DR, there was a time he remembered answering the phone and a very loud voice echoed telling him what horrific things that would be done to his mom if she did not leave the political party. His mom read his body language and sensed what had occurred. Melting into her arms, he felt helpless living in the middle of chaos. She did not want to stay in DR anymore. This is when he began to worry about his mom and learned what a strong person she was. He constantly reminded himself of this when things got hard. His mom worshiped her children and wanted to protect them, and having family in the states made her believe in the American Dream. The only caveat would be their dad would not be allowed to leave the country due to a previous legal incident.

The four of them made The Point in Salem their new home. "It was a two-bedroom apartment on Peabody St. We turned the kitchen into a bedroom, and my mom worked three jobs to scrape by. She taught us survival skills and to be self-reliant." De Pena was virtually silent around people, especially when he started wearing glasses at eight-years-old. People viewed this as a handicap. "Urkel" and "four eyes" remarks were recycled lines around the neighborhood. He distanced himself from people until one day, walking by The Point Day Care with his head held low and choked up on tears, a camp counselor could not help but stop him. He handed Manuel a nerf football. It was like a magic wand hit him. From that day on, he played football every day on the streets with his cousins The E-Train, Alex, and Edwin Canelo. He found a connection to something and grew seven inches. His football skills became his outlet and intimidated the bullies by how physical he was. He earned the respect of the drug dealers and pimps who would watch from their Audis and Mercedes. Drugs were very visible, but never pushed on him as he was encouraged to stay in school by the dealers. That's what he did. He had the genetic coding of a straight nerd getting A's and B's. Poetry was one of his hobbies. With no male role models he continued to take strides on his own while maintaining a chip on his shoulder. Running and football went hand in hand, 300 meter runs condensed the football field for him and the gridiron allowed him to set goals. He always had a hidden edge that would be ready when called.

On the snap, I faked the dive to Daley, then the counter to The E-Train, and took a three-step drop, heaving a bomb to De Pena. I was immediately hit on the release as De Pena was in a footrace with the defensive back and was tackled at the Saugus' 17-yard line for a pickup of 53 yards.

De Pena exploded up off the turf pounding his chest in

disappointment yelling, "My bad!" Walking back to the huddle looking at me, he just shook his head.

"Yo Manny, you getting slow on me with that rice and beans diet?"

"Hell no!" De Pena yelled.

Perrone instantly went into his bag of tricks, calling for the Statue of Liberty. The E-Train took the ball out of my hand and looked like he was back on the streets of The Point playing 'catch one catch all' as he juked several defenders and scampered 17 yards for a TD. Salem scored 20 points in the first 6:43 of the opening quarter and practically took the rest of the game off. Overall Salem incurred 89 yards on 11 penalties and was just 2 for 10 in third down conversions.

At halftime with Salem leading 20-0, we walked down to the baseball diamond and sat against the fence on the ground in an isolated area while the coaches held a meeting.

Perrone was furious by the senseless penalties and blown basic assignments. "Contenders go the distance. To be a champion you cannot take plays off; to be a champion in life it is about being consistent every day. Being honorable. When you say you are going to do something, do it. Look around, boys. You have made a commitment to each other." Perrone now knew the team's potential and was frustrated that the team hit the pause button.

Salem received the ball to start the second half. Mercado was getting great push from his line and picked up three consecutive first downs. I hit De Pena on a down and out for another first down. On the 13th play of the drive, Salem faced 3rd and goal and The E-Train was stopped. I attempted a 30-yard field goal into the wind which just missed left.

Saugus started to get some wind in their sails and they were moving the sticks. Downes was getting frustrated and took it out on Saugus QB Steve Poplawski as he came off the edge like a bazooka sacking him for a 10-yard loss to end the third quarter.

On the 15th play of the drive, Saugus faced 4th and inches from our 11-yard line. Marcoulier signaled an all-out blitz and stopped the Sachems dead in their tracks. With 4:27 left, Saugus got on the board. That was the first rushing TD against Salem that season. Salem went on to a 20-8 victory. With the team assembled around Perrone for post-game remarks, he did not scold the offense for getting shut out the second half, but praised the team for their effort.

Perrone was pleased his team was 3-0 in conference play. "That is more meaningful than any milestone." We might have gotten lackadaisical the second half, but Mercado was in sync, which was crucial because now there was another power back to compliment The E-Train.

As the warm October sun set on Stackpole Field, another memory was created for the mighty Witches. Salem side-stepped getting stung by the history bug as the Sachems' twenty-eight game losing streak continued.

The following Monday, Curtin picked up his morning coffee and inserted thirty-five cents into the newspaper machine. Unfolding it and opening the sports page, he spit out some of his coffee reading the headlines "Perrone gets 250th win." Tossing the paper in the trash, he continued on with his day.

CHAPTER 10

A Veteran's Cry

"Treat people the way you want to be treated and respect everyone"

~ Mike Eruzione

Autumn never slept in Massachusetts; with its rich history and beautiful countryside, it gave you a sense of completion. Throughout the year the seasons changed and one was able to take advantage of all the New England landscape has to offer. From dominant professional sports franchises to its high school rivalries that went back to 1882, it created a diversity of things to explore. New England high school football might have taken a backseat to Texas, Florida, California, and New Jersey in terms of skill, but its history and tradition was unmatched.

In 1994, again, it would be the battle of the conference unbeaten. Gloucester's legendary QB Jay Palazola's nephew Bryan would be leading the Fishermen.

Before leading his players onto the field, Perrone had one word for his players' "legacy." "The 1974 team left theirs. Very much like this team, we were constant underdogs. How do you boys want to be remembered?" History was made on this very field twenty years ago and it would be made again this day.

"Two decades have gone by. It's hard to believe it's been that long, but easy to remember," said Coach Marcoulier. Perrone called the 1974 Gloucester vs. Salem game the greatest football game he had ever been associated with. Just as baseball purists label Game 6 of the 1975 World Series "the greatest Series game ever played," Salem's "Super Showdown" one-point victory over Gloucester in 1974 deserves a similar classification.

It was a once-in-a-lifetime coaching experience. That game had everything. Both teams were 8-0. Cars were pulling in at 9 AM for a 1:30 kickoff. Gloucester's QB Jay Palazola was Notre Dame-bound and had all the makings of a Division 1 QB.

Trailing 6-0 at the half in the 1974 game, it took Salem longer than usual to get off the field and into the locker room because of the crowd. It was twenty, thirty, forty deep outside of the fence that the team had to pass through to get to their locker room. Marcoulier got to the locker room door and paused. Turning around he looked at the hill which was basically a rock in the south end zone. It was a piece of granite that rose approximately twenty feet high overlooking the field. It was covered with people.

After the coaches spoke about adjustments, Marcoulier made it a point to grab Perrone, informing him that he needed to address the team. Standing in front of the team, he preached to the players, "This game is not about you and me or Salem and Gloucester. It's about all those people out there. When you go out the door, don't look at the field. Look up on the hill and see those people on the rocks; they are cheering for you. It got me so fired up and the kids were amazed that I was not talking about football but was talking about the people, fans, parents, everyone that came to see this football game. The fans on the rocks stood cold, uncomfortable, but committed," said Marcoulier. Salem scored with six seconds remaining to win. "It was the biggest crowd I have ever witnessed at Bertram Field."

The three Salem captains Freeman, Higley, and Whitten held hands for the coin-toss. The referee tossed up the shiny 1994 coin in the air. They were ready for battle. It was a picture-perfect breezy and sunny day at Bertram Field. Salem was trying to make itself right at home on Homecoming Day and clearly establish itself as a legitimate NEC title threat. The color guard and band performed the Star Spangled Banner. With the flag blowing in the wind, Marcoulier's eyes started to tear. The American flag symbolized many things to him, but most importantly, the true meaning of being an American. Football gave him the confidence to be able to put his own life on the line for his country. He was more than a football coach. He was hero, a proud veteran who grew up as an Air Force brat and followed in his father's footsteps by enlisting in the military.

He coached kids to play fearlessly and with passion. His memories lived within him. One in particular was the chartered flight to Vietnam when the reality of going to war hit home. With over 330 lieutenants on the plane, he realized that the large number of lieutenant casualties required more replacements to be made available. The nightmares at the DMZ (Vietnamese Demilitarized Zone) haunted him every day. "The gunshots never stopped coming." As the verse of the "bombs bursting in air" played, he looked at all the kids on the field. He thought back to driving down the streets of Da Nang and seeing kids holding grenades one minute and blown to pieces the next. Often he traded fruit and candy for ammunition that the kids had found. The man always tried to analyze the situation first, be friends with the Vietnamese kids, and let them know he was not the enemy. Marcoulier has always been a decision-maker and a very good one.

With 5:38 left in the first quarter, I placed the field goal block on the right hash. The wind was blowing from left to right. It was a 22-yard chip shot and I missed wide right. The first play of Salem's next possession, Sullivan faked the toss right and went up off tackle for a pickup of 48 yards. Two plays later The E-Train took the counter and with a second effort, he broke the plane for six with 52 seconds remaining in the first quarter. The extra point attempt was blocked and for most of the second quarter, Salem was meeting Gloucester power for power.

I dropped back to pass and with the pocket collapsing, and I got sacked with 30 seconds remaining in the half. With no timeouts, Perrone signaled for the field goal team to attempt a 30-yarder. Unable to change into my kicking shoe, I would need to focus on technique. The clock ticking 10…9…8…7…6…5…4…the ball got snapped low. Sullivan placed it and I drove it through the uprights as time expired making it 9-0. I jumped up in the air. After missing a field goal and extra point earlier, I was now soaring with confidence slapping high-fives to my holder, snapper, and offensive line.

The second play into the third quarter, Gloucester tight end Vito Ferrara caught a drag route and Corey Perry timed it perfectly and flattened Ferrara, forcing him to fumble. It was the Fishermen's third turnover of the game.

Sullivan faked the dive, picked up a pancake block from The E-Train, and went 18 yards for the TD making the score 15-0. Marcoulier, realizing Gloucester needed points, switched to a 44 defense which was more conducive toward the pass. Downes got the signal from Marcoulier, looked at his wristband, and smiled. He was ready to come off the edge and he did just that, drilling QB Palazola. Whitten read his eyes as he tried to get rid of the ball, tipped it to himself, and went 33 yards for a TD. Just like that, Salem scored twice in 12 seconds to go up 21-0.

With a relentless ground attack, Salem was moving the ball up and down the field. Gloucester's defensive line was very strong and forced Salem to work for every yard. Facing 4th and 3 from Gloucester's 28-yard line, I faked the dive and with the OLB applying pressure, I threw a corner route to De Pena who made the adjustment for a TD reception.

We forced another turnover as Freeman lit up a Gloucester TE and Whitten recovered. Gloucester must have thought Halloween came early and they were playing in a haunted house. Nothing was going right for the Fishermen between turnovers and penalties. They closed out the game throwing a touchdown pass with less than a minute remaining to make it 27-8.

Our swarming defense ran its takeaway total to 21 on the season and Marcoulier would be buying five Engine House cheese pizzas for the defense. We played smash mouth football, rushing the ball 49 times for 286 yards. The Salem football team was starting to connect and was a group making a name for itself. That said a lot more than the Salem teachers union and the city.

WAR CRIES – October 17, 1994

Bright and early Monday morning as frost melted off Curtin's car, he slowly made his way to the Salem Newsstand. With his radio tuned to WEEI, he paid for the paper. He was shocked to read the front page of the sports section that read, "Salem has a Fish fry."

The sidewalks outside of the Collins Middle School were crammed with 200 teachers ringing cow bells, waving flashlights, and holding signs that read "Wanted: A Fair Contract for Salem Educators." It was the most animated rally to date with the sole purpose of getting public attention. The teachers union was adopting a strategy that had never been used before in Salem: public appearances in the community and reaching out to the parents.

More recently, a letter was sent to parents asking for their support in securing an "acceptable contract" for teachers. The letter asked parents to contact Mayor Harrington and the school committee and "tell them that you do not wish to see a disruption in the school year and that you support Salem's teaching staff and the Salem educational system." The union's message was clear: They wanted more money and were using external forces to leverage management. This was causing the pot to boil and the football team became more of a bargaining chip at this point in the season.

The following day, Perrone went along with his daily routine, opening his front door with his coffee in hand, reaching down for the local newspaper. He was startled by the headlines, nearly burning himself by spilling his coffee. Headlines read, "Teachers demand contract with raise." The union decided to take its cause to the public, issuing press releases explaining its position. The union criticized the city for giving raises to administrators, ranging from 10 to 25 percent, while not offering raises to teachers. The union also stated that salaries of Salem teachers were behind those of surrounding communities, earning between $3,000 and $6,000 less than neighboring schools. (*Salem News*, October 18, 1994)

Perrone forced himself to believe that if an agreement was not made, then the teachers would be going on strike after the fall season.

CHAPTER 11

RAY OF EMOTIONS

"Truth over Harmony."

~ Joey Gauld, Hyde School

Downes sat on an egg crate in the corner of the Bertram field locker room. His walk-man volume turned up and was listening to NAS. He loved music and used it as a way to relax. With the lyrics getting deeper, he reflected on a specific time growing up, a moment he keeps close to him. Smiling, he let out a deep laugh thinking about playing records in the living room and dancing with his mom. Touching "Mom" on his jersey, she was weighing on his mind. Standing up, he started rapping some words, but he couldn't get his eyes off the board. The words Senior Day, Respect, and 1976 looked like they were in 3-D. A part of him wished he could be walking on that field with his mom, like his fellow teammates, but the other half of him was grateful God had given him the opportunity to play a game he loved, a game that gave him a natural high. He appreciated his aunt who had become a great support system.

Salem was trying to preserve a series domination at home that had not allowed Marblehead to win at Bertram Field since 1976. With a solid week of practice, Perrone was confident that we would knock off the pre-season favorite to win the league.

On the other side of the locker room, The E-Train quietly knelt down on one knee. He was alone in his thoughts. The bullseye was on his back. Bowing his head, he began to pray for the seniors, that they could win their final home game, and pray that his ankle, hand and shoulder would hold up, allowing him to play to the best of his ability.

When the Witches took the field, they were greeted by a cool damp day. The skies were gray and the rain had stopped falling. Perrone felt, with Marblehead's speed, the field conditions would make it a slower track for them and enable Salem to do what it did best: play smash mouth football.

On Salem's first possession, we moved the ball well into Marblehead's territory. Facing 4th and 11, I signaled The E-Train in motion, he faked the dive to Mercado, and the defense bought into it, gang-tackling him. Rolling to my right I saw The E-Train open for six and planting my feet, I shifted my hips. Attempting to throw the ball, I got blindsided by a cornerback blitz. The ball popped up in the air falling incomplete as I went airborne, face-first. With a quarter pound of soil covering my facemask, Big Willie made his way over to help me to my feet.

The Witches D would be put to the test trying to stop Marblehead's running back duo, D1-bound Dan Healey and Jason Tarasuik. They had rushed for nearly 1000 yards, which was almost as many as the entire Salem High Football team.

Starting at its own 37, the Witches' fabulous front five, center Cronin, guards Higley and Dulong, and tackles Russell and Jones, went to work. This unit played with honor and glory. Five plays later, The E-Train followed Cronin into the end zone for a one-yard touchdown while the band performed the beats of *Superman*. The extra point was good. Salem 7, Marblehead 0.

The Marblehead coaching staff felt Salem's only weakness was their inability to stop the pass. It looked like they were right on their ninth play of the drive as they moved the ball to Salem's 5-yard line. Higley's hands were on his hips, Downes was pacing like a wild animal, Whitten was frustrated, and Perry was talking trash to the Marblehead receivers. The band was pumping out beats of *The Lion King* trying to inspire Salem's defense to pick up the aggression levels and play like lions instead of kittens.

On 1st and goal, Marblehead's running back took the handoff and Downes exploded through the gap, smothering the ball carrier as the ball landed into Salem linebacker Bouchard's hands.

After a Salem turnover of their own, Marblehead wasted no time moving the football down the field. Operating out of the Wing T, the ball was placed at Salem's 12-yard line, covered in mud. Freeman received the blitz signal. Off the field he was laid-back and quiet, but once he buckled that chinstrap, he was trying to bring tenacious hits. Freeman, a record-setter in the high hurdles, jumped over the cut block and timed up the double counter colliding into the running back just as he received the handoff. The ball lay on the ground and Leopoldo could smell the pizza as he dove on the ball. This incentive alone was a key motivator for some of the kids who lived on rice and beans and often went to bed hungry.

Salem led 7-0 at the half. "We did not bring our 'A' game. Respect is earned not given," Perrone told the team. "This is not just about winning and losing. It is to honor your mothers. Think about what they went through to have you. Play with sportsmanship and let your play do the talking." Both the offense and defense absorbed all the constructive criticism from their coaches.

Then Higley stood up and addressed the seniors. "Boys, this is the last time we will ever play on this field together. We are serious contenders and each week, we need to find a way to play like it. Starters, these seniors have devoted four years to this program. We need to find a way to get every senior in this game," said Higley. The team shouted with praise, and passion started to circulate.

Three plays into the second half, the domino effect was in full force as Jones pancaked the defensive end, and Freeman and Mercado bulldozing the linebacker and defensive back. The E-Train took the toss and this train burning 60 yards of grass before being knocked out of bounds inches from the goal line. The next play The E-Train scored untouched, and my point after was good, making it 14-0.

Controlling the football is the name of the game and that is what Perrone preached all week in practice. After a 15-play drive deep in the fourth, The E-Train took himself out of the game to make sure a senior got to carry the football. Jogging off the field in his mud-stained uniform, he was wearing an ear-to-ear smile. After 202 yards rushing, two touchdowns, and a 14-0 victory, his prayers were answered. Perrone displayed the meaning of sportsmanship having me take a knee 3 times inside the 3-yard line.

Salem seniors held hands and knelt in prayer at midfield after the game, thankful for their experiences at Bertram Field. "We didn't want to lose our last game here," Higley said. "It's hard to believe I won't play here again. Nine years ago I played my first game here."

Something special was being created before all of their very eyes. Perrone's job was to develop our skills, which would enable us to become more confident when we entered the real world. But what he was witnessing gave him overwhelming joy. A group of underdogs had worked as hard, if not harder, than any team he had ever coached, in terms of dedication and attendance, and came together to form a brotherhood.

Downes was the last one off the field. He was taking it all in. Turning around to get one more view of the scoreboard, he noticed it flashed on and off. He smiled and paused. "It was a way of my mom saying 'good game' and she was watching me." Hugging his aunt, he was just grateful for the moment. The thoughts of going to Lynn next week on Halloween weekend were already entering his mind but, for now, he would enjoy a hard-fought victory on Senior Day.

On Monday morning, Curtin continued his ritual of heading straight out the door to get the *Salem News*. He was well aware Salem won again, but was curious to see what the papers had to say about Perrone. "Salem earns respect, win" was displayed on the front page.

CHAPTER 12

STRIKE VOTE

"Love is the force that ignites the spirit and binds teams together."

~ Phil Jackson

LABOR NEGOTIATIONS

On Monday, October 24, 1994, both the city and union negotiating team sat patiently in the school committee chambers, located in the Middle School. Along the table, side by side, they would try to interact with each other. Paul Devlin, who was the president of the Massachusetts Federation of Teachers, sat at one end, while Dan Kulak, the attorney for the administration, sat at the other end. Turner, the president of the teachers union, was seated to the right of Devlin, and on Turner's right was Anne Marie DuBois, who was the representative from the MA Federation of Teachers to the Salem teachers union. She was Turner's direct link to whatever he needed pertaining to negotiations. To the left of Kulak was highly-respected Carl Peterson, the longest tenured member of the school committee. Mayor Harrington's seat was empty and Superintendent Curtin sat in the middle of the group.

It was a quiet meeting where the only ones allowed to speak were Devlin and Kulak. Kulak began to speak and Turner's stomach was turning as he listened to him read the city's proposal. The school committee countered with a proposal offering teachers a three-year contract with a one percent increase the first year and one percent increase with a three percent merit-based increase for each of the next two years. After reading a note passed from Turner which read "Disgusted," Devlin immediately called for a recess. Fifteen minutes later, the union rejected the offer and stayed firm with its original request for 22 percent. The school committee said it would take the counterproposal under advisement and would return with its response at the next scheduled negotiation session on November 9. The union, however, asked the school committee to meet sooner, within the week or over the weekend. The school committee refused. Disappointed, Turner exited the room. Walking down the hallway, Turner knew that the only alternative was to go on strike. With a thousand thoughts going through his mind, the only thing he could think about was the students and the impact it would have on them.

The following day at the Stellato household, we were celebrating my mother's birthday. The celebration was cut short because Michael had to attend a coaches meeting at the Knights of Columbus Hall. Even though Coach Stellato was not under contract as a Salem teacher, Perrone wanted all of his coaches in attendance.

Once the meeting got underway, Perrone did not waste any time and raised his hand asking for the opportunity to address the crowd. Standing before the assembly he introduced each coach and explained their dilemma. He emphasized that even though the season was at the halfway point his stance had not changed since the last time he spoke to the union membership back in August. He went on to make it clear that he and the coaches had made a commitment to the team, and that they would not waiver from that decision. In his speech, he touched on how coaching was directly connected to education and how it was an important part of a student's development in high school. The audience paid close attention and seemed moved by his words.

Wayne Turner closely observed the room as Perrone spoke. When Perrone finished, he handed the microphone to Turner. Wayne went on to say that teachers in the classroom are very similar to coaches of organized sports teams. Looking at the teachers who were sitting in front of him, he expressed his awareness of their abilities to be able to adapt to their students' learning styles. They had to mold their style of teaching to suit the needs of the various levels of learning. Turner declared, "Pertaining to football, you decide which kid would make a great tackle, and who would make a great guard. You make those decisions based on what would benefit the team and focus on developing each player so the team can be successful. The team plays better than they did before. Then the team executes and scores a TD and you look at the tackle making a great block, the running back reading the hole, and the QB following out his fake. The players on the sideline cheer for their teammate. You feel like a great coach. When you are in the classroom and see your students start doing well on tests or finally raising their hand in class to participate in the discussion when they have never done that before, and you are able to get some of the other kids in the classroom to become comfortable enough to finally raise their hand. Soon enough they stop skipping class, and they really begin to learn. That was my touchdown and last second victory regarding educating students. When that year is over and I see how things materialized, I am like a great season. I am a winner." Everyone in that room applauded Turner as unity filled the room.

Standing in front of the room, Turner was wearing the "union suit," as both he and Mazz referred to it. It was a dark blue pinstripe three-piece suit. The nickname "union suit" was an inside joke, being that he could not afford another suit to wear to meetings. Turner, a straight-shooter, had a sense of humor when he chose to use it. "I am in the union suit, so let's get down to the business for the day; I have Mazz's permission to wear this just in case I have to go downtown to the courthouse."

The union negotiating team called a special meeting of the union membership on October 28. Coincidentally, this was the same day as the biggest game of the season for the football team. A win would give them an opportunity to play unbeaten Swampscott. Management had to think now is the time to stop negotiating in good faith because it would force the union to strike or take what is on the table.

If they strike, they would screw their Golden Boy, Perrone. To protect Perrone and his team, they don't strike and have to accept what is on the table. Strategically, management knew Perrone had showed his hand. They knew he was going to coach regardless of what happened. This would be used as a political power play. Either way, Curtin was smiling, thinking he would get a favorable contract for the city from management's standpoint or finally get the last laugh regarding Perrone.

On the opposite side of the coin was the possibility that management did not want to negotiate in good faith and the union, realizing that, would force a strike, believing that if they were to strike now, it would be more publicized because of what was going on with the football team. They believed the public would rise up against the city administrators, therefore persuading them.

LABOR IN LYNN

Woody Hayes would have been proud of this Salem team. Many of their opponents and fans felt they adopted a "Thou shall not pass" commandment. With only 11 pass completions in six games, there were people wondering throughout the state if they had the balance and versatility to hang tough the rest of the way. The lack of a passing game did not concern Perrone, perhaps because he had a running attack that far exceeded Woody Hayes' "six yards and a cloud of dust" offense at Ohio State. The E-Train was averaging 7 yards per carry.

Perrone had much success with focusing on what his team did best and utilizing that. Opponents were stacking up the line of scrimmage. Salem still ran it. The only obstacle might be their mental state and touch of attitude.

Perrone was building a sound foundation on leadership. The root of peer pressure is at the highest during one's teenage years. He taught that it takes great leadership and the right values not to give into peer pressure. He made it a point that his players realized that their teenage years were limited, to utilize their youth because they would never get it back and to be responsible for their own actions. In return, his overachieving team embraced that concept and led by example to find themselves 5-0 in the conference. The path to the championship would have to go through Manning Bowl, and Lynn English's motto at 1-5 was "Nothing to Lose" as they tried to knock off a contender there. Bad blood was created last year after Salem won 56-0, which was the second highest number ever put up against English. "What goes around comes around" were the words from Bulldogs coach Gary Molea to his team all week. Molea did not appreciate a defensive starter, Downes, scoring the final touchdown in that last game, even if he was playing with the third unit. "They could have taken a knee." English almost knocked off league leader Swampscott. They had a big tough defense that played well against the run with great team speed and strong guys on the offensive line. But it was the Witches' night, with the band traveling with them, which was uncommon on away games. They would be bringing their broomsticks on Halloween weekend.

Higley was nervous. All 178 pounds patiently waited to take the field. English defensive lineman Mike Stackpole was on his mind, all 309 pounds of him. Higley was a lightweight but was well-prepared for this heavyweight. Mentally he could not lose, and physically he was fearless. Buckling his chinstrap, he started to breathe heavily; his hands were sweating. He refused to overlook this team. Critics looked at this game as an appetizer before the entrée which was the Swampscott game the following week. He knew better than anyone that there were no guarantees in life. Seeing his brother enter the stadium, his heart started to beat harder, bringing him to an adrenaline rush.

As the National Anthem got underway, Mercado gazed up into the stars. He shut his eyes and hummed the words. The sacrifices his mom had made enabled him to go after his dreams. She worked double-shifts seven days a week, but always made sure she was home every night to cook him dinner before she went back to work. She was a hero to him. Week in and week out he was in The E-Train's shadow. He ate humble pie, but was ready for his own coming out party. On the third play of the game, Mercado took the toss for a 5-yard touchdown run.

English went to the air and moved the ball. Facing 4th and 5 at Salem's 40-yard line, Downes got the signal, and as soon as the Bulldogs' QB released the ball, he was flattened.

The release was high, and safety Sullivan eyed it, picking it off. He returned it for a 75-yard touchdown, but flags were everywhere. It was a personal foul call on Downes for a late hit to end the quarter.

Athletes and speed are a tough combo to stop. On the first play of the second quarter, English QB Chris Connelly threw a 27-yard strike to make it 7-7.

Carlos Leopoldo excelled in geometry and understood angles. Angles on a football field help athletes make big plays. Salem, blitzing on almost every down, connected on consecutive blindside hits on the Bulldogs' QB. That forced them to punt. The E-Train knew that as the season progressed, he would need to fight for every earned yard. In the final minute of the first half, he took the toss for a 10-yard touchdown.

THE VOTE TO STRIKE

The union meeting was called after school to decide if they would strike or not. Located along the Salem Commons on Washington Square sat one of the locations rented out by the union that would hold union membership. Although 400 plus union members fit in the room, the Knights of Columbus reached its capacity. The room itself had no windows and low ceilings. With long tables set up, it resembled a banquet but, in retrospect, they were far from a celebration. With darkness growing outside, anger, anxiety, and indecision along with thick cigarette smoke filled the air. As stress levels increased, the room became cloudier with cigarette smoke. Union president Wayne Turner quietly spoke with Sergeant at Arms Gaynor Riley about taking a vote to strike. At the head table, the union leadership spoke discreetly among themselves. At this point, some teachers started to get edgy, demanding answers as to what the next step would be.

Turner felt like now was the time to strike. He prepped all the teachers of the ramifications that came with striking. He went on to emphasize that it was illegal to strike in the State of Massachusetts, and the police could come to their home to arrest them, and randomly select them from the picket lines, making them look like they were a bad person. The teachers were ready and understood there was a possibility they were going to make zero progress.

Turner informed the audience that he would like to take a strike vote seeing that almost 100 percent of the teachers were in attendance. He realized that most in attendance supported the strike. Almost everybody in the room believed that the strike would be best for them. "If you want to move forward and want a contract, we are all together, unified with the community behind us. If you are ready, I want a motion and let's see what is going to happen," said Turner.

A motion was made and a member of the union leadership stood up, making a motion that the teachers were going on strike. Another member yelled out, "I second." With discussion on the motion, Tom "Mazz" Mazzarini knew he needed to let his voice be heard. He understood Robert's Rules of Parliamentary Procedure, allowing any member at any time to call for anything by raising their hand.

Mazz's eyes moved through the room. He never took his eye off the ball. Reaching into his cigarette box, he took out his last cigarette. The room was starting to symbolize "team." Egos were left at the door and replaced with camaraderie which was something he was exposed to in his days while playing catcher for the St. Mary's boy's high school baseball team.

A former union president, Mazz learned to deal with multiple personalities through the years. Education was instilled in him at a young age and he developed an interest in History and English. In 1973 he was hired by Joe Salerno to teach English and speech at Salem High. Mazz was a fighter who got respect among his peers, never allowing the city to gain ground with regard to money and working conditions. The baton was passed to Turner who inherited these fine characteristics, but times had changed and stomachs were turning as the city stood still with regard to salary increases for teachers.

Standing up, Mazz made his way to the microphone. "Over the course of two years we have been getting absolutely no respect whatsoever from the administrative side, and it is making our job ten times harder. I think the motto of this strike should be 'Bohica,'" said Mazz. An older female elementary teacher asked what that meant. Mazz paused and yelled out, "Bohica, 'bend over,' here it comes again. Damn right, we are sick and tired of being a victim of that," said Mazz.

They just wanted the respect they deserved because of their hard work and dedication. They came to the realization that even if they lost their jobs, they were willing to put it all on the line to let everybody know, especially the city and parents, what was really going on. "We were not backing down." After he spoke, the room went wild and Turner looked at Mazz, smiling.

First a voice vote was taken. Turner could not hear any nays. Turner then announced he wanted to see a show of hands because he wanted to count, and a sea of hands filled the air. Calling for any negative hands, the room went silent and still. Standing at the podium, he wanted this to be recorded as a unanimous vote. "Are there any objections to that?" Nobody said anything, and it indicated that they were going on strike. Ironically, they would start striking on Halloween.

The strike vote upset several teachers. With extracurricular activities covered in the CBA, they had to cease them. The Math team, Debate team, Drama Club, Band, and Soccer were all shut down. The cheering coaches did not suffer any repercussions for coaching and standing by their team.

With sixty-five days left until their contract extension expired, some teachers and some citizens felt that progress could have been made before going on strike, saving the city thousands of dollars.

THE TEAM GETS THE WORD

Back at Lynn English, it was Salem leading 14-7 at halftime. Looking at the statistics, minus one yard rushing for the Bulldogs was one of the highlights for Salem. Perrone was meeting with the offense and was called out of the locker room. Waiting for him was Cindy Napier, the band teacher. Perrone did not know what to make of this.

"Ken, did you hear the teachers union voted to strike?"

Perrone stood there, stunned and speechless. Taking his hat off, he ran his fingers through his hair. His front teeth grazed his bottom lip. Frustration took over his body. Wanting to yell, he let out a deep sigh. The timing could not be any worse. He had always been able to compartmentalize. With all the compartments of the brain, he would store it away and worry about winning this game. So much for the day the fact that Perrone was celebrating his thirty-third wedding anniversary to his beloved Jan.

Salem school committee member Tom Furey sat by himself at the game. He attended as many sporting events as he could and was a big supporter of the city of Salem. The 1968 Salem High graduate was proud to be part of the Salem tradition, and always a big fan of Perrone. "Perrone was the epitome of a coach's coach. When you look into Ken Perrone's eyes, you see the best of Salem. You see Salem pride, a role model, and father figure to his players. A man with courage who kept to his principles," Furey said. Furey heard through the grapevine that the teachers voted to strike, but was far from surprised as the topic came up often at the school committee meetings. The dark cloud was seen on the horizon. Furey taught for thirty-eight years outside the city and had empathy for the Salem teachers who felt undervalued. Being an elected public official, he could not teach in the city, as it would have been a conflict of interest.

His high-road view on why the Salem teachers union voted to strike when they did was that it would give them adequate time to create the fiscal budget for the following year. The raises that the teachers were requesting would have to be in the budget by January 1995 to be funded, otherwise, they would have to go for a supplemental budget. Football season was in the middle of the perfect storm and in the black hole. Student-athletes would be used as sacrificial lambs. Furey was a part-time elected official who was somewhat naïve and behind the scenes. Most of the time, he kept out of the loop. "The higher powers, Mayor Harrington, Superintendent Curtin, and Union President Turner all knew the behind-the-scenes mechanisms and had their own agenda," stated Furey.

Back on the field a shifty punt return by A.J. Grimes drew Furey back into the game. Two personal fouls gave Salem great field position. Two plays later Mercado exploded through the 6 hole like he was coming off the track blocks going into the end zone, making it 20-7. Downes started to get amped up. His mind was bouncing back and forth from the field to the girls. With the cheerleaders chanting, "Shake your booty, shake, and shake, your booty," Downes started eyeing all of them trying to figure out which one he was going to kick it to. "I cannot wait to freak some chicks tonight."

Late in third, English was threatening and cornerback Perry read the QB's eyes, picking the ball off at the 7-yard line. Sullivan took the QB keeper around the end on third and long fighting for the first down. On the fifteenth play of the drive, Mercado was ready for dessert, taking his seventeenth carry to the house for his third touchdown of the evening. He had a magical broomstick he was riding and it was blocking back Freeman and the offensive line. Perrone went for two and it was good when I hit De Pena on a corner route making it 28-7.

Edwin Canelo's crispy clean white #5 jersey stood out and his game pants were spotless. He had never played in a varsity game, but that did not have any effect on how he cheered for his teammates. But on this particular night, when Salem went up 30-7, he thought he would get his chance. Just about every player made their way on the field that night except Canelo. A lonely feeling, with a sense of rejection, entered his thoughts. All he wanted was one play which would have been his reward for all the work he put on the scout team. "I was jealous of the other kids that played. I envied the fact they had all their family there for them as well. Playing for Perrone was what I wanted, but after that game, I lost a lot of respect for the man," said Canelo. He believed politics played a role in some of the team members not playing.

Defensive end Leopoldo iced it with a safety and, with 1:24 left, the game was suspended when English was called for the twelfth penalty, a personal foul. We were on our seven after that interception (leading 30-7) and we were told by Perrone that "Now's the time to see what you are made of." We went 93 yards and killed the clock, all hard yards. We were a blue-collar, hard-working, smash mouth team. Perrone made it clear that is what we were.

On the bus ride back, Mercado was glowing, Jones was tired, Leopoldo was excited, and Freeman sat still with that boyish smile looking out the window. Perry was appreciating the moment, Sullivan had an ice pack on his head, Downes had his walk-man on, listening to some slow beats, and Higley just stared at the full moon. Uncharacteristic things occur during full moons. The coaches were quiet. Perrone sat with his arms crossed at the front of the bus. It was common for him to hold a conversation with other coaches but not on this ride. My brother had a staleness about him that concerned me. He looked broken. I sensed something was not right.

EPIPHANY

Perrone ordered the entire team to go into the small gym for a team meeting. First the coaches met separately behind closed doors. Seven grown men sat together in silence. The room was dark, as they did not want the lights on because Perrone's migraine was in full force. When he explained to them what was taking place, it left them speechless.

What was supposed to be a happy time was bitter-sweet. The teachers strike could possibly result in a postponement, cancellation, or forfeit. Beginning Monday, Perrone and four staffers would not be allowed to coach. The Salem-Swampscott matchup in the Game of the Year was in limbo.

They practically spent more time with each other than with their families. "Gentlemen, I understand if all of you want to walk out of this room and not put your career on the line. I understand and respect that." They realized that the administration had the total line with the superintendent and it would be a fierce fight in support of Perrone. As they stood, they announced their years together with Perrone: Marcoulier, twenty-two years; Wilbur, twenty years; Elsaesser, five years; Stellato, four years; Baldassarri, six, but first season back since the Super Bowl team in 1974; and McKenna, first season back since the Super Bowl in 1974. From this moment, they knew they would only have each other. They were their own militia from this point; anything they decided to do would be done together.

The players gathered closely together, talking among themselves. Moments after the coaches met, they went into the small gym to address the team. Educating them on what was occurring was Perrone's main focal point, because most kids did not realize what was happening. "Our coaching staff is willing, ready, and able to coach. Boys, it is out of my hands. This game could be cancelled. I'll be there unless the mayor forbids me to coach."

On his way home from the game, Perrone stopped at a red light. He was fighting to get the thoughts out of his head. With the union striking now, maybe they would settle, bringing the administration to their knees. They would have the entire community backing the coaches; they would get public sentiment on their side, feeling the threat to the continued success of the team. This would give them bargaining strength. "Maybe we will be on the politically favorable side of the equation. Is this a greedy act by the union? Maybe Harrington and Curtin will give us what we want." He could see Curtin with those big glasses and his smirk, trying to get them on a technicality and blame them as well. "Your teachers are out of school; you cannot coach."

At the same time, Mayor Harrington and Curtin could be thinking we would turn it around on them. The irony is that both sides were looking at the same thing and reasoning that the other side hurt the kids. The clincher was that Curtin would finally get Perrone, but political pressure from the community would cause one side to back down. Would the union take less money and settle? Pulling into his driveway, Perrone realized he could keep the administration and union at bay because he had a separate contract to be a coach. That was his trump card, at least he thought it was.

***

Sullivan's alarm clock was blaring. His head was throbbing and it was not from the six-pack he drank the night before. It was not from the frustration of his 75-yard interception return for a TD getting called back or the cheap shots he took throughout the game running the ball. He played a pivotal role in Salem's win over Lynn English on Friday night. The Salem football team had a dark halo over their heads. They often represented a ray of hope but, in this case, it was uncertainty.

Curtin ate his Saturday morning breakfast, skimming through the *Salem News*. "NEC championship showdown is set."

"We will see about that," Curtin deliberated in his mind. His eyes scrolling down the page, he read another article entitled, "Game jeopardized by Salem teachers' strike". "Try coaching, and the ax will fall right away." Curtin's sneer summed up his thought process. Ironically he along with the other administrators culled 10-23 percent raises from the previous year; Curtin personally realized a 23 percent raise for 1994 going from $65,000 to $80,000.

Perrone was aware of the situation and wanted to be proactive in regard to getting his troops prepared. He knew the school would be locked up like Fort Knox and, after Sunday, he and four fellow teacher-coaches would be barred from using any school facilities. He held a two-hour practice on school grounds Sunday morning. While the team practiced, the teachers picketed on Salem Common during Mayor Harrington's political breakfast held at the K of C, across the street from the fabled iron fenced green. Harrington angered the crowd by slipping out the back door and driving away.

Later that evening the school committee met behind closed doors. They voted 5-2 that the coaches would be fired if they coached without being in school. Members Carl Peterson and Tom Furey were in favor of letting the coaches continue to coach. Furey believed that because the coaches had a separate contract, they should be allowed to coach. Such occurred while the teachers rallied at their HQ, the Moose Lodge.

CHAPTER 13

SOUL SEARCHING

> *"It is in your moments of decision that your destiny is shaped."*
>
> *~ Anthony Robbins*

As the school committee met behind closed doors Perrone sat speechless with his wife at the kitchen table. It was as if they were both afraid to talk. Perrone knew deep down in his heart what he was going to do. Without saying a word, Jan knew what he was thinking, and it tore her up inside to see him like this. Food didn't seem appealing to him, and he didn't even feel it if his body felt hungry. He didn't even notice the alluring smell of his wife's cooking. The kitchen was dimly lit by the old-fashioned lamp that stood in the corner of the room. Janice rubbed his neck, waiting for him to open up and begin talking. She was concerned about the stress that he had been encountering.

His life work as a coach would be ruined if he decided to coach; the writing was on the wall. He had led players and coaches for years; it was his life. He thought he had faced all bases from physical and mental adversity. After a few minutes, he chose to unlock his heart and get his true feelings out. "How on earth can I ask kids to be courageous, no excuses, push kids to the limit, and not coach?" His heart was nearly shattered. "Jan, this is ethically and morally right. How can I not be consistent in what I have taught the kids? I have come to the conclusion I am who I am standing up against all that has been brought to me." Legions of former players looked up to him. Recipients of all his coaching were in the audience. Perception had become reality. Improbable events had come true. "Sean Stellato, walking into my office as a tiny sophomore and making the bold statement that if he is the starting QB, he will lead us to the Super Bowl; The E-Train coming out of nowhere and becoming one of the premier running backs in the area; and Higley recovering the fumble in the end zone against Danvers that enabled us to hold onto a 15-13 win. These signs have connected the dots." Looking at his wife, "How can this not be meant to be? How can I not continue coaching? Now it is my turn to lead by example."

Perrone found the clarity in the form of support from his wife and coaches. All of their responses were similar: "Greatness is shaped in times of adversity; the kids have dedicated so much of their lives to playing for you." He had a profound feeling of regret that he might have to live the rest of his life thinking how he let his players down. It is a lot easier to live with something when you know it is the morally right thing to do and jump in head first with all your heart and soul. All those years of service, his pension, his seniority, his legacy, his identity…. don't we all want to leave something, a legacy, a lasting impression? That is human nature.

CHAPTER 14

HALLOWEEN... TOOTHBRUSH

"If human beings had genuine courage, they'd wear their costumes every day of the year, not just on Halloween."

~ Doug Coupland

DAY 1 of the STRIKE -
MONDAY, October 31, 1994

The most anticipated holiday, Halloween, had arrived in Salem. It presents with a carnival atmosphere without comparison. Demons and goblins were in the air. Annually a million people flock to Salem in search of some history and fright. In the month of October alone, 400,000 tourists flood the streets, resembling New York City more than the small New England city of Salem. On Halloween alone, 100,000 people jam the streets, making it impossible for the locals to get anywhere or anything done outside of the city walls. It was nearly unattainable for students commuting to Salem State University to get to class on time, or even at all. During Halloween, Salem is beautiful and family friendly. However, when the sun sets, the streets come alive. This is when the local retailers thrive off of the horror theme of the holiday. The residents of the city are proud to be part of such great local history.

The streets are well-maintained and give you that fresh New England feel. Small well-kept trees line the streets with corn husks tied to them with orange ribbon. Stacks of hay are used as barriers to give it an autumn feel. The smell of new fall leaves fills the air, supplemented with a fresh breeze of ocean air in the wind. The fallen leaves sprinkle the streets, adding the final touches of a picture-perfect feel. There is a sense of security with police officers everywhere you turn. Glancing up at the names of the stores can give you a sense you are at Hogwarts with *Harry Potter*. The local businesses thrive off the holiday and prepare for it yearlong. The clever names of the shops are well thought out like Salemdipity and New England Magic. The shops all have "Halloween specials" going on, may it be ghostly food, devil horns, or scary hair wraps.

There is array of things for a family do. The city offers a carnival, bazaar, trolley tours, street fairs, Kids' Days, Saturday movie night on the Commons, and the Kids' Parade just to name a few. At night in October is when Salem comes to life and history is told. There are museums, ghostly candlelit tours, reenactments, and the Old Burying Point Cemetery ceremonies. Samuel McIntire, the architect responsible for the mansions designed in the McIntire district, and Justice John Hawthorne, an ancestor of Nathaniel Hawthorne and one of the judges during the Witchcraft Trials, are buried in the Old Burying Point.

Walking down Front Street in Salem is a Halloween treat in itself. The cobble-stone street is now a pedestrian walkway and filled with local and international vendors filling the street in October. At the entrance of the street sits the most alluring witchcraft store, Crow Haven Corner, which has been in existence since 1972. Further down the street is Old Town Hall. Along the street there is an array of other witchcraft stores, physics, palm readers and souvenir shops. People dressed in seventeenth century clothes and costumes fill the street. It truly gives you a feeling as if you were on a movie set. The atmosphere is entertaining; down every street you turn, something ghoulish can be found. On Halloween Day people drive and sit in traffic for hours trying to get into Salem, reputed to be the scariest place in America, and to enjoy the treasure this city has to share.

THE CITY WAS ALIVE BUT THE SCHOOLS WERE NOT

The hallways of Salem High School were silent while 440 members of the Salem Teachers Union picketed. Michaud Bus Line, the city's school bus contractor, would not cross the picket line. The morning 7:20 school bell rang, but no students were reporting to homeroom. Classrooms were dimmed and locked, weekend assignments still written on the boards. Four thousand eight hundred school children found themselves with no classes to attend, but 369 of 4,800 students attempted to go to school. School administrators were on hand at every school trying to make the best they could of the situation. Essentially all those who came were ultimately shepherded home in one way or another. My fellow teammate and friend, Patrick Creedan, and I were two students that walked to school that morning. Neither of us had missed a day of school in six years.

Students had mixed reactions. "They're always yelling at us to be organized and to try and solve problems in a friendly way. Now they are doing this." Some students expressed disappointment that teachers chose to strike instead of continuing negotiations. What about the kids that were trying to learn and earn art, music, or academic scholarships? Parents supported the teachers on Monday morning when about twenty students started their own picket line in front of City Hall, carrying signs that read "Mayor Harrington, please negotiate" and "What does this teach our children?" Walking in a circle, the students were chanting "Two, four, six, eight. Why don't we negotiate?" (*Salem News*, November 1, 1994). Reports confirmed that Mayor Harrington's office was in a frenzy since he and his staff could not keep up with the overwhelming media and citizen requests for information along with managing the legal and elected official cadre involved in management's decision-making.

HARRINGTON UPS THE ANTE

Harrington had declared that he would fire the teachers for failing to work. He and the school committee dispatched Labor Counsel Dan Kulak to petition the Massachusetts Labor Relations Commission for a determination that the strike was illegal. Kulak successfully obtained the edict which, per Massachusetts statutory labor law, was to be enforced through the equity powers possessed by a Superior Court. The enforcement, per the city's complaint, was filed at the Essex Superior Court at Salem and assigned to the Honorable Elizabeth Donovan. The city sought to obtain an injunction against the union compelling the teachers to return to work. The consequences of non-compliance were a contempt action punishable by fines, incarceration, and/or other orders.

Turner, as the president of the union and named party in the enforcement action, received a summons to court to appear before Judge Donovan. That day it took Turner extra time to make his way over to the Salem Superior Court, the highest trial court in Massachusetts. He had been made aware of the courts powers of equity, ability to issue injunctions, and range of penalties for contempt. The likelihood those forces would converge at a single moment upon Turner were intimidating to him but he was resolute in not backing down.

JUDGE ELIZABETH DONOVAN

This Halloween Day was the biggest anticipated retail day for the city of Salem. Sitting in the crazed traffic streaming out of Salem for miles, Turner sat like a spectator viewing the array of people from around the world decked out in their Halloween best. However at, this time, Turner's mind went back to the strike and how long it would take for the city to meet their demands. He was quickly brought back to the present moment when a person dressed in a sixteenth century witchcraft trial costume banged on his driver's side window and pressed his face to the glass-leaving a mark. Chills ran through him. Once at the courthouse, he met with his attorney Jeffery Jacobsen and stood before Judge Donovan. Notably the court was a 200-year-old stone block edifice also resembling the architecture from Hogwarts from the *Harry Potter* series. With little dispatch, she ordered Turner to call for a union meeting that afternoon and advised them to report back to work tomorrow. Quickly, without thought, Turner responded by saying that they would be meeting as they do daily. However, he said that going back to work was not an option. After a prompt response the judge called for a fifteen-minute recess.

BRING YOUR TOOTHBRUSH

Upon returning, she repeated the same question only to get the same answer. Pausing, she looked Turner in the eyes and told him to return tomorrow at 8 AM and to bring his toothbrush with him.

She slammed down the gavel, the *bang* echoing through the ancient courtroom, and left Turner numb. With a confused look on his face, he turned to his attorney to explain what she meant. Attorney Jacobsen told him to get ready to go to jail for not obeying the court's orders. Failure to obey a court order is contempt, and contempt can be addressed by fines or incarceration. Incarceration can be assessed for a time certain, or, for a duration purged by compliance.

Upon returning home from court, his family was supportive but horrified at the same time. Later that day while Turner's family was at home, a constable arrived and served him papers informing him to return to court the next day. He was a husband and father of two. Naturally, that night he was restless and sleeping was an impossible task. His mind was racing about what he could do to get himself out of this without backing down from striking. Turner communicated with his fellow union officers and maintained that the school committee must come back to them with an offer.

DAY 2 of the STRIKE
NOVEMBER 1, 1994

Turner climbed out of bed before sunrise and started to get ready for his dreaded day. He went along with his regular morning routine and reached for his warm cup of coffee. He slowly made his way to take a nice long shower to relax and take advantage of his freedom of privacy before going to the pen. Turner reached into his closet and took out the "union suit." After dressing, Turner took one last look at himself in the mirror only to come up with his brilliant scheme—he would not back down. In preparation he rolled up toilet paper, stuffed it into his front chest pocket, and collected his toothbrush and toothpaste.

Before leaving, he quietly went into his kids' bedrooms to kiss them; he knew he was to be incarcerated. His heart was torn as he shut the front door. He was 100 percent behind the union, but at the same time, did not want his children to experience their father going to jail.

Before he knew it, he was standing before Judge Donovan once again. This time he knew what was going to happen; he had his game face on, he was ready to stand up for the teachers and let the public know how serious they were about the strike. What would the judge do? Turner reflected on the possibility of being sent to jail for the duration of the strike. The stakes could not be any higher. He stood his ground and stated that the teachers were not ready to end the strike. He scoured the courtroom for court officers whom he expected would take him into custody. He had been told of the walk down the narrow stairs to the basement where the 150 year old "lock-up" was located. There, a century and half of detainees waited, confined in an ancient steel-wired cage, bordered by mortar and brick walls and flooring until the Essex County sheriff's van arrived for his transport to the Essex County House of Correction and Jail. There, Turner had been told he would be placed in confinement with the "general population," a grim prospect. As an older white man he would be demeaned throughout the classification process, including a full body search for weapons or drugs, bunked with those having demographics of early twenty-year-old black or Hispanics "in" for drugs, stealing, and/or violence. He ultimately would be deprived of food or good bedding by "gangs" taking his entitlements, and bullied unmercifully in food or bathroom lines.

UNEXPECTED REPRIEVE

Judge Donovan firmly stated her position: the union would be fined $5,000 for every day they remained on strike. Turner could not believe what he had heard. No jail time?

She adjourned Court before Turner could get a word in. Instant relief warmed Turner's body and he felt like this was a step closer for the union. This was his brilliant scheme. He would not, and did not, back down.

In contrast, could his fellow union brothers and sisters ever really appreciate the sacrifice he had been prepared to make on their behalf? Did Turner ever think he was doing the right thing? "I do not think it is fair to say public employees cannot strike for benefits when they are being railroaded. I never had a problem with my decision. I never had doubt that the strike was going to collapse because every day I monitored that, day in and day out, I got reports from the office which were that the people were coming in and working. And, we had enormous parental support. Everything was positive. Later, when the constable came to my house to serve the contempt order citing the $5,000 per day penalty, my children (six and three) were in absolute tears because this guy was a complete jerk, giving me the papers and talking about going to jail," said Turner. "As my lawyer explained to me, a fine was an intermediate step on the way to someone going to jail," Turned indicated. Turner had been made aware of the concept of progressive discipline but its import only was appreciated after Judge Donovan spared him. Certainly, he realized the next transgression would certainly involve jail time.

Salem teachers gathered in the cold night, not for a costume party but at a time when David was standing up to Goliath. Teachers insisted it was not just the money that pushed them to the picket lines. They said it was also the lack of respect the school committee and the mayor had shown them at the bargaining table. The teachers felt their salaries should be in line with those of surrounding communities too. They felt degraded with the school committee's proposal. The teachers demanded the school committee continue negotiations during the same week. The committee refused, insisting on keeping their scheduled meeting on November 9. "That was the straw that broke the camel's back. It's the history of the attitude," Salem teacher John Fortunato said. The teachers union was very united and made it clear there would be no backing down, even if that meant Turner going to jail.

ANALYSIS FROM AN OLD SAGE

School committee member Carl Peterson's head shook as he read the *Salem News* while sitting at the dining room table, his cereal becoming soggy. Mayor Harrington's remarks to fire all striking teachers did not sit well with Peterson. Clearly this was Harrington's attempt to mimic former President Ronald Reagan's firing of air traffic controllers in 1981. Although Peterson understood where the mayor was coming from, he had different philosophies and was trying to make a point. The mayor had a very political family. Peterson had witnessed Harrington trying hard not to be pro-teacher. "I think he kind of leaned over that way. He was having a hard time with the city unions. Every mayor has trouble, particularly with public safety people. I think he wanted to show that he was tough against the unions, and prove that he himself, was personally tough," said Peterson. "The teachers proposing a salary increase and striking gave Harrington an opportunity to make a statement." From Peterson's perspective, the mayor's statements publicly hurt his image, making it a personality issue, the city against the union, as opposed to solving the deficiencies in the bargaining process. The issues were significant, but did not seem as important as the behavior.

Peterson noted the volatility the superintendent brought to the situation. In reality Curtin's criticisms of Perrone were no less a mirror image of what Curtin himself infused into the conflict. Curtin's ego and the labels of disdain he showered on Perrone obstructed meaningful discussion between the parties. He was a catalyst of additional and more intense confrontation.

With direct scrutiny on both sides, and reporters trying to become privy to inside information, Peterson stayed quiet. The mayor was adamant in speaking to the press. With just under 38,000 people observing him, he grew concerned and made a statement. As the chief executive officer he felt obligated to let his voice be heard. Due to personalities taking center stage, it was to be a monumental task to focus on the issues at hand, fair compensation being the point of debate. However the non-quantitative sideshow of "lack of respect" became the public mantra. In short, Harrington had an uphill battle redirecting the community away from the emotions that had flared.

Peterson had witnessed many changes in personnel through his tenure. Certain topics would arise that had no bearing on education that would agitate Peterson. For instance, Curtin saw himself as knowing a lot about athletics. During his time as principal, he would create controversy and feel his authority was being challenged by the coaches. Observers thought that Curtin targeted athletic coaches because he himself never panned out as an athlete or a coach. Issues arose such as access to the building during after-school hours and the use of elementary gyms for basketball practices. These concerns would constantly come up. He did not like a lot of booster clubs. Football and basketball coaches having keys to the building bothered him. The school committee did not want to pay a principal for staying at the building in the evening. Yet, practices for both sports and basketball games were played after school. The weight and film rooms were areas that separated excellent teams from good teams. This topic came up through the years, and the principal effectively policed that. Curtin's obsessions with these seemingly minimal issues cast him, to those in athletic circles, as the consummate pettifogger. Peterson's resolution was clear: "Interact with the coach, letting him know to be responsible." That seemed to be a big issue, and that carried over when Curtin was superintendent.

Peterson had a clear take on the Perrone-Curtin relationship. Peterson knew it was no secret they did not like each other. No good was said by one about the other. Peterson, as a school committee member, was asked to take a side, and there was no middle ground. Some real issues were addressed, one being the football team and whether Perrone was honestly running the program for wins or the kids. It could be done for both and either side would be a winner in that scenario. The view was that he was using the football program to enhance his image but, in reality, there was no way to build a good program for the kids without doing this. The Salem football program had a great spot in the North Shore in terms of reputation and prestige. Perrone was like Lombardi was to the Green Bay Packers.

MANY SIDES OF HARRINGTON

On the brisk fall night, the wind was howling outside. A carved pumpkin sat on Neil Harrington's kitchen table. His wife and children were all sound asleep in bed. He was nervous and animated in his movements as he made sure every door was secure in their home. His eyes were restless while looking out his office window, feeling a sense of security as he saw a police cruiser parked in front of his home on twenty-four hour surveillance. With all the stress, he was still able to sleep well at night. He learned to mentally file away any problems that arose.

For Harrington, the day had been like juggling fireballs. A death threat his wife received earlier at their home made everyone in the family a nervous wreck. He had developed a savvy on the basketball courts which aided him to be mentally tough. Insults ricocheted off him as he fielded calls at City Hall. But one in particular really hurt. A note left on his windshield read, "We know where your kids go to school; if you know what is good for them, you will stay away from the game." His eyes filled up in a combination of rage and sadness. Asking God for strength, he reached into his pocket grabbing a handkerchief and blew his nose. Slipping the note into his briefcase, he got into his vehicle and slowly drove off. Harrington was a fan of SHS athletics. He refused to be intimidated, but at the same time he was not going to be foolish. He attended several football games that season and wanted to be in attendance for the Swampscott showdown. He reached out to the chief of police, asking if he could have a couple of plainclothes officers as an escort in the event that the game would be played. His request was to be honored—escort or no escort, viable threat or not, Harrington knew he would need to be mentally poised to attend the game under the cloud of controversy and anger.

His life was somewhat surreal and he felt like he was living in two different worlds. As mayor, his job automatically made him chairman of the school committee which involved negotiating with the teachers for a new contract. But the rest of the city still needed to be run. Like a tug-of-war game, he was being pulled in two different directions. The public was encouraging him to hold the line financially, while some citizens were in his ear to give the teachers a big raise. The populace did not understand that it was not just up to Harrington. The majority of the school committee had to make the decision.

Harrington was proud to call Salem home. But people were observing from the outside what he was doing and not really understanding what was going on internally during negotiations. Opinions were forming and jabs were being thrown on the street. The irony of the situation was that most people did not know the background behind Harrington's rationale; for the decisions made, there would always be someone that would disagree. But that comes with every mayor's job and, practically speaking, could not take the time to explain every new issue to every person on the street.

With no provisions in the NEC bylaws covering a strike, Swampscott Athletic Director Dick Baker made it clear that Swampscott had no desire to play Salem the Friday or Saturday before Thanksgiving. The Witches would have to prepare without five of their seven coaches affected by the Salem teachers strike. Salem made it clear that they would forfeit, rather than play unprepared, but Baker said, "We don't want that; we want to play the game. We have empathy for Salem players, but we want to play this week." (*Salem News*, October 31, 1994)

"Why should Swampscott be punished for something going on in Salem?" Perrone asked. "Hopefully, the powers that be will step back and cooler heads will prevail. I think the kids are being punished enough without school. Let's not take away something that means so much in their lives. A game this meaningful does not happen that often. But with no football DNA, how could they truly understand?"

Propaganda was spreading like it was 1692 in Salem. But three hundred years later, a modern-day "witch hunt" to oust legendary football coach Perrone was brewing. This time Judge Hawthorne was not presiding over the trial. The Salem administration had created its own "Gallows Hill" and was doing everything in its power to shut down the football program and steal the dream away from devoted coaches and kids.

COACH, COACH, WHO IS GOING TO COACH?

There was still no indication Monday or Tuesday that Salem's five coaches on strike would be allowed to prepare the Witches for "the school's biggest game in the last twenty years," creating a cloud of gloom that hung over the game. Salem High interim defensive backfield coach McKenna was to direct the practice and was the only other coach eligible as a non-teacher in the Salem public school system. My brother, Mike Stellato was coaching the freshman squad.

How would one coach who has been with the program for nine weeks and a freshman coach lead a team?

TALENT ALONE ISN'T ENOUGH

Good coaches enable players who have the aptitude to refocus and help them play above their God-given abilities. I had a learning disability and Perrone taught me ways to understand pass coverage's, pickup blitzes, and check down to different receivers. I developed patience with his fakes and poise in the pocket.

The E-Train was raw mentally and his football skills needed some tweaking. Perrone educated him on the nuts and bolts of football physics. If you are running full speed at a stationary target, just lower your shoulder and you will pancake the defender or pick up additional yardage. The E-Train smiled, enjoying the thought of being able to hit kids and not get into trouble. He added simplicity to plays which facilitated him to understand the playbook.

De Pena was fast and could jump, and Coach Wilbur saw the gem in him. He developed De Pena's hands and taught him how to gain leverage on DBs. This allowed him to get separation and catch more balls. He learned to utilize his jumping ability and pull balls out of the sky similar to fishermen pulling fish out of water. His sophomore season, he got jacked up a lot, getting off press man coverage, but now, developed a rip and swim techniques which were moves that allowed him to get off the ball and made him more of a complete receiver.

Marcoulier was the guru of the defense. He saw a troubled, lost soul in Downes, a kid with tremendous talent who ran around like a chicken with its head cut off. He trained him to understand different methods, to be patient, and disguise blitzes. He taught him to use hands, which enabled him to shed blocks and be aware when to expect cut blocks. Marcoulier smiled when he delivered knockout blows. The kid played like a complete madman on the field, which is what Marcoulier liked. In return, Downes would sell his soul for him and loved him. "He made you responsible for what you did. He was like a mentor. I never had anyone like that before. With other coaches, if I made a mistake it was like whatever, but with Marcoulier, he went off and put the fear in cats," said Downes.

Cornerbacks Mccellon and Corey Perry had some "hood" in them and Marcoulier taught them how to channel that into a positive on the field. They did so by mugging wide-outs after the catch or forcing fumbles. Marcoulier developed Perry to protect his cushion and communicate with his fellow secondary posse. Perry was part of the transplant posse. He didn't want to leave his roots in Lawrence. Waiting to the very last minute to pack, his father promised him more opportunities. That is what he got and made the most out of it. He was slowly building a reputation as a shut-down corner. His father moved his son to a town where he didn't know a single person. "That is not easy. But now we wouldn't trade it for all the money in the world." He preached that a cardinal DB rule was to never get beat deep. Mccellon became a shutdown corner, and Marcoulier simplified the game for him. He transformed a bunch of underachievers into achievers.

JUST A STUPID IDEA

The mayor and superintendent expressed they were lining up temporary coaches to lead the team. What real authority was there to allow extracurricular activities to continue without teachers working and classes being conducted? Literally, if there was no school, no teachers, and no coaches, there was no reason for extracurricular activities like football to be undertaken. Why engage in the academic gymnastics of allowing one activity to continue, but without coaches?

The problem was that the same hypocrisy that existed during the Salem Witch Trials existed in the present. These people were going to use and leverage the community sentiments in favor of the football team to their own advantage. Their hopes for gains were: political for Harrington, revenge for Curtin, and a contact enhanced with increased benefits for the teachers. These "gains" were all mortgaged on the back of the players. The replacement coaches that the school administration wanted to hire did not know these kids, and did not care for these kids. With the schemes on offense and defense changing every year, it would have taken weeks or months for them to provide proper coaching.

CHAPTER 15

PLAYERS PACT

> "Failure is the condiment that gives success its flavor."
>
> ~ Truman Capote

The Team's DAY 2 – November 1, 1994

Perrone was conducting a coaches' meeting when he was asked to accompany a police officer to City Hall for a sit down with Mayor Harrington. Perrone's disdain for Curtin's hypocrisy and personal vendetta weighed heavily on him as the cruiser approached City Hall.

Perrone not being allowed to coach brought tremendous scrutiny to the strike. When Perrone sat down with Harrington, he thought the mayor had the power to allow Perrone to coach, which he did not. "People were trying to mix the two things together as if I could control it myself. I did not think it was fair that I was looked at as the person that was going to take on the whole burden to try to fix it. I was not the only one negotiating the contract. Perrone did not report to me, so I could not make any personnel decisions relevant to him. I would have preferred to have the matter looked at as some sort of compromise, so the kids did not suffer. But the powers that be at the time decided what they wanted to do. So, I was focused on trying to get the contract settled, hoping that the Perrone issue would go away. I think that anyone who followed sports would recognize that Perrone had one of the finest coaching minds around, but his situation got caught up in what was going on in the bigger world around him. He was wedged in a complicated state."

Perrone had a productive talk with Harrington. He walked away feeling very optimistic that he and his staff were going to be able to coach after their meeting. "Neil was a fair guy," Perrone stated. Harrington was very clear to Perrone in explaining that there was a governing body, the school committee where all the members of the committee voted. No one person had authority that would allow Perrone to coach.

Hours later, school Principal Gerald Silverman called Assistant Principal Paul Higgins to let him know what was brought to his attention about the meeting between Mayor Harrington and Perrone. "Perrone almost physically attacked the mayor and had to be restrained!" Silverman went on to tell him, "I guess, that tremendous ego got the best of him. He needs a lesson in insubordination in that he needs to adhere to the directives of his superiors." Such characterization served as the hint of the Witch Hysteria, like behavior to come.

Later that day Perrone spoke with Peterson who was on the school board. He informed Perrone that when Curtin got wind of Harrington's possible exemption on behalf of Perrone, he had a fit and went crazy at the school board meeting. "Apparently he went nuts and would not back down, even though Neil was a big man in size and Curtin was a small, man he could yell loud and intimidate people like he always did. I'm not sure if Harrington would admit that, but I feel he backed down to Curtin's demands," said Perrone.

THE PLAYERS WON'T BACK DOWN EITHER:
THE MEETING AT THE STADIUM

Phil Downes circled his aunt's living room while watching Channel 4's evening sports broadcast Tuesday night. He clenched a tennis ball harder as the sports broadcast clearly made it sound like the coaches would not be coaching. His beeper started beeping as he sat down on the sofa. Not recognizing the number, he called it back. Trying to keep his cool, he took a deep breath and dialed the number.

It was Higley. "Downes, Whitten, Freeman, and I are calling a team meeting," referring to all three captains. "Meet on Bertram Field at 8 o'clock."

Downes replied, "History will be made one way or another, Higs. We can play their game and have a chance to become the first Super Bowl champion in Salem, and if we don't play them, twenty years from now, people will look back and remember the '94' team that did not finish the season."

Some kids walked from The Point, others rode their bicycles in the cold, several piled in cars, and some parents dropped their children off and waited in the parking lot. Every kid knew what this meeting was about. Seventy deep were not brainwashed, but were broken. The glare from the parking lot light softly lit the field. When Captain Whitten asked the team to raise their right hands in support of Coach Perrone, every player's arm rose in the air like the wave at Fenway Park. It was unanimous. They made a pact as a team that they would not play if their coaches could not coach. That would go for game day as well. If they removed Perrone from the sideline, the team would strip down and leave their uniforms on the field. Another barrier that stood in their way was getting their equipment out of the school locker room and off the practice field.

"Guys, we need to break into the school and take your football equipment," said Higley.

Downes started to clap his hands. "Man, I studied MacGyver's movements and I am one step ahead of you and already know how we are going to get in," a hyped-up Downes declared. "Stars come out at night. You guys ready to do this tonight?"

The team responded with, "Let's do it!"

Shortly after, some of the team arrived. The kids who went home with their parents wrote down their locker number and combination. Downes showed off his street skills. With his back to the door, he drove the back of his heel into the back of the door and it sprung open. Like a bank heist, time was crucial; they took care of business and vanished like a ghost in the night. Certain players played the Grinch on the practice field and cleaned the place out. There would be no way this team would be backing down.

News circulated fast. Players were vocal and did not turn down interviews. This was their only means of expressing themselves. Like all the adults involved the players pondered their own "hardball" strategy. "No coaches, no game this Saturday," the outspoken Downes declared. "The whole team met, and we agreed if the coaches are not going to coach, then we are not going to play the rest of the season."

The coaches were the core of this team. They were with them when every critic had them down and out during the preseason.

"How can you play without coaches?" Freeman asked. "They were the ones that got us here, and we need them." They were not going to back down!

"Everybody is behind us," said Mercado. "It's been real tough to stay focused the last couple of days. If there is one thing positive that's come out of all this, it is we've become closer as a team." Clouds of doubt sat over the football team. No Thanksgiving Day game? For Salem fans, that would be like canceling the Super Bowl. The Salem football team would turn in their jerseys and forfeit the rest of the season if Saturday's game against Swampscott was not played due to the teachers strike. Higley was still holding onto that dream that he had since he first started playing Pop Warner, to someday play on a Super Bowl team. But that dream looked like it was fading into the abyss as quickly as midnight approached for Cinderella. Time was running out and Perrone's hourglass was almost empty. We were caught in the middle.

"I feel we were being used as pawns," Downes stated.

The team's dilemma had been one of the hottest topics statewide. Every major Boston media station camped out at Castle Hill Park, the proposed "non-school venue" for team practices. All major sports talk radio shows were dominated by the topic. On one day, both Harrington and Curtin were interviewed by WEEI sports talk master Dale Arnold who dedicated a four-hour radio show to the Salem High football situation. Arnold said later he had only three or four phone calls in all that time that did not agree with the viewpoint that "The kids were being shortchanged in this." (*Salem News*, November 3, 1994)

Chapter 16

Reality 101 Police Sirens- Administration's Cease and Desist

> *"Tough times don't last but tough people do."*
>
> ~ Tim Marcoulier

MORE MACHINATIONS on DAY 2 – November 1, 1994

Coach Perrone faced a three-headed monster that was making his life a living hell. He and his four assistants were all under contract with the teachers union and refused to cross a union picket line, yet to coach would imperil their jobs. Perrone and his entire staff had separate contracts outside of the union's CBA to coach that gave them a double-edged sword, and as expedience dictated, a shield.

The administration issued a cease and desist order that involved all aspects of the team's functional activities and sought to prevent access for coaches to fields and equipment. It included "off-site" coaching activities. The bite of the order was, at least theoretically, trumped by Perrone's second contract as a coach and Curtin's continued hypocrisy allowing student participation in football but without school resources.

With the same entity paying him on two different contracts, Perrone had leverage which enabled him to stiff-arm the cease and desist order. Fortunately for Perrone, public schools did not write coaches' job descriptions in the CBA. The CBA clearly did not provide a job description of a coach, which at the moment, was Perrone's saving grace and a loophole Perrone's legal team dissected. The "contract" trains were running on parallel tracks, at least in Perrone's eyes. He clearly should not have been penalized as a coach under the Salem educational bylaws. Perrone had a legal obligation to coach under one contract, and a similar obligation to strike under another. Perrone went with his intuition and would take on Goliath to coach his team if he had to relying on this rationale. It was an easy decision for him. Since last years' discussion with Principal Baker, he knew he was being targeted as both a teacher and a coach.

Perrone had an elevated status in the community, if not equal to or more popular than the mayor. That did not sit well with the administration, nor did the empty bottles of champagne found in the locker room after 1977 Thanksgiving Day win over Beverly or the discriminatory threats during the 1993 pre-season camp up in New Hampshire. When you are coming off an 8-2 season and miss the Super Bowl by eight points, most coaches would be rewarded maybe with a raise, not pressure from the principal to resign.

"You might have worn out your welcome," were the exact words declared by Principal Karen Baker. (*Salem News*, November 3, 1994) The students, the athletes, the fans, and the Salem football founding fathers consisting of former head coaches Fred Perkins, Reggie Wade, Harry McDevitt, Bill Broderick, Glen O'Brien, Walt Sheridan, Andy Konovalchik, and Jack Farland, were all considered by Perrone in his analysis. He would not back down.

HYSTERIA INCREASES

On the other side of the city, a different type of game with equal fixation was being played. Shouts of "We are one" echoed against the granite and brick building as a parade of Salem teachers, surrounded by parents and students, rang bells and shouted slogans. The glare of the television camera lights felt like the only brightness that had shined on the teachers for some time. This marked another day of the city's "first-ever" teacher's strike.

Tom Mazzarini walked the picket line with his head held high. Wind was cold on his face, but the fire inside channeled energy throughout his body. The support from students wanting to picket with the teachers was awe-inspiring. At times, he was fatigued from the sleepless nights. "I stayed tired but I never showed it. Our concern was about the students, but we were losing pay, which was hurting us financially," said Mazz. Approaching City Hall, the thought of losing his job remained with him. He constantly asked himself the question, "Why are we doing this?" Guilt started to sit in like a bacteria eating at his flesh. The city had hired them, and now they were willing to lose their jobs over the commitment to the kids in this city. This comes with the territory of public education. You have to work together from a united front. You cannot have a dichotomy to pitch one side against the other. "We look at that as teachers, and looking at the administrators, a great deal of people do not know what they do. They give out detentions, but they are not in the classrooms. That is what I think is important; the discipline will hold itself. We see how hard a teacher works, but does an administrator work as hard? The salaries that are given out to vice principals, principals, and superintendents are much higher than teachers. Is that fair?"

VIEWS FROM ANOTHER SAGE

John Fortunato stared into the crowd at Town House Square. Grateful for the support from his colleagues, he had one agenda to keep the negative energy out. He was a leader that preached self-esteem and self-worth to his fellow teachers. Not only was he a teacher, but he was the captain of the picket line, and head girls basketball coach. He thought back to his 1990 girls' basketball team and how they persevered to go 23-0. "Little things make all the differences," he told another teacher. "That is the same mentality we need to have. I feel it is degrading after all eighteen years of service to feel like we can be replaced like interchangeable parts," said the Salem High School physical education teacher.

Thinking back to his college days at the University of Miami and all those education classes, no one ever got him ready for this type of scenario. Begging for a raise every three years altered the equation. His focus was on developing his craft, a teacher by nature who loved his job and adored his students. "There comes a time in people's lives where they say 'enough'. That is what the union shouted. When you follow up a three-year contract at 0 percent, 1 percent, and 1 percent and come back with 1 percent, 1 percent, and 1 percent, it became the straw that broke the camel's back. It galvanized the teachers to be able to finally take that step and say 'enough'. I think the other side felt the union would accept. The city's job is to keep the taxes down. I never looked at things with anger, it is a negotiation and that is what it is. For me as a teacher, it was not acceptable. There were many contracts that I was not happy with, but once that contract is ratified and agreed to, you put it behind and move forward. I was not bitter; it was the will of the union." Comparing the surrounding communities' teacher salaries to Salem teachers, who made much lower, there was no link between them. That concrete data stimulated teachers to take the stand. "It was not the hard line mentality of the Teamsters. We were talking about kindergarten and first grade teachers who are out there standing in the cold, petrified," said Fortunato.

NON-FURY FUREY

Tom Furey's hands were shaking. He sat next to the other members of the school committee, absorbing it all. The comfort zone of the middle school chambers was not realistic as the meetings were moved to St. Chretienne's chapel, which was part of Salem State College. This was a neutral playing field. Located at the South Campus, it was private property and gave the school committee, city officials, lawyers, and union negotiating teams some isolation as the striking teachers were not allowed to picket at this location.

The lights were dim at St. Chretienne. That is how Tom Furey liked it, as his head was pounding. He was a devoted Roman Catholic and felt this destination was somewhat symbolic, as maybe the powers above could shed light on the situation. "The school committee had a lot of dead time between meetings," stated Furey. This is when he would sit by the window and pray. The stars he saw through the windows gave him comfort. With the vocal outburst by Curtin getting louder and louder, he took out his rosary beads. His mouth was dry and his lips were chapped. He knew this group needed to gain some extra spiritual benefits. He quickly stuttered Hail Marys.

The tension and egos were building up like a volcano. Curtin was turning beet red. Furey pulled him aside when recess was called. The football team, still operating and practicing, left Curtin in a state of rage.

"Forgive and forget," were the words Furey stuttered out. "Your career is on the line, Mr. Superintendent. Don't lose your perspective or your career will be washed out to sea. But like a spoiled child not getting his way, the tirade of revenge would not be denied and the moral road would be neglected."

"Let's come together and make a better school system out of it all. Perception is everything in education. That did not come about and was not in the leadership of all three (mayor, superintendent, union president). They all came with personal baggage, and disliking each other was the norm," stated Furey.

Dr. Joseph Salerno, the assistant superintendent, was a man of honesty and integrity. "Joe was silenced by Curtin during negotiations. If Curtin allowed Dr. Salerno to get more involved, it could have been smoother sailing for both sides. Harrington and Curtin should have stayed out of negotiations. They put politics above teachers and students," Furey emphasized.

As a public official, Furey enjoyed a reputation characterized by honesty and integrity. To him, the mayor, superintendent, school committee and teachers union president had the wrong goal. They forgot the role of the kids which impacted the lives of so many. Furey was a teacher outside of Salem and worked for the school committee for twelve years. He did not forget his roots. "I marched with the teachers during the strike. I tried to bring credibility and honesty. I attended all the games, and it was probably one of the most exciting times to be part of the Salem school system. Everything was going well and then the vision got blurry with the storm arriving, bringing the strike. People did not want to come down and compromise. They had their personal agendas. The Irish stubbornness of some of the people involved delayed progress several times. Mayor Harrington stayed composed but was the wrong person at the wrong time." Furey constantly urged the mayor not to lose his perspective and make this a personal situation. Stuttering, "Please, please, please, always keep your eyes on the prize, the kids," Furey stated.

Furey was trying to solicit people to take the high road, be a better person, and help make Salem a more special place. "This is what Salem is based on: a dream and doing what is right."

"I was the greatest supporter of Ed Curtin. I had him as a teacher back in 1968. I campaigned for him when he ran for state representative. I always considered him a friend and was proud to serve with Mr. Curtin on the school committee. But when I saw the dark side of a man I respected as a leader and educator, things quickly spiraled downwards. People have that Dr. Jekyll and Mr. Hyde side. I saw both sides during the strike. Here he was, an Irish Roman Catholic, and went on a tirade of hate, rage, no forgiveness, no remorse. He contradicted what Christianity stood for. I could not take that road. I saw him taking the school system down. I went on strongly to support a high road to solit a whole new atmosphere, a whole new climate for the school system." Furey revealed.

CURTIN PLANTED

Ron Plante sat patiently in the back of the room as the school committee meeting got underway. A letter was delivered to the committee members and superintendent. One of the parents of a football player, referring to the letter, asked Curtin, "What is your position, Mr. Superintendent?"

As Superintendent Curtin spoke, Plante started to sweat. Because of the recently enacted law, the Education Reform Act, all of the authority of the school board was given to the superintendent. This gave him complete authority to hire and fire personnel.

The letter read:

> We do not agree with the lessons that have been recently taught by our football coaching staff to our football athletes. We, as administrators, feel that the school climate and healing process upon return of our students should be our main focus. In our opinion the current situation surrounding our football team has the potential to seriously impact the school climate at Salem High School when school resumes. If we are to maintain the primary interest of most members of the Salem School Community, which is the safety and well being of all of our students, then we must recommend that all the teaching personnel with extra-curricular activity assignments be allowed to resume those activities.

> Before arriving at this decision, we explored all possible avenues which would allow the players to play the game for which they have been pointing toward all season.

> We have contacted Swampscott school officials and they have, as the home team, informed us that they do not want the game time or date changed.

> In our judgment, the two assistant coaches would not be sufficient to adequately supervise, instruct and coach the team.

> We want all practices conducted on our authorized fields with appropriate facilities available to our student athletes.

> All of the events of the past week have served to confuse many students and have begun a divisiveness, which must begin to heal. We hope that we can begin this process with a resounding win over Swampscott on Saturday. Our athletes have the talent to accomplish that goal.

This letter was written to Mr. Edward Curtin by Mr. Silverman, Assistant principal Mr. Higgins, Director of Vocational and Business Education Mr. Pesce, Assistant Principal Mr. Burke, Athletic Director Mr. Geswell and Head of Guidance Mr. Dan Wholley. Mr. Curtin never responded and never showed the school committee the letter. In his deposition, Mr. Silverman testified to the authors of the letter.

Plante stated, "When Curtin was asked the question from the parent, he said that he needed to get recommendations from the coaches' immediate supervisors. The aforementioned letter was written to Mr. Edward Curtin by Principal Mr. Silverman, Assistant Principal Mr. Higgins, Mr. Pesce, Mr. Burke, Mr. Geswell, and Mr. Dan Wholley. Mr. Curtin had never responded and never showed the school committee the letter. Curtin's inner circle of colleagues and high-ranking administrators identified the harm caused to the community the order not to coach. Those trusted individuals prevailed upon Curtin to change his mind. Looking back, Curtin's non-disclosure of the so-called "Recommendations" was simply insidious. This decision-making supports the contention that Curtin acted against Perrone and not with the community in mind.

City councilors were hesitant to take sides and some felt it was not the council's job to get involved. The Ward Six Councilor was supportive of the teachers trying to get a pay increase. "The teachers have to do what they have to do," she said, noting that teachers have the right to be upset in wake of recent pay hikes to administrators. "Those increases sent the wrong messages to teachers." (*Salem News*, November 2, 1994)

But all city councilors criticized both sides for allowing negotiations to break down. While agreeing that teachers deserved raises, they noted the city continued to face a dire financial picture. "Going on strike is a tragedy, but the money in the city is extremely tight and whenever a raise is given, it has to be rational," observed Councilor-at-Large, William Burns. Our council president said that both sides, teachers and the school committee alike, needed to think realistically in negotiating a compromise to end the strike. The council president went on to say that if the city honored the teacher's union request for a 22 percent pay increase, layoffs would have been the end result not only in the school department, but in other city offices. "There needs to be some reality brought to negotiations," he said. "We're courting financial disaster, and we have been for some time."

DAY 3 of the STRIKE–
NOVEMBER 2, 1994 THE CAULDRON

Mayor Neil Harrington looked at his wristwatch. It read 8:58 AM. With his hair parted to the side, he resembled the part of an up-and-coming-political figure. Reaching for the water pitcher, he poured himself a glass. Donovan entered the Salem courtroom and everyone was ordered to rise. All 6'5" of Harrington slowly stood up. He was trying to be fair and do everything by the book. Parents vented anger toward Harrington, who threatened to fire the striking teachers and replace them. "I think the mayor should walk into those schools and see the quality of education that's going on. Maybe he should think about sending his own children to the public schools," stated a Salem parent. Public schools can be great vehicles for learning. But do they really challenge our children? Harrington sent his children to a private catholic school. Judge Donovan ordered a temporary restraining order (TRO) issued against the Salem teachers union. Judge Donovan threatened that "heavy fines" would be imposed if the union did not comply. Notably, contempt of a court order could also involve incarceration.

All parties appeared before Judge Donovan. She was to decide what orders she would issue to manage the strike. The union was requesting that Harrington be present at all negotiation sessions and that negotiations be held around the clock. Donovan also set a hearing for

November 8 to determine sanctions in the event of contempt by the Salem teachers union failing to comply with the order to cease and desist strike activities. (*Salem News*, November 3, 1994)

Turner sat unfazed when the proposed order was read. There would be no backing down from the union. They were practically attached at the hip. Camaraderie, chemistry, and persistence were all part of their makeup. This was their war and they were soldiers in their own mind. This union was made up of all middle class individuals whose passion was to educate kids, earn an honest livelihood but by the same token, not to be objects of ingratitude. The union was willing to negotiate and actions spoke louder than words. While teachers were standing tall in the picket lines, progress was being made for Wednesday night at the bargaining table. The union reduced its previous demand from a 22 percent increase to nineteen percent. When the clock struck 12 AM, the union was steadfast.

Despite minor progress, LRC lawyer Tammy Bryne filed the expected complaint of contempt against the union with the request for a trial as soon as possible. "I have every reason to believe sanctions will be imposed."

Another day passed, costing the city $20,000 per day, totaling $58,000 for the week. These expenses included police overtime, lawyer fees, and salaries for non-striking school workers and miscellaneous costs.

Harrington was quoted in the paper saying that it was a slap in the face to every taxpayer in the city. "The union leadership must think that money grows on trees in Salem. We're going to attempt to have all of these costs charged to the teachers union after the strike."

The union did not blink an eye and disclosed in court that it had assets of $60,000. They displayed the highest level of courage. The union was in the zone and the intimidation of fines coming their way was ignored.

PRELUDE TO THE SHOWDOWN

At Castle Hill, Mccellon slowly put on his cleats. Emulating Deion Sanders' skills, he often tried to dress like him as well. Perry put his practice pants on, hiding under a playground slide with several teammates following his lead. Higley sat in his Jeep, listening to some hardcore Metallica, screaming out words and using his steering wheel as a punching bag. His head was beating like a drum sending shockwaves through his body. His mind never slept; he wanted this nightmare to end. Some of the players used their cars for privacy to get changed, while other players emerged fully dressed out of the woods.

Coach Marcoulier looked at Coach Wilbur, "Looks like *Field of Dreams* except in retrospect it was a real-life nightmare."

Perrone paced the parking lot at the Castle Hill playground. He thought about every scenario and hit rewind in his head over and over again. He watched the same episode of his team being shortchanged. There were twenty seniors who gave their blood, sweat, and guts. "I could not turn my back on them. It would have made no difference if we were 0-6 or 6-0; those were my kids and they deserved to play." The man did not ask for this. He wished it did not come on his watch and that somehow or someway, his life could go back to normal.

Perrone had charisma, intensity, work ethic, intelligence, dignity, and faith. Those were all traits that he used with his years of service to create his own ark. He did not look at this as judgment day, but if it was, God would see a man of righteousness in his generation, nurturing God's children by looking out for their best interests. This was a day he made a pact with God, his team, and coaches that there would be no backing down. This man ran the program tighter than an Army boot camp and was ready to go to battle. He was pointing the finger at Superintendent Ed Curtin Wednesday, after putting his job on the line to direct practice at Castle Hill Park. The newspaper read that the superintendent was unhappy with Perrone taking an unpaid leave from his teaching job every spring to accompany his college baseball team to

Florida before the season. The feeling was mutual. Curtin received a $20,000 raise and then yelled and screamed at Perrone before the season, stating the budget was bone dry and $300 for raises would not work.

LIVE TV COVERAGE

Channel 5 News sports anchor Mike Lynch sat in his 1986 gold Toyota Camry at Castle Hill. Entering the park, he could not help but recognize the street's name, Story Road. Nineteen years removed from taking his last snap as a QB at Harvard, he found his true passion in covering Boston-area sports. He had empathy for the Salem football team and appreciated the important values that are developed at the high school level. This particular upcoming game against Swampscott made it even more appealing because he had played for the Big Blue. He cherished the experiences in high school and the opportunity to be part of a true dynasty going 35-1 in his four years. "All you had to do was hand off to former NFL and Yale star Dick Jauron who played running back and watch him go," said Lynch.

Patiently, he watched kids from all walks of life make their way into the park. He did not wait for the story to unfold, but reacted as if he were back on the gridiron with that same passion and analytical skills he had transitioned into his career.

CURTIN'S CULT LEADER ACCUSATIONS OF PERRONE

After hearing the Channel 7 interview and Ed Curtin compare Ken Perrone to Jim Jones and David Koresh, Lynch agreed that there was similarity between the accused (Witches) in 1692, and to Curtin comparing Perrone to cult leaders.

Lynch's reaction was clear, "I always felt that Ed Curtin made the whole thing personal. That changed the whole dynamic of everything. When you make something personal, you are on a mission. You just want to keep your thumb and foot on that person. Curtin did not keep it at a professional level," said Lynch.

Stepping out of his car he could feel autumn in the air, but a major storm was forming before him. Tears were shed and uncertainty painted all over the kids' faces. Moved by the huddled players, Lynch walked closer to it. He could feel the team's inner strength being formed. A football lay a few feet away with a folder next to it. The letters MIAA (Massachusetts Interscholastic Athletic Association) stood out like the courage the kids were defining. He instantly thought about that association which governed, coordinated, and promoted education-based programs for high school students. As the administration and police made their way to the field, Mike Lynch only shook his head with disgust. "It was so off base. Curtin, the athletic director, and the administration belong to the MIAA. One credo of the MIAA is to provide lifelong and life-quality learning experiences. You tell me that everything Ken Perrone taught that team, everything he was trying to accomplish with those kids during those turbulent times was providing leadership, lifelong and life-quality learning experiences. That is exactly what the MIAA is looking for. Curtin and the Salem School administration were members of the MIAA, yet they did not adhere to the MIAA credo," said Lynch.

Lynch had the ability to observe as a credible sportscaster who was named Massachusetts Sportscaster of the Year, a father and former Division I two-sport athlete. He scribbled the words "confusion" and "collateral damage" on his notepad. It was certain the kids were looking for leadership, stability, and a place to belong. "Ken Perrone and football gave them all those things they were looking for. They belonged on the football team, they had leadership with Ken Perrone, and they had stability being with their teammates while the town was polarized with the teachers out on strike and no school going on. You can always make up lost time in school; it's done every year with snow days. You can always make up a test. You cannot make up a game against

Swampscott with 12,000 people. It would be impossible for the kids to make up that experience in their lives." Mike Lynch made multiple trips down Story Road to the practice field and was extremely impressed at how this team was holding it together.

SIRENS STIR MCCELLON

Jamon Mccellon sat in denial on the cold aluminum bleachers at Castle Hill playground. His dreadlocks were going in every direction like fireworks exploding in the sky. His eyes were closed listening to Redman's "Time 4 Sum Aksion." He was always keeping it east coast old school which represented his roots. He did not want to open his eyes, praying these nightmarish feelings would go away and wishing they were unreal. This was his shelter, holding his sanity together; his emotions were as fragile as a house of cards. He was terrified to open his eyes. The police sirens were getting closer as his tears started to fall.

When reality hit, he was afraid that this dream season would vanish like he did at eleven years old on that cold December night when he boarded a Greyhound bus out of the housing projects in New Britain, Connecticut. Those sirens brought back lurid memories of the ghetto where he stayed with his mother and two little brothers. On welfare, they struggled to get by, but most of the family's welfare check went toward his mother's habit of crack and cocaine. He lived scared, hungry, and cold. His mom would go missing weeks at a time, leaving the family with no heat or electricity. The warmth of his heart kept his brothers alive. "We did what we needed to do to survive. We had the same mother, but all three of us had different fathers, none of them anywhere to be found. She would only return with sketchy men in all hours of the night." All he wanted was love. In his dreams, his dad held him in his arms, telling him he loved him and that everything would be okay, but in reality, he was MIA. Never in his life.

He knew there had to be a better life. He was always an articulate kid with a vision. Delivering papers and keeping the clock for basketball games at the local Boy's Club enabled him to save a few dollars. Sitting in awe and keeping score, he would watch future New England Patriot Tebucky Jones ball out against grown men. This gave him the strength and resilience so that he, too, could succeed in sports. There was only one way this could happen: He needed a new beginning. "One night a man was in our room looking through drawers, holding a gun. I slept with the little money I had. I needed to go and sensed something bad was going to happen."

With kids, it is about progression, but he felt like it was a battle just not to regress. "It was a constant course in Regression 101." Not telling anyone, he headed up to Lynn, Massachusetts, to live with his grandparents. "It was a fresh start." They were churchgoing Baptists that restructured his faith.

Lynn is a city in Essex County. The population was 92,519 (1990 Census). It was located about seven miles north of downtown Boston and 4.2 miles south from Salem. He enrolled at Pickering Junior High in East Lynn. The surroundings were better than the projects, but not by much. Gangs were on the corners and violence was in the air. He turned to the gridiron, and the East Lynn Pop Warner team gave him all the makings of a complete family: support, connection, trust, empathy, respect, and goal orientation.

With four high schools in the city, and being a hands-on type of kid, he chose Lynn Tech, a vocational technical high school. It did not take long for him to realize that he needed to always watch his back. One night he attended a party on a Friday evening with several friends from the football team. An altercation between groups of kids resulted in a knife being pulled and a former football star getting stabbed. Later that year his mom wanted to make amends; she was tired of running from the demons.

At times he veered off the road of righteousness and searched for ways to express himself. One way was "art," as many kids from the hood would call it, but the Lynn law enforcement agencies looked at as "graffiti." Graffiti can be used as a gang signal to mark territory. With the tag name of "Swiss," he was known city-wide. Caught in the act, he was arrested and charged with defacement and vandalism.

Mccellon required some structure; he needed a guardian angel. His mother started dating an area football coach. He was well aware of her past demons and took a liking to her kids. Realizing how much her boys were into sports and being a former coach under Ken Perrone, he believed a move to Salem which was just over four miles northeast from Lynn was in their best interest.

They all moved down to The Point. The living arrangements were tight. They lived in a three family on the top floor. He shared a room with his brothers. Deion Sanders and Jerry Rice were his idols, and Rice's poster was taped to his wall. He kept his scrapbook under his bed, and from time to time, he would take it out. He recalled the C-team Pop Warner tie-breaker against Salem like yesterday. Lying on the floor, he started tossing a football up in the air in disbelief that he was going to be part of the Salem team. A couple of months went by, and just when he felt his relationship with his mother was starting to prosper, she picked up old habits. The situation with his mom left him saddened and shaken. "I was completely broken and wanted to have that tight-knit relationship with my mom. She basically neglected me for drugs." He needed a shoulder to cry on and, after enrolling in Salem High, he received a double dose.

Salem offered a counseling program which helped him therapeutically. Coach Perrone and the team embraced him. Jamon had been diagnosed with a learning disability in high school. It went undetected and caused him to struggle in school. During elementary days, no one was assisting him in his education. He was not a diligent student and never took it seriously. He did the basics to get by. He made a commitment to himself to stop smoking blunts and start locking down wide receivers.

Football was a means to an end, but it was also providing an education in life. Burdened by his mom's past and her lack of empathy, football was his shelter and provided a shield. He opened some eyes in his first-ever start against Peabody playing determined and fearless. Like a flower, he blossomed from his coach's nurturing, and his past mental wounds started to heal.

SIRENS STIR THE TEAM AND COACHES

With the police sirens getting closer, the team could have ran away as if they had something to hide but just like on the field, they were prepared for the invasion by the Salem Police Department, administration, and anyone else.

Tears of disappointment streamed down Jamon's face. He did not take this team for granted. He loved everything about it. He did not feel lucky, but blessed, to be a part of it. "We were a tight group. At first there were all different types of personalities, but we grew past that and everyone cared about each other. To me the mayor and superintendent hated Coach Perrone for the simple reason that he had more clout in the city than both of them put together. Bruised egos are tough to repair. Maybe if they compromised with him and took the time to sit down, they could have learned something about leadership," stated Mccellon. "All I had to hold onto was football. I cried for the simple reason that I thought our coaches were going to get arrested. This team was the closest thing I ever had to a family. I am not sure if Curtin understood that or cared. All he preached was doing things on principle. I guess he never got educated on loyalty."

CANELO'S FAMILY

Edwin Canelo slowly biked up Read Road. The two-mile ride to and from practice was challenging with his equipment on. One of his boys, rapping some beats, was hitching a ride on the pegs. Making his way onto Story Road, he was amazed by what he saw. Every major New

England news station had broadcast equipment at Castle Hill Park. The street was like a reality TV show unfolding before their eyes. They camped out at Castle Hill Park, similar to committed season ticket holders trying to get tickets to see their team play in the Super Bowl. Coach Perrone was being interviewed; the team captains were speaking to reporters. The questions, "What are your thoughts on the strike? Will there be a game?" came out of reporters' mouths as he walked by, but the questions did not register.

Pausing, he continued to walk. Most of his teammates were standing together, looking confused. At this point in his football journey, he realized it was more than just a game and it meant something to him. The strike united this team and brought out the best in every member of that team. He saw egos disappear, attitudes fade, and empathy internally sweep through everyone affiliated. "It opened my eyes and made me want to excel more in a sport. I wanted to be somebody on the field. This transformed lives. What the administrators were doing was wrong. Why not let us fulfill our dreams? They were trying to take the best thing going for us and stop it. Football became an actual family to me, teaching me teamwork and character," said Canelo.

GESWELL: A GOOD MAN IN A BAD SITUATION

Athletic Director Bob Geswell was a quiet, honest and behind-the-scenes type of guy who lived a life of integrity. November 2, 1994, was the page on Geswell's office desk calendar. The last school bell rang, but the corridors were empty. He had made a number of calls throughout the day, trying to line up volunteer coaches. Painful muscle spasms ran through his back. Multiple sclerosis was starting to control parts of his body. His left leg tingled and burned. A cease and desist document sat in front of him as his hand shook with a pen in it before he signed the document. Twenty years of thoughts passed through him. He recreated the thought of walking down the corridors and seeing some of the kids in the special needs program which affected Geswell. But at times, seeing some of the athletes that understood they had a duty to give back to society because of the way they were brought up and the lessons they were taught while being members of athletic programs was very gratifying when he witnessed these athletes making others feel important. He had loyalty to the administration, and he had loyalty to the kids and the program. Geswell had always tried to do the best he could. "I have seen a lot of people in Salem do what they thought was best for kids, and they have been criticized for that. In terms of education, whenever you tell a person they cannot have or do something, you get labeled as being against kids. That is the criticism you deal with in education, while being involved with kids."

His allegiance was with his superior, Superintendent Ed Curtin. How could you fault him? He was just taking orders. "Respect" is the word that came to heart when he thought of Curtin. "I think Mr. Curtin wanted what was best for the kids: to get the strike settled as quickly as he could. I think that was his main focus. In my eyes he was a good guy and I think his intentions were honorable. I have seen him do what's best for kids many times over and over again," said Geswell.

ASSAULT ON CASTLE HILL

Police cars and trucks entered the park full force as if someone had been murdered. Wearing their riot gear, the SWAT teams took their positions. The police dogs growled and barked. At that point the team thought everyone was going to get arrested: the coaches for holding practice and the players for breaking into school and stealing their equipment.

Mccellon felt the same type of sadness that punctured his heart when he cried himself to sleep, waiting for his mother to come home and for his dad to show up on his doorstep one day. The players arm locked and formed a barricade circling the coaches. Feeling the strength from his team, Perrone emerged from the circle and approached the administrators. Silverman, Geswell, and Higgins delivered a letter to Perrone at the beginning of practice. The letter was from Curtin. He accepted it with glassy eyes and a heavy heart. The letter read like legal document. It was phrased as a cease and desist order. Even though the letter was written like an injunction or temporary restraining order, it was issued outside of the court process. Looking back, Curtin implicitly was trying to install in the coaches the same fear that the teachers union was exposed to in court. That implicated big fines and incarcerations. This was just another subtle way Curtin was using the overall situation to pressure those coaches into compliance, Curtin's compliance. The memorandum read: "Please be advised that we are directing you to cease and desist from any and all athletic practices with the Salem high football team until you return to your teaching assignment."

"All assistant coaches who are striking teachers are also instructed to refrain from their coaching until the above conditions are met.

"Those coaches who are not teachers are further directed to conduct all practices on the upper field of the high school, effective immediately. Refusal to adhere to this directive will be considered as acts of insubordination, and will be subject to further disciplinary action.

"Consistent with the policy of the school committee, you are not authorized to conduct athletic practices if you are absent from your teaching position on a given day, unless approval has been given in advance. As you continue to be absent from your teaching position due to an illegal strike, you are directed to cease all coaching, monitoring, or supervisory activities."

***

Cameras were in Coach Wilbur's face; reporters were asking him questions. WB56 sports director Frank Mallicoat approached him. Wilbur was at a loss for words. Intimidation defined his emotions. The presence of the school officials, the law, and the simple necessity of keeping his job put him in an unpleasant state of mind. At forty years old he had his entire career in front of him. He had taught with passion and coached with poise and dedication. Wilbur truly cared about the kids and played an operative role in molding them to develop in grade school and have the mentality to get up if they got knocked down. He was proud to be a part of something so special and embraced the opportunities that were given to him. "We all decided together to coach, not knowing what the ramifications were going to be," Wilbur said.

CHAPTER 17

POLITICS

///

> *"When at a young age you learn to face your fears, that makes the difference between people being champions and people not being champions."*
> ~ Evander Holyfield

DAY 4 of the STRIKE – NOVEMBER 3, 1994

Perrone sat in his home office. It was 5 AM and he could not sleep. Dust settled on his 19" TV, the Swampscott vs. Beverly game VHS inserted in the VCR. He wrote in his notebook and watched the defenses of Swampscott. Trying to exploit any gaps they might have, he paid particular attention to the first half as they were trailing 10-0. The phone rang at 7:05 AM.

It was Coach Marcoulier, "Coach did you hear the report on the WEEI radio show?"

"No," said Perrone.

"They stated that *The Boston Globe* correspondent B.J. Schecter confirmed that you would be fired in Town House Square at 1 PM."

Pausing, he sat back in his chair and took a deep breath. "Well I guess it beats getting a horse and carriage to the Gallows."

This is how the accused witches were transported in 1692. Walking out of the room, he started to feel pressure throughout his body. Sitting down on the sofa, he reached into his pocket and took out a nitroglycerin pill which he took to prevent heart attacks.

The man just wanted to coach his team.

CONTINUED TV COVERAGE OF PRACTICE:
NO MOVEMENT ON PERRONE

Practice was conducted for the second day under the glare of television lights as reporters waited patiently for something stranger, something crazier, or something more ridiculous to happen next.

Despite an early morning meeting involving Principal Silverman, Athletic Director Geswell, and Assistant Principals Burke and Higgins, no disciplinary action was to be taken against Perrone and four other teacher-coaches. This actually led to speculation that Perrone and company would be allowed to coach.

Mayor Harrington was unwilling to make any commitment. "I don't know who will be coaching the team Saturday. I am in full support of the game being played. I hope the kids play."

For the moment, the indecisiveness of the administration gave hope to the team and exoneration for the stealing of the equipment to continue practicing.

The rumblings remained low as this was a big-money game. Perrone said, "All the administrators had to say is we forfeit and there would have been no game."

Players stood in the outfield at Castle Hill with a look of amazement on their faces. The entire area of grass had been lined the night before. On the 50-yard line, the words "Good Luck" were written. The support from the community had been tremendous.

I played catch with De Pena. Higley took in mental reps from Coach Marcoulier. At the beginning of the week Higley felt like a professional athlete because of the scrutiny from the media: no school, just football. "As a young athlete, I looked up to Perrone for what he did by putting his career on the line. What he taught us was that he was not doing it for himself; the reward was seeing his players succeed. Building young guys into great men is what he did, and that is what it is all about. They were going to take that away from him. I did feel we were used as pawns by the administrators, union, and coaches; everyone had their own agenda and we just wanted to play football," said Higley.

The E-Train took a knee on the grass. The park was secluded by woods, and negative ions were in the air; this would be an ingredient that helped everyone stay balanced and focused on the task at hand. The coaches and players were all living in the moment, not sure what was going to happen next. It was all a mystery. They were all little boys at heart, playing a kids' game.

Practice was like a calm sea compared to Wednesday's circus. This enabled the players to prepare for less-than-favorable conditions. "It was nice, finally getting a day where I was not harassed," stated Perrone. "Monday we had no practice, Tuesday we accomplished zero in forty-five minutes before it rained, and Wednesday was so windy, making it tough to pass and kick the ball."

Perrone's first priority was to honor the teachers. He never thought once to cross the picket line without the teachers' blessing to coach. Brockton High, Tewksbury High, and Belmont High were just a few of the high schools that went on strike during the past twenty years. Those strikes occurred during the football season and exceptions by those schools' superintendents were made for the athletic programs to continue participating in extracurricular activities. Brockton AD Tom Pileski said, "All the teams were allowed to continue with their coaches, and the idea was that the kids would not be hurt by the job action. Neither side prevented the coaches from coaching." No exceptions were being made, however, in Salem's case. Salem could have drawn on the precedent established in the Brockton, Tewksbury, and Belmont situations.

It was in this context that Curtin agreed to the infamous interview with Boston's Channel 7 John Dennis. Curtin professed Perrone to be "a cult figure." "We're very concerned about young people being manipulated and led astray, and what comes to mind is Jim Jones and Waco (David Koresh)," Curtin said. "I hope the Salem public and Salem citizens think about that."

Dennis then asked Curtin, "So you are equating what Ken is doing on the football field with that kind of cult?"

"I think so," Curtin replied.

Dennis also asked, "Do you think Coach Perrone is fit to coach this football team and should be coaching this football team?"

After a lengthy pause, Curtin said, "No." (*Salem News*, Friday November 4, 1994)

MANY SEE BEHIND THE REAL CURTIN

Mazz's hypothesis rested on the great personalities the coaches and teachers had. The dedication and camaraderie developed between the teachers and coaches were all positives, but poison to Ed Curtin. Curtin did not like that. He wanted to be the one to embrace all that, and despised seeing others have it.

At Perrone's compound he was not using the cult tactic of sleep deprivation. However, he himself was deprived of sleep, averaging two to three hours a night which left him weary and perturbed, but he remained focused at all times. He was managing a surplus amount of news media calls, and then he went to the picket lines where he was putting in the same amount of energy as he did when coaching, while supporting the teachers union.

That day, Perrone held his coaches' meeting on picnic tables before practice got underway. With no chalkboards, he literally drew up plays in the dirt, and using blue puff bags as Swampscott players, he was implementing a game plan that allowed his players to comprehend his points and prepare for battle.

Armond Colombo, the famed Brockton coach, followed the controversy in Salem and said, "For them to say the football team could play without five coaches is idiotic. It would be the same thing to say maybe the schools can run without a superintendent and a principal. Let the teachers just do their thing with no direction, no leadership."

"I find it absolutely appalling that any school superintendent would equate a football coach to a cult leader. If anybody up there should be in trouble, it's the superintendent for making that absurd remark." Jack Welch of Ipswich said, "The Massachusetts State Coaches Association fully supports Perrone. What they (the administration) should have done is call off everything and forfeit, but they didn't have the guts." (*Salem News*, November 5, 1994)

Watching the reruns on Channel 7, Perrone started laughing as he heard Curtin compare him to a cult leader. "The guy is sick; here I am in my twenty-second year, have great evaluations from the administration, and he makes that statement."

Everyone who knew Perrone realized the type of person he was. The next morning, walking into the hall where the teachers' meeting was held, Perrone received a standing ovation. Many union members were shocked that the leader of the Salem school system would make a comment like that.

Being the face of the city, Harrington watched Curtin, a very educated man, compare Perrone to a cult leader. Why would he do that? "I don't know why. There was a lot of stress involved. Tempers were flaring at various times and things got emotional. "I would imagine that in retrospect, many people wished they might not have said certain things," said Harrington.

After Curtin's first filming of the Channel 7 interview, there was a malfunction in the video camera and the video did not take. Dennis returned to Salem to do a retake, and he gave Curtin the opportunity to avoid repeating the cult leader remarks previously uttered about Perrone. As Ahab did, Curtin stayed firm in his blind rage for his

1994 Salem High School Super Bowl team

Owa, me, and my mother Gloria - 1992

Doug Flutie and I at a Flutie Autism Foundation fundraiser - 2006

Mercado (20) leads for The E-Train.

The "Mad Dog" Marcoulier

Salem students picket City Hall during the strike.

Perrone served cease and desist before media presence.

The ultimate act of defiance at Swampscott: Coaches Wilbur, Baldassarri, Stellato, Perrone, Elsaesser, Marcoulier, McKenna

Jamon Mccellon reacts to police escort and delivery of cease and desist to Coach Perrone.

Supplied with stolen equipment, the team prepares for its offsite illegal practice at Castle Hill Park.

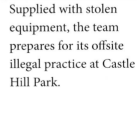

Coaches confer before telling team they will ignore cease and desist.

Higley (67), Daley (33), and Downes ("Mom" on left shoulder) come up with a big stop.

Big gain on broken play against Swampscott.

Coach Perrone and wife, Jan, expressing the conflicting emotions of the career jeopardy attached to the Swampscott win.

Celebrating the Swampscott win.

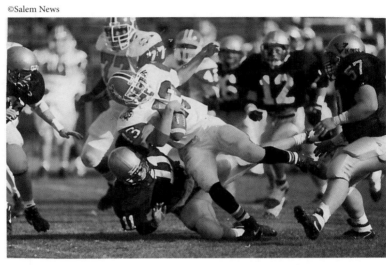

The E-Train gains ground with Jones (77) clearing the right side.

Perrone improvising the miracle play against Winthrop.

Cronin and Jones celebrate
with De Pena after miracle TD
reception.

Coaching staff
during Beverly
game

Perrone protests last minute Beverly
score on controversial play.

Another late game play selection by
Perrone to seal miracle win at Beverly.

The handoff to win the Beverly game. Cronin (55) powers open the hole for game-winning TD.

The E-Train (43), Mercado (20), De Pena (83), Dulong (61), and Jones (77) after winning TD over Beverly.

I am taking it all in after Beverly miracle.

Perrone with
Pep Cornacchio,
Salem's greatest
fan

Firing a pass during the Super Bowl.

De Pena (83)
and Dulong
(61) open up
a hole for The
E-Train.

The fearsome DL Higley gets a sack
in the Super Bowl.

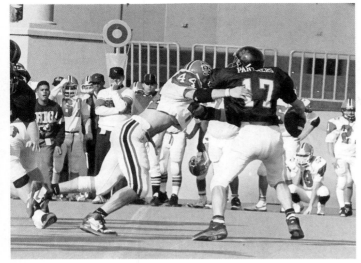

Relentless LB Downes (44) in Super Bowl action

The E-Train in Super Bowl action

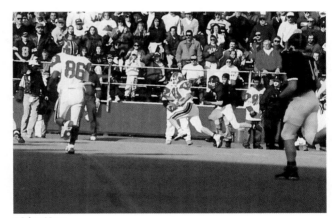

Stellato to De Pena (83), complete concentration

Cronin led the offensive line from his center position.

Agony of Super Bowl defeat

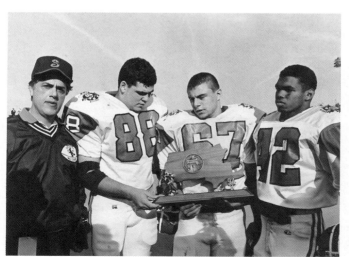

Perrone with captains Whitten (88), Higley (67), Freeman (42) holding the runner-up trophy

Hall of Fame induction with my family

The resurrection
of Owa's cross
when I returned
to Miller Field.

With my family
at Good Harbor
Beach

©Christine Mallette

Always reaching
for the sky

©Christine Mallette

My true road
dog, Sly

nemesis: Ahab, the white whale, and Curtin, the football coach from Maine. Knowing his quotes would be disseminated in the mass media, he had time to reflect on the full meaning of what his declarations would do to the community. He deliberately premeditated the full scope of the treacherous image he wanted to re-convey.

Curtin, like Ahab breaking the compass, could not resist the temptation and, for a second time, regurgitated all of the verbal venom against Perrone he had earlier conjured.

Wayne Turner had his two minutes of fame and, unlike Curtin, emphasized that the real problem with the strike was that the students were missing school. Turner stated, "I never heard Ed Curtin, Harrington, or school committee member Andrew Lippman mention anything about students during the strike. Harrington threatened to fire all the teachers, and Lippman was always screaming at me when I went to any of the schools and spoke to people who were yelling, 'Why are you doing this? Why are you making a strike?'"

I would shout back, "Your bonehead idea regarding merit pay has not brought any light to the situation."

Day 5 of the Strike: November 4, 1994

Optimism was in the air between the Salem Teachers Union and the school committee. Both parties broke bread at the bargaining table Friday. However, any attempted resolutions took a step in the wrong direction. "The session opened with the committee waiting three hours for a counterproposal that was to be presented at the start of the evening. In response to the counterproposal, the committee offered its response in the form of counterproposal which the union summarily rejected." (*Salem News*, November 5, 1994)

The teachers were playing a version of Russian roulette as they were due back in Superior Court Monday. They needed to demonstrate why they should not be held in contempt of court for violating a judge's order to end the strike. Later that day, the Salem teachers union was cited in the Salem Superior Court for contempt of court.

Mayor Harrington and colleagues on the school committee had grossly underestimated the extent of teacher dissatisfaction with the last contract and the offer they had on the table as of a week ago Friday. It did not take Harrington long to discover that finding competent personnel to replace hundreds of teachers out on the picket lines required more than putting an ad in the paper. Two elementary principles of contract negotiations subscribed to by municipal officials was that: 1) It's better to seek a wage freeze and claim poverty than insult someone with an offer of a one percent wage increase; and 2) if you don't have any money, it's not the time to seek radical changes in the collective bargaining relationship like tying wage increases to improvements in students test scores. (*Salem News*, November 5, 1994)

The Salem girls' soccer team had the goal to win a state title. Unlike the football team, Charlie Maihos' soccer team had been left alone by the media and school officials. His decision to coach, like Perrone's, received the blessing of the teachers' union.

Perrone and Maihos shared the same belief. "You have to do what your heart and head tell you to do," said Maihos. "If you are any type of coach, the kids will always be first." Maihos was sent home on Monday. Tuesday's practice was held indoors at the school so he could not attend. Wednesday and Thursday, he ran practice at Memorial Park.

Standing on the Bertram Field sidelines, he waited patiently for the opening round of the Division I North State Tournament to get underway. It was a picture-perfect day until he was greeted by the Grim Reaper and given a cease and desist order. It was the same type of letter that Curtin gave to Perrone. How does that help a team's psyche moments before a game? Coach Maihos coached his team, Salem won 2-0 over Peabody and now Perrone had company within the Salem Administration's list of "Most Wanted Men." Perrone was notified at practice that Maihos was served papers, and the administrators would be making their next stop at Castle Hill Park to pay him a visit. Perrone stood still and braced himself for the worst. Standing by his team, he feared this was the last chapter in his story, and symbolically it would end on Story Road where Castle Hill Park was located. A vehicle carrying administrator's assistant principal Higgins and athletic director Geswell parked several feet away. They slowly approached him and gave relatively good news. Perrone was told he could not ride the team bus to Swampscott for the game, but assistants Coach Stellato and Dick McKenna were allowed to ride it.

He was given the impression that nobody would prevent him from coaching the Swampscott game. Turning to his team, he gave them the thumbs up sign and yelled, "Guys, we're all set, baby."

The team was put through a light workout without pads. Adversity had not completely evaporated as the team headed over to Salem State College and watched films of Swampscott for the first time.

"If they come to take me away, my team will take their pads off and there won't be a football game," said Perrone. "As I told the team, it doesn't matter if we win or lose. The second we take the field, we've won." (*The Boston Globe*, November 5, 1994)

Bob Geswell lay in his bed, trying to sleep. Stress refused to leave his body. Reading helped relax his mind. Sitting up in bed, he was startled as the phone rang. Softly, he said to himself, "It's 11:30." Answering the call, he heard someone breathing heavily on the end of the line. In a deep voice, they asked to speak to Bob. Confirming it was him, the person went on to disclose how they were going to ruin his life and Bob would get his if he attended the game.

In a very opinionated society, people often forget there are two sides to every story. Ignorance is created when society refuses to address the root of the problem. Geswell took orders, went to work, and did his job. He did not reach out to anyone for lucidity. It was a very degrading time in his life.

With reputations and credibility going up in smoke, Geswell knew this was not making Salem a better place. It was less than twenty-four hours to game time. He was all worked up and thought back to earlier in the day when he arrived to an empty house, upset and disgusted. Once he got comfortable, the phone started ringing, thinking for sure it was another harassing phone call, he decided to deal with it now rather than later.

A soft sweet little voice said, "Hi, Grampi." It was his three-year-old granddaughter.

Taking a deep breath, he tensed up to hold back tears and he got sentimental as tears came out of his eyes. It put everything into perspective and made him realize at that very moment what was important in life.

CHAPTER 18

MEDIA BLITZ AND POLICE ESCORT

"To be a winner in life and on the football field, you must come to terms with God first, your teammates second, and yourself third."

~ Ken Perrone

LATE AFTERNOON, DAY 5 of the STRIKE

It was Friday, November 4, the night before the big game. The clock struck five. I walked up to my dad and said, "I am ready to go now." The two of us drove over to Blocksidge Field in Swampscott and decided to take a walk on the field.

Swampscott is an affluent town in Essex County located on the North Shore, twelve miles up the coast from Boston. It is known for its high school football. Coach Bondelevich's era was equivalent to the Red Auerbach dynasty had while coaching the Celtics. The Big Blue captured ten Northeastern Conference titles and had eight unbeaten teams under him. From 1967 to 1972, the Big Blue went a combined 54-1. He coached several former NFL players, one of them being Dick Jauron.

Bondelevich had to say this about Perrone: "He is a hell of a coach. He makes things equal. He is one of the finest coaches I have ever seen.

Ken will always give you problems because of all he does. He is a master of deception. He can take advantage of players and make them a lot better because he can confuse opponents." As a point of comparison Bondelevich mastered the task of building a high school football program from the youth program to the booster club. He developed the youth program coaches. He asked them to use his play book, terminology, drills, and teaching methods. He encouraged independence in thinking, but maintained a line of propriety when players ascended to "his" ranks. He cultivated parents and businesses to donate time and money to enhance the banquets, promote the cheerleading squad and band, create programs and attract media attention. Bondelevich was idolized in Swampscott as he literally defined the community with his football team. Perrone was nothing short of another Bondelevich. Both lived with the maxim that success breeds contempt, a motivating force that can rear its ugly head through anyone at any time.

During the past summer, I spent nearly every day training nowhere else, but here on Blocksidge Field. Swampscott High School's program was the most dominant in the state's 112 year history of high school football. When it was all over and done with, I choose to believe that getting my reps in here on their home field was me acting like a dog who pisses on a spot to mark it. Yes, I was making a statement, unknowingly, about a claim to be made.

The sun shined bright and the heat and humidity combined to create an outdoor sauna. The well-groomed, closely-trimmed grass resembled a country club fairway and looked nothing like the crater-filled field it would be in a few short months. The wooden stands were worn down, and well used.

Although the crisp autumn air was still three months away, I knew that these dog days of summer were when football champions were made and unsung heroes were born. With shoulder pads and helmet on, I buckled my chin-strap and was ready to compete against Drew

Bledsoe if I had to. I knew my time had come. After all, my grandmother had told me as much. Coach Perrone had made his point very clear at the final meeting: The QB position was still up in the air. Pat Ryan wanted the job, but I coveted it and, unknown to anyone–perhaps other than Owa–I would not be denied.

My father, Patrick Stellato, dutifully sat in the stands every Saturday morning, videotaping me. The father who shaped me into the man I would become was committed to helping me fulfill my boyhood dream of becoming the starting QB and leading the team to the Super Bowl. Having lost his own dad to leukemia when he was only eighteen compelled him to want to share in my journey.

Chris Carroll, A.J. Grimes, and De Pena were my receivers for the summer. Carroll had played with my older brother at Salem High and was fighting to see the field at Sacred Heart University. Grimes, a gifted wide receiver from The Point, was like a golden retriever, obsessed with running down any ball that got close to him and then sprinting back to deliver me the prize he'd secured. I was convinced Grimes must have been a dog in another life.

Carroll ran a dig route and the ball came in low. "You are dropping your elbow," my father yelled from the stands. A no-nonsense type of guy, my dad made it very clear to me that he would give me every opportunity to succeed but under one condition: I would have to handle constructive criticism if I wanted to improve.

Hitches, slants, and curls, wheels, digs, flags, sprint-outs, posts, and fades were a combination of routes we rehearsed repeatedly. The competition was fierce as we worked specific game situations: third and long, red zone, and my favorite, the last minute, hurry-up drives with it all on the line. I developed instincts to react in these situations that would either mold or handicap younger athletes. I watched Doug Flutie's heroics on a weekly basis. I emulated him by putting myself in similar situations and thrived off pressure.

Any dropped balls or bad routes earned the receivers extra sprints or push-ups and the same would go for poor technique or badly thrown balls. With every ball tossed, I would utter the name of the teacher who told me, "You will never play QB for Salem High." I was motivated and inside, a flame was burning bright. I couldn't tell if I was sweating from the 90 degree plus temperatures or my desire to succeed. Using my brothers as benchmarks, I knew at a young age how quickly careers come and go. I refused to be another has-been and knew Owa was right, that I would be part of a legacy. The QB challenge was something I fed off. I knew in my heart that success on the field was a key to open many doors, and that the gridiron was a place where souls were lifted and dreams come true. I didn't want it any other way. What did it matter if others were bigger, stronger, faster, or smarter? No one would outwork me. Those are the values my parents instilled and those are the values by which I live.

The sun beams on my body as I continue to sprint on the field, 40s and gassers. Less and less oxygen was reaching my head. Winded, I felt thoughts going every which way. Dry mouth and nausea start to take control of me. Then the single image of my goal lit an internal flame, igniting the mental toughness. I was in the zone. No one had a clue just how badly I wanted it. The solitary thought lived within me, quietly pushing me on. The three of us were running our last 40-yard sprint, but for me it was not just about running to get faster; it was a lot more complex. Chris Carroll's priceless impressions of Johnny Most, the Boston Celtics play-by-play announcer, would fire up Grimes and me. We would get one play with time running out. If it wasn't successfully executed, we would have to wait until the next workout, usually after I had thrown 200 plus balls. The blister on the index finger of my left throwing hand throbbed but I was in the moment and ignored the pain. I was at the only place I wanted to be. Others were hanging with friends at the beach or recovering from a party the night before.

As we threw pass after pass, I scripted it out in my mind. At the time I was so focused, I could have easily been convinced that we were in the final drive of the big game, playing before a stadium packed with rabid fans. I could hear the play-by-play commentator in my head, as if I were sitting in front of a TV watching someone else's game. "Sean Stellato is under center with Grimes split out wide." As I prepare to take the snap from center, I can see the ghost of Stan Bondelevich, Swampscott's all-time greatest coach, pacing the Swampscott sidelines. "The crowd is on its feet, going wild. Salem's down five with only four ticks remaining on the clock. Stellato takes the snap from center and sprints out left. Grimes almost effortlessly parts the secondary like the Red Sea. Feeling pressure, Stellato heaves a pass to the back of the end zone where Grimes makes a diving shoestring catch. Stellato thrusts his fists into the air as the Salem faithful erupt. The skinny kid who had never been given a chance has led Salem to Perrone's first state championship!"

And then, the rapid echoes from a clap, followed by my father's booming voice yelling out, "Never let this moment leave your mind," brings me back to the present. It was an almost out-of-body experience, as if my dad had just experienced the surreal game-winning pass with me.

The beach is a place where people rest and roast. The sun may be hot but that isn't the only burn you can get there. The resistance training you receive from running on sand is guaranteed to give your leg muscles an instant burn. I spent time reflecting and training at Good Harbor beach in Gloucester. It was on the Good Harbor beaches where I found the call that so far had eluded me on the football field. I used nature's power and the rhythm of the ocean to find my inner strength and beat. Isolated from competition sixteen miles north of Salem, I hit my three and five step drops into the beach sand and sprint out passes kidnapped my focus. The beach became my substitute football field where I managed to develop areas of my body I hadn't known existed. My older brother Eric wanted his kid brother to succeed so he volunteered his time to catch balls and be my moving bullseye whenever he could. On that score, we were always close, but the bond we cemented on those long, sweltering summer days had begun the summer before with the passing of one of our closest friends, Jody Ryan. That year it grew even stronger as Eric pushed me to succeed. Jody had died tragically in a car accident, and when Eric heard the news, he cried so hard that he scratched the cornea of his eyes.

"He made everyone smile that he came in contact with," my brother would say. Losing Jody taught my brother and me a lesson that we would carry with us our entire lives: laugh and love. In that hectic beach workout summer, we did.

Eric, a former bruising tailback for Salem's 1991 team who dreamed of being the next Eric Dickerson, was 5'11" at 240 pounds with 4.57 speed and possessed what seemed like superhero strength, had the ability to turn his dream into a reality. "I let girls and booze stand between me and my dreams," he would tell me. "You're not going to make those mistakes, least not on my watch. And you're not going to slack off in the classroom either." Even without his adolescent distractions, my brother's grades would have derailed his football career, and he was bound and determined to save me from his fate. His heart was big, and he showed me unconditional love, convinced I had what it took to succeed where he had fallen short.

Gallows Hill, where the accused witches were hanged 300 years earlier, was another familiar place I made part of my training regimen. The landscape, the steep rolling hills give off an eerie feeling from its history as a location where witches were hung. Gallows Hill was a frightening place to me. My brother played on my fear to get me to train even harder. Being the naïve little brother I was, I allowed him to play a game known as "Running Scared." Eric had so much fun with this, he couldn't resist inviting our oldest brother, Michael, to join the "fun." Eric and Michael led me into the woods—blindfolded, alone and in the dark—and taunted me with tales of the haunted grounds and bears that lived in those woods. They would leave me there with the blindfold on and have me to count to 100 before I could take it off. After counting to 100, I would take the blindfold off and shoot out of the woods like a lightning bolt with my brothers watching and laughing. This, they had me convinced, would up my running speed. The crazy thing is, even as they put the fear of God into me, I was so desirous to be stronger and faster that I was a willing accomplice in the game of brotherly love.

I snapped back to reality as it was no longer summer, but the day before the game that would prove whether or not all those reps paid dividends.

"Son, how are you feeling?"

"Anxious, but ready. Dad, no one thinks we can win this game. You have read the papers, they think there are too many distractions."

"Channel those words into faith. This is a home game for you. You threw hundreds of balls this summer to Chris and AJ, ran tons of sprints, all with the music from *The Natural* playing in your head," stated my father.

Seconds later a shooting star shot out of the sky.

"That is for you. Do you believe?"

"With all my heart and soul, I am ready for this," I stated softly.

Slowly taking it all in, I made a stop by the bathrooms which were connected to the locker rooms. Walking by the Big Blue locker room, some of the players were laughing out loud and making the remark, "I am going to hit Rodriquez so hard, he might speak English. They should check his birth certificate; he looks twenty-two. Can their QB even see over the line of scrimmage?"

JUDGMENT TIME

Our boosters were holding a football rally at the Salem Commons. I made my way through the hundreds of people who were gathered to support the program. Spectators were dressed in red; it showed why red is known as being the most emotionally intense color. Heartbeats were beating faster as the entire football team wore their red game jerseys. Parents, students, and residents unaffiliated with the team were walking up to Perrone and embracing him. They were voicing support for him. One Salem resident screamed out, "You are doing the right thing. You stood by your team and your team stood by you." Red is an extreme color and it characterized the road they were traveling.

Ken Perrone was on a never-ending roller-coaster ride; he was not losing his stomach on steep hills, but on every step he took. Several hours earlier at practice, he was informed by Athletic Director Bob Geswell that he had permission to coach the game. But the good news proved to be transitory.

As 5 o'clock came, with his anxiety levels peaking, Perrone was approached by an administrator informing him he could not coach.

In the glare of three different television cameras, a bold Ken Perrone stood in front of his team, revealing to the crowd gathered that unless he died tonight, he would be coaching his football team. This was no cult meeting, but a leader putting his team's dreams and desires above his own. It was not about putting football above academics. Memories, goals, dreams, and structure were alive. These can often be accomplished through sports.

Although the rally lasted for an hour, I stood there, savoring the moment, taking it all in. With the brisk fall air hitting my skin, the smell of the nearby ocean put me into a state of relaxation. I looked around, imagining what it looked like at the "Commons" in 1890 when Salem played its first game against Beverly. Walking along the path, the statue of Roger Conant stood out, giving me a sense of pride for my city. I knew how much Perrone believed in the team, and the surroundings helped me focus.

SATURDAY, NOVEMBER 5, 1994
GAME DAY STARTS WITH MOM

I awoke early on Saturday morning. I instantly noticed the glare my helmet was making at the edge of my cot. A piece of paper was hanging off my facemask and read:

> *Since you can see over the line, maybe the shine from the helmet will blind the defense.*

> *- Dad*

The game ball next to my helmet had been rubbed with a dry towel to release any oils on the ball. This was similar to one of Flutie's tactics. My older brothers remained sound asleep in their bunk beds as I tried to be as quiet as a churchgoer at a Sunday mass listening to a sermon. Stepping off the cot, my cleats were shining like they were just shined by Gagnon Shoes, known as the most reliable cobbler in the city. As my mom prepared her homemade French toast, the aroma of the vanilla filled every room in the house. She took pride in everything she did and always put her family above herself. "There are no traffic jams in going the extra mile." That quote was engraved on the wall in our kitchen. She sipped a cup of coffee, looking out into the horizon at the sunrise. She was grateful to be in this very moment. She felt blessed to be alive. Going the extra mile is exactly what my mom would do for her family. It is a gene that was passed onto her from her mother that paved the way to motherhood. She stayed old-fashioned, but knew a thing or two about fashion. Deserted by her father at the age of four, she never used that as a crutch on her journey. Her mother worked night and day to keep her two daughters and son together. "She never let her kids do without, and I was grateful when she met someone as special as my stepfather."

Closing her eyes, her mind instantly went back in time. Loud thunder exploded throughout the sky. Scars lay as deep in her mind as her heartbeats. The memories started to unfold as if the gunshot was fired right before her eyes. The wind gusts created noises in the walls that kept her paranoid, thinking back to the apartment in Revere where rats the size of cats used to keep her awake at night by gnawing at the walls. My mom would lay awake, trying to fall back asleep. She, at times, felt entrapped and relived the episode: five bullets, one for each family member. A true nightmare.

Her anxiety as powerful as the thunder in the sky, she sat up and tried to erase the thoughts from her mind, but as the thunder got louder, her thoughts got stronger. Part of her has never left that apartment. Part of her was stuck in that very moment. How brave her little brother, sister, and she were that May night. All three of them shared a room. Her mother and stepfather lay sound asleep. Her stepfather's brother Joe apparently did not care for the new additions to the family. He entered her parent's room with a shotgun and bullets for the three kids, Shirley, who was mom's mother, and his own brother. My mom was awakened by a loud yell. As she entered her parents' room, she witnessed her stepfather getting shot in the chest. Her stepfather fell to the floor, lying motionless with splashes of blood on the walls. Paralyzed with fear as Joe DeStefano pointed the gun at Shirley's stomach, my mom and her siblings barreled into him causing the gun to go off into the ceiling. He then started beating their mother with the gun. Pregnant, Shirley was doing everything to shield her stomach. The gun jammed and my mother's intuition assisted her in running out of the room to dial 911 as her brother and sister ran outside.

With bills piling up, they eventually became homeless and had nowhere to go. They were taken in to live in a funeral parlor. Shirley suffered a broken arm and a contusion to her eye, while her husband passed away three years later as a result of the shooting. The baby, my Aunt Laurie, was born with a handicap as result of the trauma Shirley received to her abdominal area. Joe was arrested and got off on insanity.

"To this day I have nightmares about that night, my stepfather lying in a pool of blood. After the incident, he would often have gun pellets pop through the tips of his fingers." At the same time, she cherished the memories and sacrifices her mother made which allowed her to fulfill her dreams.

She opened up the gates to her heart and supported her sons. She wore my photo clipped to her jacket and my number three was painted on her cheek. She was always a kid at heart, but also a true mom's mom who would speak her mind and would step in the ring with Mike Tyson to protect her boys. She reminisced with me about how my toughness came from her. My mom liked to sit high in the stands, with her eyes closed, praying in the silences of her soul that the football gods would protect her son from any injuries.

Her pre-game ritual was a little different than mine. I was a surprise baby and born years after my parents thought they were done. My mom would tell me that I was her "fountain" of youth before I took the field. She would take my hand and kiss it, making sure the lipstick stuck on my skin. It was a symbol that I would often look at on the field that enabled me to find motivation when adversity was in the air.

FINAL PREPARATION

Coach Perrone arrived with his staff a little earlier than usual to go over some schemes. Coming into the game, Salem had allowed only 56 points, and Swampscott had scored 183. The football locker room was already starting to bounce from the bass of the music. Captains Whitten and Higley called teammates up to the bulletin board. "Have you guys seen these newspaper clippings?" they echoed.

The Boston Globe's prediction read "Too many distractions, Big Blue rout 40-8." Some of Higley's motivation came from his dad who would buy the papers and read quotes from other teams.

Swampscott was a very balanced team with very good athletes, a big offensive line, and had a great coaching staff. Tom Beatrice, a former Swampscott star, Harvard running back and current

Swampscott offensive coordinator, did not let the strike distract his football team. They isolated themselves from the media and focused on the game by going about business as usual. Beatrice had played and coached in many big football games. He agreed with Perrone's decision to coach, and his coaching philosophy was to do what is best for the kids. To bail out because of a political issue between a teachers union and administrators was ridiculous. "I would have never bailed out. I had no doubt in my mind that Perrone would coach his team. The thought of other coaches coming off the streets to coach that team is nonsense. Anyone who has ever been part of a football program knows that it does not work. You need the leadership, and the person who has been there from day one. An example from my own experience was my senior year of high school. My coach's wife passed away, coincidentally, the week before the Salem game. Ron Cochran took over as interim head coach. It was a one touchdown game and that definitely affected us that week. The intangibles provided from the coaches covering for Bondelevich had a great effect on us that week. For anyone to even suggest for someone to step in and adequately do the job for the kids knows nothing about team sports in my mind. Stopping the extracurricular activities, to me, is representative of the destructive power of the administration to a certain extent. The administration's line is that we are going to lock the fields up to further our interest to the detriment of football, soccer, or cheerleading teams, to me, is again ridiculous and totally inconsistent with the whole idea of education. If they have a problem or issue about wages and salaries, negotiate it out but do not lay it on the feet of the kids. I feel very strongly about it."

Beatrice went on to discuss that, "Team sports structure kids' lives. Football intensifies it for a couple of reasons. It is one game a week instead of several. So the team works the entire week to play one game as a team. It creates certain intensity, plus it is a physical game. A player is challenged mentally and physically throughout the practices and games. The team sports aspect of it is so important to kids' education it is irreplaceable. My most pleasurable part of coaching was always watching the kid who came in as a freshman who was insecure, didn't have a lot of self-confidence, did not know how to put on the equipment, and was a little timid. Then this kid goes through the program, gets knocked down, gets back up on his feet and gets a pat on the back along with some words of encouragement. He goes through the program and comes out of it as a graduate of the school, more secure and well-adjusted. The kid is ready to take on bigger and better things, having been part of a team and having developed a feeling of worth and the ability to succeed. Going through the program and facing those types of things is unique. So, having the administration saying we are going to take you away from it or we are going to suspend it was totally contrary to the whole idea of education."

"Every local paper has us losing," said Higley.

The soft-spoken star running back spoke up, "This train has a lot of power and is ready to roll," said The E-Train.

FRIENDS FOR LIFE

The team made their way down to Gallows Hill Park to meet Perrone and staff, as they were still not permitted on school grounds. Upon arriving at the park, I still lacked confidence that the game would go on. Looking at several of my teammates, I think they were having a mutual feeling.

But when Perrone began to speak, the sense of doom changed quickly. The team started to show a tremendous amount of enthusiasm. "Gentlemen, close your eyes and hold hands. We have all different walks of life on this team. I want you all to put each other in your thoughts and prayers. Look around, look at your coaches. We sacrificed our own livelihood for you because it is all about you." Tears strolled down his face, "This team has more character than any team I have ever coached. Now it is time to form one." He asked the team to head back to school which they did and in violation of the school facility use prohibition.

Hand in hand, the captains led the team into The Pride Room. It was holy territory for any former, current, or future player. Many would argue it was equivalent to the Peabody Essex Museum.

I was the last player out of the room. I could not help but stare at the wall which featured team pictures that went back to the beginning of the century. The 1974 picture stood out like the painting of the *Mona Lisa*. I walked up closely, taking the photo out of my helmet. It was the one I found on the stadium steps almost a year earlier. I put the picture next to the one on the wall and repeated the words from my dad, "Train your mind, body, and soul for moments like this."

Moments later, as the team made their way out of the field house, hundreds of fans starting cheering. It was a motorcade. Police sirens were on. Two yellow school buses were lined up behind the police cruisers. Squad cars and motorcycle cops lined up behind the buses. We were receiving a police escort to Swampscott's Blocksidge field for police protection. To some it resembled more of a presidential visit. Seeing this no one could ever have imagined that the head coach was equated to Jim Jones and David Koresh. The outpouring of community support was representative of the public consensus that the characterizations were false. No one pinpointed as the root of societal evil could muster such positive karma. Said differently, it was the white whale surfacing to take on Ahab.

The bus ride over was the most calming part of our week. It was just our team and our thoughts. I sat near the front of the bus. I had the game ball in my hands. My father's words recycled through my head, "Train your mind, body, and soul for moments like this." Higley visualized punishing anyone who wore a blue and white uniform, and Downes' motor was running like the beats from his Walkman. Downes had Swampscott's Woodfork on his mind and his mother in his heart. It was all a heartbeat away. Mccellon always sat in the front of the bus to honor Rosa Parks. She paved the way for people like him to go after his dreams. The E-Train had his eyes closed and the back of his head resting on the seat. He was simulating big plays. De Pena sat in the back of the bus with his helmet on. Palming a football with his long fingers; football was his compass and this ball was his outlet that allowed him to dream big. We were all ready to come off the bus flying.

It was a beautiful fall day with Indian summer maintaining its grasp on New England, with the temperatures running abnormally high, 74 degrees for an autumn November day. Stands on both sides were overflowing with supporters, and the field was roped off for a standing-room-only crowd. Media from across the state line converged on the visiting team's sidelines in a feeding frenzy. Fueled by the highly controversial teacher's strike, you could see those forming opinions: Salem football coaches have ignored the administration's cease-and-desist order to stand shoulder-to shoulder with their team. The jury was still out. One thing was for sure: The game was huge, but the event was even bigger. There was such hot interplay between sports and politics, Sports Channel had selected us as the high school game of the week to be televised nationally.

Mike Lynch slowly walked through the Swampscott locker room at Blocksidge Field. Several different formations were written on the board. The coaches and players were in positional meetings. He sat in front of his old locker and saw the 1970 team photo. Examining it very closely, he looked in the eyes of every former teammate. Pausing, he zoomed in on his coach. The joys and the memories lived within him from those years. Thousands of athletes compete each year but only a limited amount get a chance to live out childhood dreams and play for a championship. So much wisdom had been created through his experiences playing high school football. He was familiar with the strikes at Brockton and Tewksbury and how professionally they were handled. Lynch observed that Perrone gave the kids a sense of belonging, a place to go after school, and an experience that they would never forget. This was something they would cherish. One thing is for certain, it brought the team together more than any two-week pre-season camp; you can have all the pep talks, all the jokes and laughs, but that week brought this team closer together.

The size of the crowd resembled a Thanksgiving Day atmosphere. Lynch instantly thought back to the 1969 Thanksgiving Day game. Trailing 14-12 in the final seconds, Lynch hit a 21-yard field goal, giving the Big Blue its third straight undefeated season, twenty-seventh win in a row, and Class B title. Channels 4, 5, 7, and Sports channels were doing pre-game preparations. Walking onto the field he grabbed a football, rubbed it into the ground, and tossed it to one of the water boys. It was game time.

As the Salem team made its way out of the locker room, the team stalled and had a hesitation that concerned the coaches. The players seemed in awe due to the size of the crowd. With over 12,000 strong, there was no turning back. They were ready to march like soldiers and fight like gladiators.

Coach Perrone huddled the team up and said, "The field is 100 yards, the goalposts are 10 feet high, and this ball is the same ball that we have used all season. Witches Pride forever, men." The team started to make its way onto the field at the same time the Salem mayor was entering with his three bodyguards. This was a complete adrenaline rush for the team. They knew the mayor did not support their coach, their team, or their dreams. If it was three hundred years earlier, he probably would have had Perrone hanged on Gallows Hill.

Higley walked with beats from "Crazy Train" in his head; he liked Ozzy Osbourne. Before games he always made it a point to locate his brother. This would be challenging because the sidelines were packed, but this became part of his pre-game ritual. His brother was always on his mind. He thought back a year earlier when he played Marblehead. He spent the morning before the game in the hospital with his brother. He had just had surgery to amputate his legs and was experiencing phantom pain. His brother's face was perspiring, and with tears in his eyes, he looked at his kid brother and said, "Make them feel some pain too." Mark went out there and knocked kids around like he never did before. After the game, cutting through the emergency room, he saw the Marblehead QB that he collided with and knocked out of the game being treated for a severe concussion. Every game he played, he had that mental picture of his brother lying there in pain. He channeled any aggressions into whoever was on the other side of the ball. Spotting his brother at the edge of the field gave him a sense of joy. To him, he was in his backyard, this time with his idol watching closely.

While the team waited on the sidelines, several players started to get edgy and grew concerned when their coaches were nowhere in sight. "Man, what if they had second thoughts? This is their lives, careers at stake," stated Joey Freeman.

Moments later the Salem fans erupted.

AN IMAGE FOR ALL TIME

In a form of solidarity, Perrone and the coaches, arms locked together, ran onto the field in unison. His staff showed they were all in this together.

Coach Perrone walked up before the game started, put his arm around me, and said, "Sean, if they put nine in the box, we are going to throw the ball." My eyes opened wide as I knew, only completing eleven passes in my first seven games, I would just have to make the most out of this opportunity. Looking to my left, legendary *The Boston Globe* sportswriter Bob Ryan was on the sideline and was all business. He had the inside scoop on all subjects connected with sports, especially our league, and he stood a few feet from Coach Perrone, speaking into his tape recorder. This past week the bigwig Boston sportswriters had focused their attention on high school athletics only to criticize Perrone for staying by his players. With the heart of the NHL lockout and MLB strike, these sports journalists were covering this story even closer.

Fans could have just as easily spent the day at one of the beaches that line Swampscott's shoreline, instead they are here in Blocksidge

Stadium, where it feels like the storm is about to hit. It is clear who the Salem fans are. The packed stands are humming like a beehive. Supporters hold up signs painted in the team's red and black colors, and scream, 'You're not alone' and 'Perrone for Mayor.'"

Meanwhile, I'm watching Salem's elected mayor seated high up in the stands surrounded by an army of bodyguards. I turn to Canelo. "Yo, Canelo, yo," I call. I always use that line with him, he prefers it. "What's all the security for?"

He cocks his head over to my side. "Code for protectin' 'im from threats, death threats he's gettin'. Curtin' wants to destroy us. Mayor's behind 'im. No lie. Bet on it."

MAYOR WITH BODYGUARDS

My mouth is dry and I don't want to think about it. I'm a teenager and baffled by how much political paranoia is distracting me and the team. The city may be in the midst of one of the most heated political debates in its school system's history, but all we want to do is play football. A loud booing from the stands grows, creating a disturbance. Players look up. While I stare straight ahead, grinning like a witch's cat, it seems that the mayor is the target. One guy thinks this a good omen. Much to the team's surprise, given that the mayor is a polarizing figure who isn't there to support us, it becomes clear that his presence provides the motivation for our team to get back to the business of football.

Swampscott won the coin toss and elected to defer to the second half.

On Salem's first series, we moved the chains for a first down and then were forced to punt. Big Blue got a quick first down. But then Swampscott's QB had trouble with the center exchange, resulting in a fumble and Salem recovering on Swampscott's 34-yard line. We picked up consecutive first downs thanks to running back Freeman. We brought the ball to the 8-yard line and got stuffed three plays in a row which set up my 25-yard field goal. The kick split the uprights 3-0 in favor of Salem. Undersized offensive lineman Dennis Dulong was playing possessed on special teams and laid the boom on the returner. This was done after losing his helmet, running down on kickoff. By this time, the Big Blue had the jitters out and was ready to unleash its high-powered offense. With another QB center exchange going bad, however, defensive end Leopoldo jumped on the fumble as if it was his acceptance letter to Tufts. This gave the Witches the ball at the Big Blue's 24-yard line. Salem faced a 3rd down and 1 from Big Blue's 20-yard line. I took the snap and picked up 6 yards for a first down. On 2nd and 9 of the next series, my ball sailed out of the end zone. On third down, I jogged to the sidelines to get the play. At this point I looked up into the stands and spotted my dad. This motivated me because I knew how much my dad believed in me.

I addressed the offense, "Jet Right Sprint Out Pass. Joey, get to the goal line." The line, led by Big Will Jones and Jeremy Cronin, did a great job allowing me time to roll out to my right, square my shoulders, and throw a dart to Freeman who fought for a yard to break the plain for the score. My point after was good, making it 10-0 Salem.

On Swampscott's next possession, Downes came up with a great open field tackle, which forced Swampscott to punt again. On Salem's next possession, The E-Train started to make his presence felt by grinding out yards. The band playing super beats became a motivating factor for the Witches. On 3rd and fifteen from the Swampscott's 28, I rolled out and saw tight end Whitten settling on a curl route. I threw on the run, hitting Whitten in the hands but the ball fell incomplete. Inside I wanted to yell. I knew we needed to play almost perfect to win this game. Swampscott took over on downs. With a sense of urgency they moved the ball at will to Salem's 7-yard line. On fourth and goal, blitzing LB Whitten made up for the drop and sacked Swampscott QB Todd McShay to close out the first half with Salem leading 10-0.

Perrone stressed execution and more points to his team. In addition, the master motivator touched on the foundation that had built this team which consisted of brotherhood, pride, and courage. "All you guys are fighters, and as long as you stick to those three words, victory will be always within. Go win this game. We want it more."

Right before the second half started, one large sign was held up, stating "Hang Perrone, the real Witch." The team knew they were in a modern-day witch hunt. Their coach was their leader, mentor, and friend. This team was going to do whatever it took to win this game.

Walking on the sidelines, Perrone was trying to keep it together and was blocking everything out except his players. He was moved by the fan support. A group of men started chanting, "You are not alone." The beat got so loud; he took a step back to turn around and saw thirty members of his 1970 National ranked Brewer High Witches leading the beat. They were all wearing their old Brewer game jerseys. Perrone's eyes started to moisten, "If I am such a bad person, why are all these people supporting me."

On Swampscott's first possession of the second half, Sullivan intercepted McShay's pass and gave the Witches the ball at midfield. On 3rd and long, I hit Freeman on a well-designed screen pass for a first down. The Swampscott defensive end leveled me, hitting me under the chin and breaking my chinstrap. Climbing to my feet, I was stumbling and seeing stars. Two plays later, we turned the ball over.

Swampscott completed consecutive passes. Whitten got the call 44 Notre Dame, which was a blitz. His eyes opened wider; this kid loved contact. The pressure was on McShay, and Salem defensive back Perry made his presence felt on 3rd and 10; he jumped on a stop route diving and intercepting the pass. Salem was effective in blitzing and disguising it as well. Changing their formations confused their pass blocking. This caught Swampscott off-guard and forced McShay to hurry throws and throw off his back foot. Marcoulier had scouted McShay and knew he did not like to spend a lot of time in the pocket.

"It seemed," said McShay, "as if they had a guy blitzing on every single play and sometimes two or three people."

In his mind, Downes was back on the streets in Lynn with a "nothing to lose" mentality. Marcoulier saw other gaps in the Big Blue turned "black and blue" offense. Their receivers all year had free releases and dictated how they ran their routes. Not today. Marcoulier lined up Downes on their star, wide receiver Woodfork. He physically abused him all through the game, but Swampscott had other arsenals in their attack. "We were well aware of the situation and the rumors that we might not play. However, I think we went about our business in the same manner as we had the entire season. We were jealous that the players in Salem did not have to attend classes. I think the SAT test that Saturday was probably a bigger distraction or fear for a lot of us," Woodfork stated.

Salem was trying to keep the ball out of Swampscott's hands. On 4th and 2 from midfield, running back Mercado exploded through the hole like a rocket. Jones and David Russell were dominating the interior line opening holes that were key for Salem to control the time of possession. Salem faced a crucial 4th and goal from the five. With Salem fans screaming 'field goal,' Perrone decided to go for it and Swampscott was all over, stopping them at the two.

Swampscott's offense needed to move the ball, but Salem's D was as stingy as it was playing all season. It's cease and desist defense did a great job of blitzing and Swampscott was having trouble adjusting. On third and short, Downes intercepted a McShay pass, giving the Witches the ball back at Swampscott's 25-yard line.

With 9:25 left in the fourth quarter it was 3rd and 8 and I was Mr. Cool walking to the line of scrimmage. It was the same side of the field where I developed my skills all summer, living this very moment, in my mind. In the classroom I visualized this moment, in practice I visualized this moment and lying on my cot before bed I visualized this moment. I had dreams about this moment. Using the crowd as my energy, I was a stranger to this type of game but was leading the team like a seasoned veteran. Many critics view experience as a leading factor to be successful. I looked at it as just a word that was overrated. Opportunity equals experience. Pausing, as I got under center, I saw my brother Eric standing at the 20-yard line in front of the roped-off area. He stood out in a crowd because of his physique. Eric has always kept his emotions to himself, but this day was like Christmas morning for him. He was enjoying every second of it. I took the center exchange and faked a dive to Mercado and with a blitzing Swampscott DE I hung tough in the pocket tossing a 24-yard TD pass to The E-Train. With my vision blurred from getting a finger in the eye, I let out a fierce yell of excitement. Offensive linemen Cronin, Jones, Russell, and Dulong did a fine job in allowing me time to set my feet. This was a once in a lifetime opportunity and I was making the most out of it. The extra point was no good, and Salem was leading 16 to 0 midway through the fourth quarter.

Swampscott was considered one of the top-ranked offenses in the state for a reason. They took back some momentum, picking apart the Salem D and scoring with 4:54 to play. Downes was down. He lay on the ground, yelling. He was suffering from extreme muscle cramping. He played on pure heart as his crippling leg cramps got worse, but Downes wouldn't think of voluntarily leaving the field; if Perrone wasn't giving up on the team, then he wouldn't give into the pain. This was nothing compared to the physical abuse he'd taken as a kid from his late stepfather. Rumor on the street, although Downes denied it, was that his stepfather stole someone's garage full of vinyl records and was found dead the next day with a CD stuck in his mouth. Too bad, but his demise meant Downes was free to join the team and play the game he lived for. His father apparently got wind that his son was making a name for himself from the exposure the team was receiving and attended the game. His dad ran out of the stands and onto the field. Holding his son's hand brought light to his condition. Downes felt a sense of closure for the neglect he received as a child. This was a big deal for him, as it was the first time that one of his parents had ever seen him play football. The kid had uncontrollable excitement for the game and fed off large crowds. "If you were booing me, I am doing my job. If you were cheering for me, I am still doing my job." With a fist of soil from the field Downes slowly limps to the sidelines. Going for the two point conversion, Salem blitz forced McShay to throw an incomplete pass. Linebackers Whitten and Parsons led the way but were celebrating too early as Salem got called for defensive holding. The second attempt, an off-tackle run, was successful, making the score 16 to 8.

An onside kick was recovered by Salem's Bouchard at midfield. Salem's offense knew if they could move the ball, they would control their own destiny. They did, but stalled at the Swampscott's 25-yard line. Turnover on downs as Salem punts.

The ball was spotted at Swampscott's own 25 yard line. Swampscott's band is making its presence felt. Their QB McShay intends to orchestrate one of the biggest comebacks in Big Blue history. The stage was set for McShay to lead his team to victory and become a hometown hero. Perrone has put his career on the line to coach his team, and unlike the story in *Back to the Future*, for him and for us there is no turning back. The E-Train stood on the sidelines wishing he was part of the defense that had to make a stop. The team was his family and the field was his home. His boy Canelo was by his side, looking in awe at the packed crowd; he had never been part of something so big. Swampscott's fans were elated when a 19-yard completion brought the ball to the Salem 21-yard line with 22 seconds on the clock. Swampscott immediately spiked the ball to stop the clock. A play later, after another completed pass, Swampscott was at the 12-yard line. With the clock stopped for a measurement and only ten ticks remaining, I took a knee to glance at it and count the seconds tick away. I was feeling a sinister panic. Here I was watching my nemesis take his team on a 63-yard drive, seemingly at will, and all I could do was watch…helplessly watch. I fought back the despair, turning instead to faith, pleading with God to let our defense dig deep and pull out just one more stop. Surely the defense wanted this win as badly as the screaming offense, and surely they could pull it out.

Higley stood with his hands on his hips and shot a quick glance over to his brother sitting in his wheelchair on the sideline. His brother's face lit up, and he threw a high-five. Higley was inspired and dug deep. The referee signaled with his hands that Swampscott was just inches shy of a first down. Fourth and inches with no timeouts left, there was time for just one last play.

The play was signaled in to McShay, and Swampscott got in their alignment. Woodfork wanted the ball and knew McShay would try to answer his plea. Our defense lined up in a Cover 3, putting Perry one-on-one with Woodfork, split wide to his left. On the other side of the field, Mccellon was hoping to make the play of his career. Everyone on the sideline was on one knee, clutching each other's hands. Perrone had his feet firmly planted on the ground, hands fastened on his clipboard, coolly taking a deep breath. He seemed at ease, despite internalizing his great anxiety. He was like a father to Mccellon. He cared deeply for the rootless player, helping them discover a world they'd never imagined, that's the way he was. With his intense connection to Higley, who he encouraged to help his paraplegic brother when no one else seemed to care, and with Mccellon, who, it was said, lived in an environment of hellacious addicts and drunks, there's no way Mccellon will let Perrone or the team down. Mccellon saw his little brother drinking from a water bottle on the sideline. Vivid memories flash through his mind that brought him back to the projects of Great Britain, Connecticut, where he would sneak into neighbor's yards to fill up and steal a bucket of water. This was done so he and his brothers could wash and brush their teeth when their water was shut off as they were on the verge of being evicted.

There were over 12,000 fans on their feet, roaring, and McShay dropped back to pass. Pressure crashed down from our defensive end

their salary, they look for another job. In any private sector job, raises are not routine. They are based on merit and the company's ability to pay an increase.

The local Salem Evening News pointed out the following: No private sector job has tenure. An employee must comply with company standards day in and day out, or they were terminated. Teachers in Salem had some of the finest benefits offered to any workers, including health care benefits, ample holidays, sick days, enviable retirement payouts, and vacation days. Their work days were shorter and they worked only 180 days a year.

Had the educators really done their due diligence on a realistic contract offer? What they were asking for could have a negative, long-term, financial effect on the city. "Any teacher who expects anything other than a salary increase based on merit is teaching a poor lesson of responsibility to their students," one of the committee members stated. (*Salem News*, November 8, 1994)

***

It was Thursday, 5:45 AM, November 10. Half-filled coffee cups and a box of Ziggy's donuts lay open on the table. Ash trays were overflowing and cigarette smoke lingered in the air. Mayor Harrington stood up and handed school committee lawyer Dan Kulak a sheet of paper that read "Final Offer." School committee member Carl Peterson whispered something into Kulak's ear. The administration and the union sat in separate rooms. The six members of the school committee sat side by side weary, but filled with optimism that an agreement would be reached that evening. This group was advised to be careful of what they said outside of those walls. A mediator sat in the room with them.

Down the hall sat the fired-up union members. The school committee was well aware of their arrival because the union let their presence be known as they loudly entered the building after attending their rally. The union negotiating team was strategically constructed with a teacher from each of the learning levels, sixteen teachers in total. There was representation from elementary school which covered kindergarten through grade 5, middle school, Chapter 1, which gave special education to students in need and high school 9-12. The union lawyer Jeffrey Jacobson sat to the right of Turner. Turner felt tension finally taking over his body as he passed notes to Devlin. His head was throbbing and his neck was stiff; stress filled his eyes. Jacobsen sat, writing on a piece of paper.

During a recess, Jacobsen and Devlin stepped into a closed room for privacy at St. Chretienne's, while Curtin and school committee member Lippman relocated into another room. The main issue on the table was merit pay and the "No Reprisal" clause. Lippman and Curtin wanted merit pay. The teachers union felt the reason why Curtin wanted it was so he could weed out the teachers that he did not want. Since Curtin had the ultimate control of what students the teachers taught, they feared that Curtin would go as far as putting teachers with troubled students in order to make the teachers look incompetent and want to leave. "Over 25 percent of the school was minority with a language barrier, and these students trying to deal with cultural differences presented another issue for the teachers regarding merit pay," said Turner.

Fifteen minutes later, both sides returned. The issue that was agreed upon by both parties was the "No Reprisal" clause. This was language the union wanted in writing before they ended the strike. The clause stated no teacher could get fired for having any involvement in the strike. The coaches were not covered under this because they had a different contract as a coach. Turner stated their contracts as coaches were never negotiated at the union table with the administration, and it was always their decision for that to be the case.

Turner went on to state, "I think those guys believed that they could do much better if they went individually and sat down with the school committee and Ed Curtin. They felt that they could get their own deal done because they were good coaches and at the time were winning. They thought that was to their advantage and would always be the case and the people that sat across from them would always respect them because they did a great job. We, the union, would tell them there is going to come a time when that is not going to happen, whatever the reason might be, no money, etc. No matter how great you are or how well you work with students they are going to say, 'no way.' We also made it very clear to them, especially a few of us, that we did not trust Mr. Curtin. If he decided for any particular reason at all that you were doing something wrong or not doing what he told you to do, he demanded that you do it. If you didn't do it because you knew it was wrong or wouldn't produce the results he thought it would, he would get you, period. We had people that would recite things that Curtin would say."

Turner, in reflection, emphasized Curtin's obsession with avenging prior conflicts with people, illustrating this odd penchant by saying: "Like, I had a disagreement with Ed Curtin and he has never forgotten that. He would say, remember back on December 6, 1975, you said this about that and you were wrong. He would come after you forever until he got his reprisal for that. We informed the coaches that they needed to understand this and they were like, no, we are not doing it and will stay under separate contracts."

Both sides had been debating through the night for the past eleven hours. At this executive session, the school committee "Had significantly altered" its proposal to teachers and would wait for the union's response. The union and school committee, mutually, were trying to reach an agreement before the point of no return. Furey looked at his watch. It read 6 AM, and moments later, the meeting was adjourned.

Later on that morning, Mazz's phone rang. Turner was on the other end, informing him of the progress that was made. Mazz went on to say he was concerned about Curtin. "With your schedule in your contract, Curtin could have you walking the corridors all day long. That is the type of power he has over us. He would have you made an outcast by the administration; they would not speak to you. We look like the jerks making your life miserable." With his voice getting louder, he referenced the amount of great teachers Salem had lost over the years because they did not want to work for the man. Ever since he became superintendent, things had gotten worse because he had the power to hire and fire you right away. "Stubbornness and not negotiating fairly is what Curtin is all about," stated Mazz.

"Relax, Mazz, the negotiating team wrote the language on the 'No Reprisal' clause and merit pay was flushed down the drain." Turner went on to say, "I don't think Curtin even thinks about the kids. He thinks about the guy standing in front of him; he is looking at Perrone and he does not like him and here is his chance to get rid of him."

"What interests me, Wayne, is Perrone is a good guy, good teacher. He has developed a lot of people. Curtin is very jealous of that and something I can't understand. Why would you be jealous over success with students? He wanted to be the one in the light. He could not stand when someone else was very successful and popular."

"Curtin dreamed of being what Perrone was and he was just a wannabe, a terrible athlete and really never liked anyone that was a good athlete," said Mazz.

The proposal they had worked out over the past eleven hours outlined an 11.5 percent pay increase that would cover three years, with 3.5 percent of the increase in raises connected to school improvement objectives to be decided by a combined group of teachers and management. The new tender made no reference to SAT scores. The offer consisted of eight out of ten components of a plan earlier proposed by the teachers union. Harrington made it very clear this would be his "Final Offer" to teachers.

By Thursday afternoon, city officials were perturbed when they heard that union leaders still had not informed the union membership of the school committee's proposal.

The Coalition for Excellence in Public Education, a sub-committee of United Parents of Salem, strongly supported connecting pay with performance. The coalition issued a statement calling for more accountability from the teachers and criticized the view that Salem schools should not be judged in the same light as other school systems because of the number of children from minority or economically disadvantaged households. "Professionals are held to exact standards of excellence. If teachers want to earn the salaries of other professionals, they, too, must be able to do difficult jobs well and achieve high results in the face of adversity," the coalition said in its statement. The coalition stated that public opinion was heavily weighted on the side of performance raises. There was even some disappointment that the offer was not more rigorous.

Turner realized he had some grace time to make a decision. By law, the union had five days after the provisions of the contract were presented in black and white and circulated to the entire membership. "The membership was hoping for more money and some would like a change in the language," Turner said. (*Salem News*, November 14, 1994)

News started to spread through the city, and teachers were outraged because the mayor had notified the press of the details of the latest contract offer before they learned about it. An enraged Turner felt the mayor was using the newspaper to win over public opinion. The mayor made his point very clear from the beginning that they did not negotiate through newspapers, but at the bargaining table. After another marathon bargaining session on Sunday, they reached an agreement. Changes were made from the city's "Final Offer" to favor the teachers.

CHAPTER 20

THRILLER AT MILLER

> "That's the way I like it because there's no time to have nerves about it. You just run out and do it."
>
> ~ Doug Flutie

Manuel De Pena slowly made his way into The Point neighborhood. His hands were frozen and his nose was running. He was hoping his sister turned on the portable heater. He passed through Prince St. Park and paused. He reflected on a spot where his athletic journey began. He used the scars on his hands and forearms as a timeline for those battles. Skills were developed and lives were transformed on those grounds. Sitting on an old park bench, he removed his glasses and closed his eyes. His mind traveled back to winning races at Shetland Park as a boy, visualizing making plays in the next day's games against Winthrop. He couldn't help but think of last year's loss which still irked him. A middle-aged Hispanic man limped through, walking his dog.

Noticing it is Manny, he called him "Manolo," his nickname as a boy. The man exclaims, "The pride of The Point; paving the way for young Latinos to go after their dreams."

He couldn't help but crack a smile.

He climbed up the front stairs, skipping one step that was cracked.

He felt anxiety coming on and sat on the front porch to decompress. A copy of the *Salem News* lay on the ground. He grinned as he knew his mom was following him closely. She was his inner strength. He never regretted his upbringing but always thought about how different life could have been if he had a father figure on the home front. He looked up at the moon and pondered its beauty, amazed by the thought of someone walking on it. He was determined to do something great. All this made him think of his mom. Every time she dropped him off for games at the high school, it hurt because he wanted her there. "I just wanted her not to worry about me. My cousins got deported because they were drawn to that fast money," said a soft-spoken De Pena.

Walking into his room, he immediately sat down at his desk. His room was practically empty with no TV. Music constantly played in his mind which he referred to as the soundtrack of life. The materialistic possessions never came, but the love and faith were constant. His rice and beans placed on his desk were getting cold. His stomach loosened up and the smell worked up his appetite. He dug his spoon into the dish and savored every bite of it.

He took out a pad of paper from his back pack and started to draw an elephant. *Amazing animals*, he thought. Looking through his bag, he pulled out a football which was his holy grail, as well as his favorite book, *The Celestine Prophecy*, which had allowed him to create his own spiritual awakening. Reading was another outlet for him. He often read the beginning of the book where the male narrator discussed the insights on a manuscript dating back to 600 BC. De Pena was drawn to history and understood its role in creating change. His football team was traveling that road.

Closing the book, his bookmark fell out. Staring at the date August 28, 1992, the word Jesus was weighing on his mind. De Pena reached out at him. Instantly, he was overcome with sadness and grabbed the football, the one prop that was helping him create his own movie. His nephew was pushed off a subway platform in Manhattan and was electrocuted. Lying on his bed, he tossed the football in the air and extended his hands. The feeling of the ball was a sense of therapy but the memories were engrained in his mind. De Pena set up a wall and would not get close to anyone because he did not want to feel the pain when they died. Each ball he tossed up got him even more relaxed. His eyes got heavy and he placed the bookmark and ball under his pillow. Similar to the Tooth Fairy, he yearned for the football gods to comedown in full force to answer his prayers.

Destiny may be seen either as a sequence of events that are inevitable and unchangeable, or seventy individuals choose their own destiny by choosing different paths. This team felt they could play with anybody in the state, but only if their coach was at the helm.

Winthrop was a true spoiler for Perrone's teams dating back to Troy Staffia in 1983. Then, in an odd tactic, they had changed game uniforms at halftime only to lose a heartbreaker 14-12. The 1992 and 1993 Winthrop teams rolled through the NEC. Salem vs. Winthrop 1993 was a tough loss for Salem, in contention to win. They had a late-game field goal attempt and Perrone decided to use a kicker who had never kicked in a game before. It showed and the kicker kicked the top of the ball which hit the long snapper in the butt. It would have placed first in football bloopers.

***

The strike continued into the following week and the students were still out of school. The mighty Witches traveled up to Miller Field to play the Winthrop Vikings.

A pre-game ritual is something athletes do before sporting events to help them prepare mentally before they perform. I started a pre-game ritual when I was in the eighth grade. I would watch *Why Eagles Soar*, which was basically the Doug Flutie highlight film. One specific play known as "The Pass" was used against the Miami Hurricanes and was the play that defeated them with no time left on the clock. That play paved the way for Flutie to win the Heisman, awarded to the top college football player across the country. This was a play I witnessed back in 1984 with my dad and has stayed with me since.

Winthrop, Massachusetts, is the home to Mike Eruzione, who scored the winning goal in the 1980 Winter Olympics to beat Russia in hockey. He just happened to be at the football game.

The air was very stale at Miller Field with a sky punctuated by planes above the field in low altitudes, preparing to land at nearby Logan International Airport.

Salem kicked off first. Our team got off to a slow start and came out flat. One of Coach Perrone's main concerns was a letdown. The team was coming off one of the most emotional weeks in the program's history. Downes ran down the field like a heated missile blasting into the kick returner, knocking him on his back. Winthrop moved the ball to midfield and was forced to punt.

Grimes waited patiently for a punt at Salem's own 10-yard line. With the punt sailing away from him, he, at the last second, did something uncharacteristic and tried to field it. The ball bounced off his cleat right into a Winthrop player's hands at Salem's 8-yard line. Three plays later, an inside counter Winthrop running back Michael Palmer scooted in from the 3-yard line. The point after was good.

On the ensuing kickoff, the ball was kicked away from Grimes, who ran after it. As it was about to roll into the end zone, it came to a complete stop at the 2-yard line. Being a playmaker, he looked up to see if he had room to run and lost sight of the ball. With Winthrop players closing in, he kicked it out at Salem's own 2-yard line. On Salem's first possession, I pitched the ball left to Freeman. He was hit by Winthrop's outside linebacker. On impact the ball bounced out and Winthrop recovered at Salem's 10-yard line. It was mostly sunny skies and the only cloud in sight was the one over Salem's sideline.

On third and goal, Winthrop called a quick toss and scored. The extra point was good, and just like that, Winthrop was leading 14 to 0. At this point, confidence was low and heads were down. It was a week after one of the biggest wins in the program's history, and the Witches could not get airborne on their broomsticks.

I was as energized as I had ever been, trying to get the offense motivated. We had no focus and Winthrop was trying to play the spoiler.

We got the ball back and went right to the ground with a toss right to The E-Train, who picked up twenty yards before getting upended. Two plays later, Freeman fumbled. Winthrop recovered again at Salem's own thirty-five. Perrone tried to keep his emotions cool, but immediately gave Freeman an earful.

Higley was struggling. He was getting cut blocked and took himself out of the game. It wasn't like him to ever do this, but mentally, he needed to refocus. F-bombs were being thrown like grenades during a war, and fingers were being pointed. Adversity was knocking, but the Witches had to work to reverse the turnover spell that the Vikings had put on them.

Grimes was down in the dumps. He had some mental lapses but the kid's hands were as reliable as you can get. Catching footballs came naturally to him. Leopoldo was furious. He knew the defensive unit had to play nearly perfect for the rest of the game to get back into it. If not, they would go down as just another Salem team that could not win the big game.

Salem's defense forced Winthrop to punt, taking the ball over with a vengeance. The E-Train picked up sixteen yards off the right side to bring the ball to our 37, fighting for the extra inch. Two quick pitches and The E-Train got the ball to midfield. Perrone decided to go up top. I faked the dive to Mercado, counter to Rodriquez, and tossed a bomb to a streaking De Pena, but it sailed just out of his reach. I grabbed my helmet with frustration. On third and long, I rolled left and threw a 40-yard pass to De Pena who was open up the left sideline for a sure six, but it slipped through his hands, falling incomplete. A groan came from the crowd as we were forced to punt.

I ran toward De Pena as he slowly walked off the field. "You just have developed a case of amnesia," I whispered in his ear. "We both laid an egg so far. It is behind us. We have a lot of ball left. Chin up and keep getting your separation. I will find a way to get you the ball. You need to attack the football. Do you hear any fat lady singing?"

The defense settled in and found its comfort zone forcing Winthrop to go four and out. Salem got the ball at midfield and went to its ground game. I could just observe from the sidelines as Perrone alternated QBs. It felt like an emotional roller coaster, but I bit my lip and put my cheerleading face on. Perrone used the Latino connection with Mercado and The E-Train slashing through the Winthrop defense. On the fifteenth play of the drive, they faced a crucial 4th and goal.

Perrone burned his final timeout of the half with 30 seconds remaining and put me back in the game. "Sean, sell the dive and tell Manny to delay his release into the flat."

Listening to my general's command, I floated a 7-yard TD pass to an open De Pena. The two point conversion was no good and Winthrop went into the half with a 14 to 6 lead. We had played our worst half of football all season, but managed to stay in the game.

Halftime in the Salem locker room, you could hear a pin drop. Coach Perrone looked each player in the eyes and did not say a word. You could see the frustration in all of the player's faces and feel the emptiness throughout the room.

Moments before the team was going to step out of the locker room, with his back to the team, he turned around and yelled, "You are better than this team. Is this where you want this dream to end?" Perrone brought the team over to the window. Silence was back in the air. The only noise that lingered was another plane going in for a landing. "Boys, look at the kids playing on the field. So innocent, having fun. That is what we do. We have fun, and this is a kid's game. The E-Train, look at the stands. The crowd is a lot smaller, it is colder outside, the mayor is not around eating hotdogs with his bodyguards, the superintendent is tucked away in his compound plotting his next move. They want to shut us down. Nobody is carrying signs supporting us and the Boston media is not covering this game. Look at the scoreboard. We have one half of football left and can control our destiny. I believe in this football team. I love this football team."

This was our moment. We were on the brink of a complete letdown and the Witches were ready to reverse the spell on Miller Field that would be talked about for generations. We had time to reflect during halftime and brewed up some witchcraft that would make fans ponder if this team really did possess some special powers.

"Please take a knee, hold hands and repeat after me: God first, my teammates second, myself third. Let's win this for everyone in this room because we truly believe in each other and that defines a team, gentlemen." The team's energy just went off the radar. Lockers were getting punched, heads were being butted, and it was complete chaos. Perrone silenced the team, "Helmets on, but no one buckle your chin-straps." Seconds later, he stood up on a bench and nodded his head, and at once, they timed it perfectly. All you could hear was the sound of seventy chin-straps snapping at once. It was another defining moment for this team. The switch was flipped. A moment united us into one team.

Heading out of the locker room, I could not help but notice Winthrop legend and Olympic Hockey gold medalist, Mike Eruzione. I wasted no time and ran over to him, "Hi, Mr. Eruzione."

He responded, "Please call me Mike," and stuck out his right hand.

I thought, *Wow, he just shook my left hand.*

"Good luck, kid, and go play some football."

Did he give some of his Olympic gold medal miracle magic to me?

In 1999, *Sports Illustrated* named the Miracle on Ice the "Top Sports Moment of the Twentieth Century." With all sports, the intimidation factor can contribute to the outcome of competition. The Soviets were heavy favorites had gone 27-1-1.

"We knew how good we were and it was going to be a tough game. Our coach, Herb Brooks, said it over and over again, 'Play your game'. We were worried about ourselves not so much them." Skating down the ice, the puck came across to Eruzione. When he shot the puck, he thought it was going in: the goalie was screened and it slid smoothly between his arms. It was surreal when the horn went off; Team USA went on to win the Olympic Gold medal.

Salem received the ball first and went four and out. Winthrop engineered a drive that ate up almost the entire third quarter. They scored on a 14-yard TD pass and followed with a successful PAT which put them well in control with a 21 to 6 lead.

"At that point, I really didn't think we would be able to come back," said Perrone.

Salem got the ball back and marched down the field with a combination of running and passing. With 8:07 remaining in the fourth quarter, The E-Train made it 21-12 after an 8-yard jaunt. Perrone went for two and the conversion rush was successful making it 21-14.

Salem forced Winthrop to punt on its next possession and the Witches took over on their own 22-yard line. Rodriguez picked up a crucial first down on fourth and two at the Winthrop 46. On the next play and, recognizing nine defenders in the box, I audibled for Grimes to run a dig route and connected with him in stride for a TD. The Salem sidelines were celebrating like it was New Year's Eve, but it was short-lived as a yellow flag lay at the line of scrimmage. The referee signaled illegal procedure on Salem, which brought the TD back.

This proved to take some of the momentum out of Salem as we got stuffed on fourth and one on Winthrop's 30-yard line.

Words were exchanged and a Winthrop player stood over Rodriguez, screaming, "Bewitched, to knock off a true champion you need to whip them on their field and that's how you make a champion die. The conference title has to go through Miller Field, not this year, baby."

Pain shot through Rodriguez's ankle as he limped off the field. Stunned, his head was spinning from the collision.

The clock read 1:48 left in the game, and the concern of defeat was visible on the Salem's players' faces. Too weak to attend her grandson's game, Owa sat in her little chamber by the window to get a clear signal from her portable radio. As the Winthrop defense stopped The E-Train, she held her rosary beads and started to pray, not for a win, but for Salem to get the ball back.

With one timeout remaining, Salem needed a miracle and they got one when linebacker Garrett Parsons came up with the hit of his career, stripping Winthrop running back Paul Ferrara of the ball. "Mr. Clutch" Corey Perry recovered the fumble at Winthrop's 25, with 1:14 to play.

Salem's flame was rekindled and I looked at the big picture: A loss and this dream season was over. But the Salem Witches would not back down. Murphy's Law haunted us for three periods, during which most everything that could go wrong, did. But the tide was trying to change.

Perrone grabbed me and asked what play I liked.

"Let's keep it in the air."

Perrone smiled and called a pass play which was complete for 11 yards. The offense had a sense of urgency and ran to the line of scrimmage as if they were running Phase IV in practice. The next play was an incompletion. On 2nd and ten, I rolled left and started scrambling, the ball popped loose from my hand. I went after it on my hands and knees. Everyone at Miller Field who witnessed the play thought for sure Winthrop recovered. My mom's head was down and she refused to look up as her fingers were crossed. She would be able to tell what happened by the reaction of the Salem fans.

I found a way to come up with the ball, cradling it with 25 seconds left. She sighed and rose to her feet. Perrone signaled the team's final timeout. On 3rd and ten, a screen pass was set up perfectly, but Winthrop's defensive lineman burst through the A-gap. Realizing a sack would end the game, I scrambled as I started to get tackled. I threw the ball into the ground with flags going every direction.

Intentional grounding was called, which stopped the clock with four seconds left. If there was ever a divine intervention, this was it; a game cannot end on a penalty. Walking to the sideline, the ball was placed at the 30-yard line. I had a brief moment to think about my idol, Doug Flutie. I closed my eyes and thought, *He did it, why can't I?*

He never did the narration as a kid of the clock winding down and throwing a bomb to win the game. "Always 4th down, you never punted. You were always throwing the ball to the end zone. You were running around, buying time trying to let someone get open and then throw it the length of the field. It had been rehearsed thousands of times over the years for sure," said Flutie.

The pressure, the season on the line, and dreams that would last a lifetime were all at stake. In my mind I had been in this situation before on the streets of Witchcraft Heights where I was molded.

It was 4th and 30. Perrone examined his clipboard as if he were getting ready to give the State of the Union.

"Coach, do you remember what I told you when you asked me what my favorite play was and why?"

Puzzled, Perrone stood in silence staring into my eyes. Perrone nodded his head, indicating yes.

Softly I said, "Coach, this will be the play that will get us to the Super Bowl. Jet Left Sprint Out Pass, X skinny post."

Perrone, amazed by my confidence, changed his own strategies. With his hand placed on my shoulder he uttered the words, "Go get it."

The huddle was in complete silence and players were holding hands. I looked each lineman in the eyes and stated with a voice shaking with fear, "Look at the scoreboard, boys." It read four seconds, lit up like a shining star on a Christmas tree. "Manny, you are in a track race, keep it skinny, split the defenders, and find the back of the end zone."

Eruzione stood in the back of the end zone at Miller Field. Miraculous moments and close games are a part of sports that he cherished. This brought his thoughts back to Lake Placid when he was part of the Miracle on Ice, and it was a tie game with the Russians in the 1980 Winter Olympics. "Any athlete out there could take matters into their own hands and make the most out of their opportunities." He knew firsthand that miracles can happen. As the ball left Sean's hand, I saw it as a coined being tossed in the air," said Eruzione.

The script could not have been written any better. With all eyes focused on me, I faded back to pass, and hung tough as Winthrop's defensive linemen applied pressure. I went through my reads. "The safety is cheating over, keep it skinny, front of the goal-post." But in my mind, I was throwing to De Pena the entire time. De Pena headed up the DB. As he broke I released a tight spiral that looked overthrown. High and long, the crowd grasped in shock, a few long seconds in which everyone froze. As the ball was coming down, Winthrop's safety was closing in. De Pena was flying down the field. He realized more speed was needed. He pumped harder as the ball started to descend. De Pena, looking over his right shoulder, realized he needed to make the adjustment and did. Never taking his eye off the laces, he looked over his left shoulder making an acrobatic adjustment and felt the hard leather in his hands, cradled like a baby, as he was tackled to the ground.

A scary thought entered my mind, *One more play, down 21-20. Any flags on the ground?* Quickly I examined the field as the Salem sidelines erupted with joy. Realizing no penalties, I got down on one knee and gave praise to the Man above. "With Christ, all things are possible." Looking into the sky, I could not help but notice a cross of clouds above the field. As I walked to the sideline, I looked up into the stands and pointed to the two people who instilled the confidence in me, who taught me to have dreams: my parents.

With no time left on the clock, there was no debating that a tie was not an option. They were going for two. Perrone looked stunned, like he was in a fairy tale. He uttered to me, but the words could not come out. His breath was taken away. After a slow, deep breath, he ordered,

"Tell The E-Train he has the golden ticket."

With misted eyes, I addressed the huddle, "Guys, three yards puts us one step closer to the title. Elvin, we all have our tickets punched for The E-Train Express and are ready to ride through the goal line. Jet Right Toss on one, Jet Right Toss on one, ready break."

The E-Train took the pitch. In his mind, no one could stop him. He had been down a road no Winthrop players had ever traveled. His dad did not want to know him, but life was going on. He was playing with a chip on his shoulder. Freeman graciously went into motion, each step getting him closer to the goal. The E-Train's life statement was 3-yards away. He could not help but think of his three-month-old son watching him from the stands. As I pitched him the ball, his pupils started to dilate, heart racing as determination defined his face. After he caught the pitch he sliced towards the goal line. At that time he resolved to create a legacy for his son. This culminated one of the most dramatic victories in Witches' annals. Cronin, Jones, Russell, Higley, and Dulong made it all possible. If it was the NFL, they would all be deserving of Rolex watches. They made it possible for me to work some Eruzione/ Flutie Magic.

Pandemonium took over the Salem side of the field. Hugs, high fives, yells, and tears were felt. A miracle had transpired in front of their very eyes. It was a feeling kids have when they dream. It was a lot deeper than winning a football game. Hope with a sense of satisfaction that everything the coaches had put on the line and all the work the players had put in was for something. They had dug deep into their inner souls to find a way to overcome the adversity they faced that day. Some of these players had already lost so much that was out of their control and were now standing up for something that they could contribute to that ended in a positive way. The fear of losing the game for some was no greater than the experiences they went through every day of their life.

Eruzione believed that sometimes things are just predestined and some things are just supposed to happen. He followed the story of Salem closely; he agreed that Coach Perrone was doing the right thing by standing with his team and protecting his kids. Despite the consequences to himself, Perrone believed that the place for him was with his players and Eruzione agreed. The feeling was surreal. It was a once-in-a-lifetime feeling, one that is cherished within your heart.

The celebration was on, or let's say fiesta, for Rodriguez, De Pena, Leopaldo, Mercado, and the rest of the boys from Santo Domingo in the Dominican Republic. Fans were cheering, cheerleaders were jumping, players were embracing each other, and the coaches were in shock. Like a game of poker, they had gone all in with no regrets.

"There was no way we were going for a tie," said Perrone. "We wanted to win and we were playing to win all the way. These kids are fighters. They'll give you everything they've got. I can't believe this, but you could almost feel it coming…then we got the darn fumble. It was a finish like I never been involved in; God must be a Salem High football fan. Somebody loves this team. We had help from upstairs." (*The Times*, November 14, 1994)

"I was never religious until this football season," tackle David Russell offered. "After this I really believe there is somebody behind us, backing us. This was miraculous. This was unbelievable." (*The Times*, November 14, 1994)

Higley kept the faith and never thought the guys around him would let this team lose. "We had the guys to get the job done. Players stepped up and adversity is what we overcame." This team lacked veterans, but had players with heart. Unselfish play is what it comes down to. Players were not worrying about what other kids were doing; they were patient and things opened up.

I stood in the end zone with my hands on my hips, trying to digest the events that just took place. The sun beamed on my face. It felt like a dream; it was a dream. Reality had not been completely digested. But then again, it was a dream came true, "Throwing one of the most illustrious touchdown passes in Salem High Football history." (*Salem News*, November 14, 1994) In one sense, logic dictates that a single event, the lone occurrence, is not subject to the laws of probability. In other words one can, by preparation, affect outcomes when he has a number of chances at that event or occurrence. In retrospect the prospect of completing the once-in-a-lifetime, historical touchdown pass is statistically remote. There are too many variables that undermine the likelihood of achieving such result.

On the other hand, there is a common thread that, in my view, ties together those athletes who achieve the unimaginable. That characteristic is imagination. Those, like me, that can be lost for hours imagining, being in that one in a million situation and come through with the big play. More so as a youngster, my friends and I routinely ended all our games on the last second miracle play. Being an eternal optimist and believing in the interconnectivity of things, I cannot help but think those childhood dreams and backyard Hail Mary plays positively impacted the outcome in this game and helped defy the odds established by mathematics. Call it an extension of mysticism that Salem has branded.

The E-Train, nearly hospitalized from the impact of the pig pile celebration, walked toward me, his eye-black smeared on his cheeks. He had a long day's work, rushing for over 200 yards and two TDs. We both had career days, but it was more than that. Although we came from different walks, we had a genuine friendship, a bond and an appreciation for each other's abilities. The E-Train was like a brother to me. He had my back, in and out of school. At times I was going to get punked by the older crowd, and he stepped in.

He stuck out his hand, "That's teamwork, double SS."

It sure was. At the same time, we knew this was the greatest day of our lives.

It was more than a QB and RB appreciation for each other; it was an entire team. Cronin and Jones were giving out bear hugs. The team was connected at the hips.

Coach Perrone found his QB and said, "Destiny, Sean!"

"Call it what you want, Coach, but we are truly America's Team," I responded.

Walking off Miller Field, Eruzione gave me thumbs up. At that point, it hit me. I was touched by an angel, and Eruzione had sprinkled some of his magic on Miller Field.

I was soon greeted by former *Boston Herald* and current *Salem News* reporter Bill Kipouras and Cary Shuman of the *Daily Item*. "The team has the heart of a lion, said Kipouras and let's just say that Sean Stellato works Flutie Magic."

I responded by saying, "No, our team showed some true Witchcraft Magic."

After a drawn-out, eight-hour bargaining session, the union membership met on Veterans Day at Knights of Columbus Hall which sat along the commons. Teachers from all of the city's eight public schools were in attendance. They all sat, waiting to hear the latest offer from the city. Turner, surrounded by his negotiating team, drank water to clear his throat before he started to address the audience. Regardless of what was negotiated, it was clear that he was not going to be able to satisfy everyone in that room. The once quiet hall turned into an uproar as Turner slowly read the proposal, teachers began to yell out remarks. It was obvious that the teachers were not happy. Every eye in the room was focused on Turner, silenced with anticipation of what was yet to come. Some of the teachers sat patiently with their arms crossed, keeping to themselves, while others had a hard time controlling their emotions.

The Salem Teachers Union approved a tentative agreement by the school committee which would bring a close to the two-week strike. This would allow schools to reopen Tuesday.

Finally, the strike was over. In the end, the fourteen days of picket lines had been dragged out, and the teachers were ready to get back into the classrooms.

The city offered the union an 11.5 percent wage increase package, linking a portion of the increase to student performance. The latter component was an area that stalled negotiations the last two weeks, and the final vote almost failed because of it. This part the school committee felt was essential to be implemented.

John Fortunato was one of them. He had sobbed at his basketball team banquet, giving awards out and saying goodbye to his seniors. This was no different, and he held back tears thinking about this, the second longest teachers strike in state history. The strike lasted fourteen days. No matter how unified this group was, people were hurting. Families were struggling financially, and their innocent students wanted to be educated. Fortunato did not feel there was any malice on the part of the teachers, the administration, or the mayor. "It was a negotiation, and I was proud how the union stood up and conducted ourselves, but I wish we never had to go through with it." They never had envisioned there was going to be such fallout, but it was just the way it played out. To him, it was the greatest gift to teach students. It was never about subject matter, but about the values that are brought out through coaching and athletics. Life lessons were given and the ability to stand up for your own value set was important. In life, it is always easy afterwards to be that Monday morning quarterback and say, "I did not see how this would play out." But you do what has to get done at the time. Regardless of what was negotiated, it was clear that Turner was not going to be able to satisfy everyone in that room.

Gaynor Riley was smoking a cigarette in one of the front rows. He realized it was going to be close. It was the first time it felt dicey in the hall. Teachers were taking turns getting up and expressing their feelings toward the negotiating team. Riley reached for the ashtray to put his cigarette out. Sipping his coffee, he slowly made his way toward the microphone to have his say. Pausing for a moment, "I worked with those people on the negotiating team for years… if they say that is the best they can do," he yelled out, "believe it." The debate was lengthy and, shortly after Riley's remarks, they took the vote and it though was far from unanimous, it was over.

Later that evening Riley received a call from Turner, telling him that he was not sure about the union's decision but Riley's comments were appreciated. He went on to tell him that he thought he made the difference. The union showed poise during the strike. They could have easily let the state union take over. But the state did not know the complete makeup of the union. By the state coming in, they would have totally controlled the strike and shut down the sports programs. Halting sports would have been utilized as a leverage play. The union was not going to let this materialize, and stayed vocal. This was their town and their students. Fortunato thought if the state took over and there was a hard line, this would have created issues and they would not have been united. "To Perrone's credit, he gave a fair warning to the entire union in August. Unfortunately, I think the other side used that to try to hurt us, but in the end it backfired in an indirect way, and helped us in that we went from their proposal of 1 percent, 1 percent, 1 percent, to 11.5 percent," said Fortunato.

In the face of the daily stress of the strike, the heavy "contempt-of-court" fines and other costs of the strike the union still faced, picket lines, and angry rhetoric between the union and mayor, the majority of teachers decided to end the strike "for the kids." Turner said he believed the job action was worth it. "I think we gained in the salary area. For too many years, and this is the reason behind the strike, this membership had felt ignored and trampled on. I think a new attitude will prevail. This is something I hope never to do again," Turner said.

Mayor Harrington stated, "Our position has been that we have a responsibility to the community to not only improve the schools, but to improve measurements people can understand and appreciate. This contract was more than just money. It was about restoring faith in the system."

The material pertaining to the linkage was changed during

negotiations. The school committee's theory of tying salaries to student SATs left them feeling insulted. They were able to stiff-arm that demand and no language was linked to salaries and test scores.

They saw eye-to-eye on creating a committee of five people elected by the school committee. They would recognize and agree upon school improvements. If those goals were reached each year, those would be escalators for teachers to be compensated at higher levels. This new committee could be utilized to build trust between both sides, but the real challenge would be the healing process moving forward. Sour grapes still hung off both vines.

Superintendent Curtin and other administrators preached, "Now it is a time to heal." Curtin, like Ahab, was fixated with his white whale of Perrone. He sent out a post-strike memorandum to the school department staff members that did not hide his resentment of the coaches. The telling paragraph read: "Other students will want to know why they are expected to obey laws and rules when adult role models have not. As educators, we can take this rare opportunity to teach important lessons about complex issues such as labor negotiations, municipal finance, civil disobedience, and rights and obligations of citizens in a democratic society."

Curtin, by his statements to John Dennis, in my opinion, failed to measure up to the expectations Curtin himself set for the adult role models he cited in this letter. He divided the community by casting the indictments of Perrone's character in such irresponsibly extreme terms. He, like Ahab, led his charges with decision-making motivated not by clear-thinking objectivity, but with hate. The real measure was reflected in the community's response, a tremendous exhibition of support to the football program's collective conduct. Unfortunately, as the judge and jury of the Witch Trials were incapable of understanding the illogic of the witchcraft accusations, so did Curtin and his followers with their failure to appreciate the "healing" and genuine good generated by the team and coaches.

CHAPTER 21

WILL ONE MORE MIRACLE HAPPEN?
THANKSGIVING FOOTBALL

> "Winners, I am convinced, imagine their dreams first. They want it with all their heart and expect it to come true. There is, I believe, no other way to live."
>
> ~ Joe Montana

Rivalries make sports even more exciting. Whether it was the Celtics vs. Lakers in the '80s, Red Sox vs. Yankees, Patriots vs. Dolphins, or Salem vs. Beverly, fans enjoy them. Media eats it up, players love the hype, and coaches will try to pull every trick out of the hat.

There were lazy days at West Beach in Beverly Farms during the summer of 1994. Salem players had listened all summer to how Beverly was going to give them a beating.

John West had left the land in his will to the residents of Beverly Farms and Pride Crossing. With a compelling history, this private beach was the location for the Farm Pride 4th of July fireworks, which had been showcased for more than a century. This very unique place was visited by seventeenth century author Nathaniel Hawthorne from Salem. Artist Fitz Henry Lane painted a masterpiece of the beach in the 1800s that was bought for $3.85 million in 1997.

In addition to taking crap of how Beverly won the Thanksgiving game the year before with a 20-14 win on their home turf, these Salem kids looked at West Beach as a historic resort and an opportunity to eye some girls and toss the pigskin around. Salem's season had already been worthy of a spot in the Guinness Book of World Records. Was Salem, with a conference record of 8-0, a team of destiny after its heart-stopping victories over Swampscott and Winthrop, or a team of luck whose good fortune was about to end?

There was nothing much at stake except the outright Northeastern Conference, which for Salem meant a share of the title for Beverly, and the NEC's berth, and possible home field advantage in the Super Bowl. A Swampscott victory over Marblehead put the Big Blue in both the title and Super Bowl, but only if Beverly beat Salem.

The stage was set. With the series going back to its first meeting in 1890, the ninety-third meeting would be a game for the ages. Salem would not travel by horse-cart over the Salem/Beverly Bridge with twelve players like it did back in 1890. They had seventy warriors who were one personality escorted by The E-Train. They were to travel the same path that legendary Coach Bill Broderick took with his teams over Kernwood Bridge separating the two rival cities. The players, realizing this could be Coach Perrone's last game, were as focused as if they were competing for the gold in the Olympics. But then again it was their Olympics and, for most of them, it was the biggest stage that they would ever perform on.

Vandalism in both cities was common leading up to the Thanksgiving Day game. Curtin had come up with a solution in 1984 when he was the principal of Salem High school called Bridging the Gap, an annual ceremony atop the Salem/Beverly Bridge, the primary connection between the two seaports. This brought both teams together along with fans so as to turn the focus to the up and coming game rather than vandalism.

**

Thirty-five, then I shifted the towel to find an unmarked spot. Thirty-six. I was sitting at the edge of my cot getting my fifty rubs on the game ball another game day ritual.

My grandma came in the room. "Is that pigskin ready?"

"I am almost done," I replied softly. "Owa, is it okay to be nervous?"

She responded, "You would not be normal if you were not. You are a seasoned veteran and leader. This group symbolizes the true meaning of what it takes to become a team. I believe in you and will be with you in spirit tomorrow." She grabbed my hand, "The joy you have given me has extended my life and has given me strength." With goose bumps popping through my skin, it was a defining moment for me. With glassy eyes, she reached over and hugged me, whispering in my ear, "Your grandfather would have been so proud of you." It was a hug of a lifetime and connection that would live in my heart forever.

Later that evening and before bed, I made my way downstairs where my grandma lived. I had one more thing to share with my Owa, but it was too late. She was sound asleep. Putting the covers over her, I noticed a note by her bed stand with her late husband's Pasquale's picture covering a portion of it. Curious, I opened it and realized it was a letter from her doctor.

Once I started reading it, tears started to fall on the letter. It was revealing that one of her heart valves was deteriorating and her time was limited. It was dated six months earlier. The proud lady did not tell anyone. That was the type of lady she was. She never wanted to be a burden; she was a true angel. This completely shocked me. The majority of teenagers think people live forever.

I was sad, but realized that focusing on the positive and influencing the things I could control was the way to manage the reality associated with the note. As a defense mechanism to the crippling effect of Owa's condition, I focused, at least in the short term, on beating Beverly and leading the team to the Super Bowl. I believed this would be the only natural remedy that would give my grandma extended hope and strength.

I walked closer to her, pausing, and then whispered in her ear,

"This one's for you."

Making my way up the stairs and into my room, I needed some fresh air. Opening the window and glancing up at the sky, I noticed it was flooded with stars. Then seconds later, I witnessed three shooting stars. Chills shot through me; I knew this team of destiny was ready to play the Patriots if they had to. We were dreamers, believers, and achievers.

I felt blessed to be alive. I often thought back to several months earlier, the barrel of a 9 millimeter semi-automatic placed on the back of my head. "Wrong place at the wrong time," I heard the statement religiously from my parents growing up. Following the 1994 senior prom, I had attended a post-prom party as a sophomore at the Carriage House, a motel off of route 1 in Peabody. Minding my own business, several African Americans just walked in the room and stared the small group down like animals looking at their prey.

Looking me up and down, they signaled for me to go outside. At this point my intuition was telling me something bad was going to unfold. As they started to make their way outside, I jumped over the bed and ran into the bathroom trying to use it as an emergency exit. Attempting to lock the door, it did not lock. The window jammed shut.

"Oh man, I am done."

Before I could apply pressure to the door, three of them pushed it in. "Why you running scared, white boy?"

The glare from the gun made it visible. They went into my pockets, took my cash, ripped my gold chain off my neck, and grabbed my beeper off my hip. Frozen in fear and looking into the intruders' eyes, I saw hatred.

"Turn around."

With the gun placed to the back of my head, I was paralyzed with frozen emotions. Somehow I found the courage to yell out "Please, Please." Seconds later, this gang from Philly disappeared into the night. Nearly passed out from fright, I sat on the floor weeping. Running my hands through my hair, I was in complete shock. Sitting up, my #3 gold football charm fell to the floor. My parents had given it to me a few weeks earlier. Picking it up I knew the number three was going to be my lucky number.

High in the stands my father glowed with pride. He had a connection with me that symbolized unconditional love and support. That is something every child yearns for, but many do not receive. Don't most sons look for that from a father? To be embraced with a real connection. Most fathers put tremendous pressure on their sons, to succeed and accomplish things they could not. They try to live through their sons, depleting any love for the game that their child has developed over the years. My dad lived for me and J. lived for my dad.

My dad had a different approach. It was a dream come true for both of my parents when I was named the starting QB. He never envisioned in his wildest dreams it turning out this way. Not back in Somerville, where he had first lived on the second floor of a two-family home. He had grown up with two great parents. His dad had come from the old country to live the American Dream, starting in a shoe factory and eventually owning a shoe store. His mother came from Scranton, Pennsylvania, and was compassionate and hard-working. She worked in retail sales.

Not until he was back in Somerville did he realize his true potential. In a densely populated ethnic pocket, he fought often to protect his own turf. During the 1950s, he was a rebel alright, but unlike James Dean, he did not have a cause. It showed with his school grades, coasting by and going through the motions to get his high school diploma. With both parents working over eighty hours a week, he lacked structure. Going against his parents' wishes, the headstrong seventeen-year-old thought he would find "it" by enlisting in the military. In 1957, he entered the Navy. He knew if he did not get off the streets, something detrimental was going to happen.

The military did educate him and gave him an A+ in Independence

101. Stationed in Virginia during the fall of 1958, he received a call from his mother that would change his life forever. "Your father was diagnosed with a terminal illness. We don't know how long he has."

At eighteen years old, he thought he knew everything. The military gave him an honorable discharge so he could help his family survive. The fun-loving man, Pasqual Stellato passed away a few weeks later. "I grew up quick. I was supporting a household." One regret lingered for my dad: He never got to know his dad as a man.

He was hired by Laboratory for Electronics (LFE) in 1958 doing entry-level work in its Boston location. Electronics was an area that interested him. He had a vision and with his work ethic and street smarts, he knew he could climb that corporate ladder. Working efficiently, getting in before sunrise and leaving after sunset, did not go unnoticed among his co-workers. He worked the entry-level position for four years and was eventually promoted to manager, the highest level in his department.

He still remembers meeting my mom like yesterday, a warm spring night in May at the Italian American Club in Everett. He had attended a dance with a friend. Sitting at a table, he could not keep his eyes off this beautiful young blond.

Finally she approached him and said, "My name is Gloria and, by the way, if I waited for you to ask me to dance, I would be waiting all night." She broke the ice and it was a match made in heaven.

The following September, they married. Living like Spartans with no furniture in a one-bedroom apartment in Revere, he knew there had to be a better way of life. Both coming from one-parent families, they knew as a team together they could achieve the American Dream. Picking up another job at Siesta Sleep Shops was the answer, and a quicker way of buying a new home. He worked from 8 AM to 5:30 PM at LFE, and then went directly to Siesta Sleep Shops and worked until 10PM. He worked six to seven days a week. Looking back at it, he didn't know how he had done it. But he had an inner drive. He never took his eye off the ball. He wanted a family, he wanted success, and he wanted to live the American Dream. There could have been quicker ways to make money and corner's to cut, but that was not him.

Four years after getting married, my brother Michael was born. In 1968, he decided to leave LFE and go work the second shift at KLH (High End Audio Manufacturer). This was a career move which enabled them to buy their own home.

Salem was the last place on earth he thought he would end up, but it had all the makings and conveniences you look for in a place to raise a family. In addition, it had quite a history behind it. Witchcraft Heights was a new development that caught their eye. It was about a half a mile from Gallows Hill, our practice fields at times where the witches were hanged

By the late 1970s, he traveled from Boston to California every two weeks. Staying at five-star hotels, dining at top-shelf restaurants, and the weather made him fall in love with California. When the company merged with Infiniti in 1980, he was immediately offered a job on the West Coast. Being the family man he was, and his other half refusing to leave her mother, he declined the offer. This was a real risk, but my dad was a go-getter and transitioned when obstacles came knocking like when his father was dying; he transitioned when he was working night and day for peanuts; and he transitioned to the one bedroom apartment in Revere with no furniture.

Like a priority free-agent on the open market, he was recruited by Doorman & Bogdonoff, a start-up electronic company in 1981. In just three years, his career was thriving. He was promoted to vice president of manufacturing. Part of the package was a brand-new Jaguar and exotic business trips all over the Far East. His father fought to survive the great voyage from the Old Country to Ellis Island. His life might not have been the American Dream but it was his dream, living proof that all things are possible if you have enough drive and faith.

Through his journey my dad never forgot about his roots, a kid at heart, a little throwback with a touch of being unorthodox. He would reflect on his younger days of selling papers at the Boston Garden. He was exposed to greatness at an early age, witnessing possibly the greatest dynasty in all of sports and using that as a benchmark on how to live his own life. The thoughts of drag-racing Celtics legend Bill Russell on the Lynn-way or protecting his turf in the Ville (Somerville) were part of his chemical makeup. He would not take what he had for granted, but would cherish the family he helped create.

He was forever grateful for the genes he inherited that instilled a work ethic that was very strong. One factor that marinated in his mind through the years was the void he had with his dad not ever being involved in what he was doing as a kid, because he did not have the time. He made a pact with himself that he would give all three of his sons every opportunity to succeed and make the time to be there. He would help shape all their destinies, enabling them to dream. But there was something about his youngest son that was different from his older brothers.

Thoughts of the Swampscott game were almost impossible to imagine. "National TV, the atmosphere, player of the game under those circumstances they were fighting, Seven Wonders of the Week." He never imagined in his life something like this happening. "A fairy tale, I watch a lot of movies and at times, I had to stop and then realized we are in a real-life movie with no actors. After Sean threw 'The Pass' in the Winthrop game, I was in complete shock. It was the most exciting game I have ever witnessed. Sean held it together and had the mindset to get it done. He wanted everything, to play against the best, to develop his skills at camps, the ball in his hands. He wanted to be the best." My dad was not surprised that when I put my mind to a task, others should take notice because there was a good chance that I was going to accomplish it.

Even after some storybook endings to games, it was hard for my dad not to be bitter about the strike. "The political game was out of their control. It was personal, and you cannot fight politics."

In a sense he felt he could relate to these kids with how he had to grow up fast when he had lost his dad at a young age. "The reality of the situation is these kids were students who were being taught by teachers every day. They were supposed to teach the difference between right and wrong, encourage them, and be individuals who could direct them into the correct career path. In a lot of ways, they are role models in certain situations."

"The mayor, superintendent, athletic director, and school committee made the rules and had the authority to make decisions. Their first responsibility should have been for the students and their well-being. They did not take that into consideration. Perrone did, and I don't know what he was going to gain in his own mind by sticking with his students. It was not going to put more money in his pockets, and it was not going to put him in a better place with the school committee. He knew that. Your teenage years are fragile and lay down the foundation and instill confidence that can enable kids to do the right thing. Don't take a U-turn or go down a side path that brings you to the point of no return. The administrators and school committee dropped the ball and felt it was necessary to make an example of these professionals. The right thing to do was to coach that team, stick with those kids, and educate them with regard to standing up for what they believe in. It was Leadership 101. When you have biased, non-football individuals in charge, it is a race with no finish line."

With all his sons having gone through the program, he had become a faithful Salem football fan. He went to all the games early to make sure he had a bird's-eye view to videotape. He attended every boosters meeting on Monday nights. He volunteered his time at the annual Heritage Day parade in which the football team marched every August. He stood in the stands at Miller Field cheering and feeling like he was dreaming as Salem pulled out one of the greatest comebacks in school history. He wore the same black booster sweatshirt to every game and confessed part of him was living through me. I was doing something he had never done in Somerville. I appreciated my dad, and cherished our connection. I wanted him there every step of the way. He was absorbing it all and had his ticket punched for wherever this team would bring him.

**

On Thanksgiving morning the outside temperature read 18 degrees. The winds gusted and the windows cracked. The kitchen stove in The E-Train's apartment was left on to generate some heat. A can storing some rice and Goya beans rested on the coffee table. Red's Sandwich Shop was a popular breakfast spot, but was not in the family budget. Elvin's mother was off to work to get paid time-and a-half on Thanksgiving morning. This would be a different holiday for Maria Rodriguez. She would be allowed to leave early to go see her son play football for the first time.

Elvin needed to fetch his own breakfast. "Damn, Victor, you used all the milk. Guess it will be water in my cereal. Ghetto." he mimicked. *The train got to be ready to ride today*, he thought while eating his breakfast.

With no police escort to Hurd Stadium and the strike behind the community, these kids were able to go back to living like regular teenagers. Adolescence comes and goes like the holidays, but these kids all grew up very quickly and realized life was more than just a game. Curtin's accusations about Perrone and the strike had ignited fire in their hearts. The injustice associated with them motivated them to achieve, to focus on the positive and good in society. We, unlike those killed or incarcerated with the little chance to be heard in Salem Village or Judge Hawthorne's court, had prevailed in the latter day court of public opinion.

Coach Perrone wanted to make a point and do something out of the ordinary. His last trip to Beverly needed to be a memorable one. The team itself was very quiet throughout the field-house; you could sense that they were getting ready for a physical battle by how they marched onto the bus, as if they were entering another galaxy. The bus brought us first to Bertram Field. Perrone ordered the entire seventy players off the bus and onto the field. Stepping off the bus he gave each player their home red jersey to put on.

The man employed Vince Lombardi-type motivational tactics. The scoreboard lit up which left the kids puzzled. Then under Salem, it read 15, Visitor 13, with one of the coaches announcing, "Salem 37, Lynn Classical 7. Salem 20, Saugus 8. Salem 27, Gloucester 8. Salem 14, Marblehead 0. Salem 30, Lynn English 7. Salem 16, Swampscott 8."

Downes shouted out, "One team, baby, one team."

"Salem 22, Winthrop 21."

Coach Perrone started walking toward his team with tears streaming down his face; in his mind he wanted to believe he might be back, but in his heart he knew the venom the administrators possessed would slowly kill him. He, like the accused of yesterday, would never back down, admit guilt, and save his job.

Standing in front of the players he slowly reached into his pockets. He pulled out a red piece of paper on which was written a poem. With his head staring toward the ground, he was trying to hold it together. He was broken and his livelihood was on a tailspin of destruction. Coach Perrone was no politician, but a genuine man. Often coaches preach that they are sincere and put certain desires over their own, only to change their stance overnight. Taking several deep breaths, he spoke the words, "Don't quit. When things go wrong as they sometimes will, when the road you're trudging seems all uphill, when the funds are low and the debts are high, And good fortune seems to pass you by, When care is pressing you down a bit, Rest if you must but don't you quit. Life is queer with its twists and turns, As everyone of us sometimes learns, And many a fellow turns about, When he might have won had he stuck it out, Don't give up though the pace seems slow, You may succeed with another blow. Often the goal is nearer than It seems to the faint and

the drawing board.

Beverly's third possession was no better, getting stuffed on three straight plays. Downes was playing with a vengeance and was just looking for someone to hit. He made it a point to play through the whistle. With Beverly punting and their running back not paying attention, jogging down the field, and admiring the crowd, he should have thought twice about that as the raging bull Downes knocked him almost up into the stands. Downes let out a roar as if he were king of the jungle. At that very moment he was. Years of struggle, anguish, and adversity were built up like a volcano and erupting all over Hurd Stadium. In his mind everyone that came in his vision was his step-father.

Salem needed to establish a drive and control the clock, but two straight offside penalties put our backs against the wall. On third and twenty, I rolled left and threw a perfect ball to a streaking De Pena on a dig route. Manny headed up the DB and ate up his cushion. The ball hit him in his hands as the Beverly DB fell down. But the ball dropped to the frozen ground, and De Pena's head went down as if he were a young child scolded by a parent. He walked slowly to the sidelines. Caught up in his emotions after dropping his third pass of the game, his body gestures defined his confidence. The kid was from the island of Santo Domingo. This was a culture shock for him with the differences in climate. Coming off the reception of a lifetime the week before, he was frustrated and angry as he made it to the sidelines. He wrestled his red Newman gloves off his hands and threw them to the ground. Manny was a fierce competitor and had high standards for himself. He spent winter days at Palmer Cove, which is a park located down The Point, catching balls year-round to prepare himself for moments like this. At 6'1" and 165 pounds, De Pena had a lanky physique with long arms and was fearless as he crossed the valley of death (middle of the field). His glasses gave him a distinguished look as he ran like a deer.

Beverly got the ball back with just over five minutes remaining.

After picking up 8 yards, they faced a critical 4th and 2 at the Salem 47-yard line. Salem changing up schemes sent the "house," and it paid off big dividends, gang-tackling Beverly's Jimmy Fultz for a 1-yard loss and taking the ball over at their 46-yard line. Energy was coming from the Salem sideline and the Salem fans were on their feet. It was like a heavyweight fight and what it came down to was who wanted it more. Salem took over the ball with one agenda, and that was to move the chains and this game was history, but Beverly had a different plan and stuffed us on three straight plays, forcing us to punt with 2:39 in the game.

Beverly got the ball back at their 31-yard line. On 1st down they picked up 6 yards on a QB keeper. On 2nd down Beverly was called for illegal motion and Salem declined making it 3rd down. They called a QB draw, picking up 5 yards, making it 4th and 1. I was getting antsy as I looked at the clock and saw 1:31 remaining. Beverly burned its final timeout.

Salem loaded the box with 9 defenders. Whitten, limping up to the line, knew a stop and it would be over. He looked over his left shoulder and got the signal from Marcoulier: 44 Stack blitz. He touched his thigh pad which indicated for Phil Downes to blitz through the A gap. Defensive tackles Higley and Daley lined up allowing Whitten and Downes to have a clearer path to blitz. Beverly was in a two back set. Whitten eyed-down Beverly running back Jason Peters like he was prey, and Downes, was ready to run through a wall if he had to. Jim Fultz would be the only person in his way. On the sideline Perrone, paced back and forth. When the ball was snapped, it was like time had stopped. Fultz took the ball and was blasted by Downes. Downes, wearing a cast, had a tough time wrapping him up but Fultz fell to his knees, landing on top of a Beverly lineman. Higley was lying on the ground, and looking up from the turf he thought Fultz's progress was stopped. In reality Fultz's knee had never touched the ground as it rested on human flesh.

All the other Salem players stopped, thinking the play was over and were celebrating. De Pena's knees buckled. His emotions took over as he screamed and wanted to trip Fultz. With the weather conditions being brutally windy and cold, he was convinced it was over. His hands were like rocks as he tried to dig deeper.

Perrone and company felt like their hearts were all going to stop beating as Fultz descended from the top of the human pile and raced 65 yards for a TD. Beverly was now leading 13 to 10.

Beverly fans were literally pinching themselves as Fultz crossed into the end zone. Reacting as if they had won the game, they went into a frenzy; standing on top of cars and buses, antagonizing Salem fans and players.

One particular Beverly player was taunting Higley. Higley calmly reacted by saying, "I don't know what you are celebrating for." The kid just looked at him as Higley went on to say, "You guys left too much time on the clock."

With the Salem fans in complete shock, I channeled my energy into the remaining time on the scoreboard, 1:19. The question was did Beverly start the post-game party too soon?

An entire team hinged upon what seemed like a single play. Facing elimination with 1:19 remaining, Salem had the ball but needed to move the ball 80 yards into the wind. With the wind at the QBs back, passes went 10 yards beyond their targets. Fielding a pass, punt, or kick was like catching an icicle dropped off the Bunker Hill monument in Charlestown. The wind gusting to 30 mph throughout the game causing the 17,500 fans packed into Hurd Stadium to feel as though they were frozen sardines in a can.

The field was almost completely frozen, so each step had to be carefully taken as if you were trying to walk on an ice rink. The E-Train returned the kickoff to Salem's own 20-yard line. First play, my pass was deflected and fell incomplete. On 2nd down, a streaking Rodriquez was tackled running a fade route and yellow flags fell from the sky. Pass interference was called moving the ball to the Beverly 44-yard line. The Beverly fans were irate, feeling it should have been offensive pass interference.

On 1st down, we called a screen pass to Mercado. Mercado stumbled as the ball sailed just out of reach. Perrone called the same play on 2nd down and Beverly was all over it. On 3rd and 10, I was drilled by a blitzing linebacker. I let out a scream that could have been heard in Salem. It was a noise that reflected pain with a touch of frustration. Slowly and painfully climbing to my feet, I grabbed my left knee. Beverly players hovering over me whispered, "Not in our house, baby. We are not at West Beach anymore, Hollywood."

The Beverly fans were on their feet chanting, "Panther pride! Panther pride!"

How could I, a teenage kid keep my composure at a moment like this with more than 17,500 fans going wild? The clock was ticking and time was running out for Perrone's and Salem's dream Cinderella run.

Coach Perrone burned a timeout with 36 seconds. I limped to the sideline, each step getting more challenging. My eye black smudged and hands frozen, I believed this team had one more miracle left. This is where I dreamed of being and there was no turning back. Perrone was as focused as he had ever been and could feel the echoes from legendary Coach Bill Broderick, who put the program on the map and had more last second wins than any coach in school history. Both of us realized this could be the last time we stood together on the field. The pressure could not have been any greater, and the fans were as energized as the players on the field. It was time to cowboy up and to do my best impression of Joe Montana with a touch of Doug Flutie. Approaching Perrone, the blood on my knee concerned my coach. Perrone was fifty-nine years old with his once jet black hair turning gray. His face looked tired, the dark circles under his eyes resembling the dark cloud hovering over the program. Perrone took his hat off and let out a deep breath. He was more passionate and creative than ever, fighting a political battle he could not win.

Perrone's energy was unmatched and his motor was always on. He often woke up in the middle of the night, as he dreamed up some plays that would beguile defenses. His livelihood challenged and scarred, it took a toll on him. Tired and overwhelmed, the man poured his heart and soul into the city of Salem. How about some loyalty—the man was not making millions. He was an educator and coach who made his players believe in themselves and live by a commitment to excellence. He was a true man of God. The man resurrected a dying football program and put it back on the map. Broderick was smiling down from above. He could have worked a combo of all David Copperfield magic and official Salem Witch Laurie Cabot's spiritual powers, and it would not be enough to win this political battle. But a win on the field would put memories in his players' hearts that no political group could take away.

He went to his clipboard and pulled out a folded sheet of paper, resembling a treasure map in my eyes. It was a designed play he named "Golden Boy." The moment was surreal, as if I were an actor in a Hollywood movie, feeling like I was touched by a greater power. "Golden Boy" was Perrone's nickname for me when I was playing back in his Pop Warner days. "Get outside the tackle." The plan was to get De Pena the ball on a skinny post, but utilize Rodriquez as option two. "Make sure you emphasize backside protection. Tell Mercado to pick up any blitzes."

"Got it, Coach," I replied.

As I made my way back on the field, Perrone called me back. "Golden Boy, go get it."

With my eyes full of fire, I addressed a focused huddle that looked at this as relief to what they had been up against. They were now in a place where things got done on heart and skill, not egos and politics. Approaching the huddle, I saw it looking perfect. A tightly-wound circle. They held hands, no pretenders, but true contenders. There was a feeling of warmth and brotherhood in the huddle with eleven hearts forming one.

I saw focus in my center Cronin, passion in Russell, toughness in Jones, glory in Higley, sacrifice in Dulong, faith in De Pena, pride in Leopoldo, tenacity in Freeman, drive in Mercado, adversity and heart in Rodriquez, and I felt destiny within my heart. My teammates were from all walks of life—the ghetto, single parents, bankers, business executives. They fought for everything they got and I exclaimed, "Guys, the next 36 seconds for the rest of our lives. De Pena, their DBs have been bailing the last three plays. Read them and flatten your route if they cover it like the previous plays."

Football was in our entire DNA. The play was called in the huddle and all eyes were on me like I was leading an army. The clap that broke the huddle was crisp.

With 4th and 10 from the Beverly 44-yard line, more than 17,500 fans were on their feet. 36 seconds would feel like an eternity.

Owa could feel herself getting really nervous as she sat in the basement in Witchcraft Heights with her portable radio by her side and her Saint Joseph Daily Missal clenched in her hands. Turned to page 619, she started to pray:

"Oh God, on the summit of Mount Sinai you gave the Law of Moses, and by means of your holy angels, you miraculously placed there the body of Blessed Catherine, your Virgin and Martyr, we beseech you, that, through her merits and intercession, we may be able to reach that mountain which is Christ, who with you, all things are possible." She added, "Lord, help these young men reach their own mountain and beat Beverly." She slowly started to pace back and forth. This was one of her true joys in life, seeing her grandson lead his team and live his dream. She wanted to experience every joy with him. She was fighting to prolong her life as long as possible. The faith and devotion she possessed was unmatched.

Athletic seasons were hard and weighed on her through the years.

It had been a way of life since she married Pasquale Stellato. Back in the 1940s and '50s, she followed her son Frank's boxing career, from the silver mittens, golden gloves, All-Navy championships, Olympic trials, and to his amateur fights at Dilboy Field in Somerville where he won ten straight fights. As an amateur he fought in the Golden Gloves All-East Championships Tournament in March of 1948 on the same card as Rocky Marciano, where Marciano was beaten by Coley Wallace. This would be the last loss in Marciano's career. Frank then engaged in epic battles with welterweight champion Tony DeMarco. However, it was difficult to remember any fight or season more emotional than this football season.

Downes got on his knees and started to pray. I walked to the line with focus and confidence; I was now a veteran. The players were not fazed by anything: the yelling crowds, the clock, the weather. They were on such an emotional ride the last three weeks that they were able to navigate through it all and focus on the task at hand. They were focusing only on going undefeated in conference play and going to the Super Bowl.

I lined up under center and saw gaps in the Beverly defense. I took the snap and rolled out to the left. Rodriguez was double-covered and I realized I would not be able to get the ball to him. Poised, I then looked to De Pena, who started to flatten his post route.

There was no doubt De Pena was the fastest player on the team. He realized development was part of the process and was determined to be that all-around wide receiver. He wrote about it, thought about it, and always believed dreams come true. He was in the place of his childhood dreams. It was not coincidental but destiny to be in that position. But the struggle had been as real as his thoughts while adversity had constantly knocked.

Beverly safety Jim Fultz started to come downhill. Feeling the pressure, with ice in my veins, I threw a 30-yard strike over a jumping Fultz's head, and De Pena displayed great concentration. Bobbling it like a water balloon, his eyes were fixated on the ball as he never removed them from it. He hauled it in at the 14 before being dragged down at the Beverly 4-yard line. An enthusiastic and resurrected De Pena exploded up off the ground with his fist clenched in the air. A powerful and joyful eruption came from the Salem side of the stadium. Realizing the game was far from over, I signaled timeout to the referee.

The E-Train stared into the thousands of fans. He noticed one in particular: his mother, Maria, who was watching him play football for the very first time. Rodriguez had waited for this day to come, but not any longer than he waited in his cold stairwell as a young boy for his dad to arrive to bring him sneakers, so he could get rid of the ones that had holes from being too small. The kid had huge "father" pain deep down inside. He had never been accepted nor embraced the way he needed to be. No TD, pancake, or championship could ultimately heal this emptiness.

Perrone displayed paternal characteristics toward him and, in return, the kid had empathy for his coach and supported what he was doing for his football team. Being abandoned as a child by his own dad, he found security in the fact that his coach would not turn his back on his team. His is but one vivid illustration of how wrong Curtin was about Perrone, and how the educational experience was enhanced by participating in inter-scholastic competition.

Rodriguez dreamed about this day and only wished his mom could have been in attendance more, but being a single mother she could not afford to take any days off. The kid had made major progress since seventh grade when he could only eat fruit salads just to keep him at the playing weight so he could play on the A team in Pop Warner.

The most scrutinized and followed game in the state, it was all on the line. He wanted the ball. He wanted it for his team, his mom, and every Dominican that came to this country for a better life. In his mind, and always with him, was the thought of college. It would give him an opportunity so many of the boys would never see: a college scholarship.

Everyone in the stadium knew he was getting the ball. He took the handoff from me and fought for 2 yards.

Perrone burned the team's final timeout. With seconds remaining, every Beverly and Salem fan was on their feet, but it was the Salem fans chanting, "Witches' Pride, Witches' Pride!" The echoes could be heard all over the stadium. It looked like a smoke show with the cold air circling the Salem side.

De Pena looked at Rodriguez, "This is it. *Ya llego la hora.*"

Rodriguez's eyes were opened wide, staring down the Beverly defense as it was his heavyweight opponent. He stayed hungry, mentally and physically. Success was in his realm; he was starting to understand what the American dream was and when you want something you just need to go get it. Salem lined up in an "I" formation.

I started the cadence tight, rotate. Freeman moved from a wide split to align in a Stake I formation putting Freeman and Mercado in front of The E-Train. It was the Latino three-headed monster. Blue, on hit, Rodriguez took the handoff and barreled through the four-hole. The surge from the line gave him leverage to find the end zone.

In a split second, he transformed from a boy to a man.

The Salem fans went berserk. The Beverly side was a concrete wall of dropped jaws. The end zone was like a scene from the red carpet. Picture flashes were going off; news cameras from all over New England were live on the field filming the celebration.

I exploded up in the air with one finger pointing to the sky, letting out a yell for the ages. I felt complete. My boyhood dream, my prediction, had come true.

We were going to the Super Bowl.

Extending Owa's life stayed on my mind, I could not wait to see her and tell her how much I loved and cherished her. I ran towards Perrone, embracing him with a hug like father and son. We both started to sob.

"You lived up to your word; we are going to the Super Bowl. Now go boot that extra point!"

***

Riding back on the bus to Salem, excitement was in the air. Players laughed, slept, rejoiced, and all let the sunlight beam on their faces through the foggy bus windows. The anticipation of the turkey and mega TV reruns on Channels 4, 5, and 7, gave them a feeling of euphoria.

Arriving back at school, Downes led the Super Bowl Witches' Shuffle, "When I say "Super, you say Bowl, Super, Bowl, Super Bowl, Super, Bowl." It was a beat that would be preserved in their hearts and minds forever.

Theordore Roosevelt once said, "It is not the critic who counts; not the man who points out how the strong man stumbles, or where the doer of deeds could have done them better. The credit belongs to the man who is actually in the arena, whose face is marred by dust and sweat and blood, who strives valiantly; who errs and comes short again and again; because there is not effort without error and shortcomings; but who does actually strive to do the deed; who knows the great enthusiasm, the great devotion, who spends himself in a worthy cause, who at the best knows in the end the triumph of high achievement and who at worst, if he fails, at least he fails while daring greatly. So that his place shall never be with those cold and timid souls who know neither victory nor defeat."

This was Coach Wilbur's favorite quote. He felt it embodied the spirit of a competitor, someone who will take the risk and lives life to the fullest. The truth of the Roosevelt quote permeated the environment surrounding the post-game celebration. On one hand you had all these young men who realized the full benefit of being in "Roosevelt Arena." On the other hand, we could envision the void in the lives not enriched in the spirit of participation of human endeavor. Part of me felt sorry for the strike participants as they had a void in their life for not having an experience like we just realized. They were fixated on the trivialities of "living." They were cursed to experience the mundane as their greatest slice of humanity. The experience of striving for and achieving what my team accomplished at Beverly that day was a slice of life that everyone including Curtin, Harrington, and teachers should have realized because such experience would have eliminated the pettiness of their behaviors.

It is now no surprise to that combat veteran of our wars that people are grounded in values we admire in society. Experiences from that season added perspective in my daily life. My teammates and I acquired a lifelong gift of being able to order priorities given the stress, trauma, and challenge presented by our season. I truly feel sorry for those who Roosevelt targeted in his poem as never having exercised courage to compete. Win, lose, or tie, you come out better for it.

This is where our ivory tower educators simply did not understand the lifelong impact and positive experience that interscholastic athletic competition brings to fulfill that person. It was then as a teenager in the trenches that I felt more mature than the leaders and participants in the strike. I had acquired enough maturity through my life experience (admittedly limited) to appreciate my teammates and, at that time, we could claim greater maturity than they. From that day to now, I truly feel sorry for all of them.

The grand irony is that these people acted on the basis that they were creating a system to help make Salem youth more mature. But rather it was in their squabble over the system that they made us more mature. The lesson is to live life, not just live.

Chapter 22

Super Bowl
Dreamland

///

> *"Most important thought, if you love someone, you tell him or her, for you never know what tomorrow may have in store. Remember, tomorrow is promised to no one."*
>
> ~ *Walter Payton*

The excitement of the Super Bowl was sprinkled all over the city as if it were Disneyland in Salem. Making my way into Witchcraft Heights, my beeper started to beep. It was home. Figuring my mom wanted to see what I wanted for dinner, I did not call the number back. But as my gray Chevy Turismo slowly made it up Puritan Road towards my house, time completely stopped. Blinded by the lights from police cars, fire trucks, and the ambulance, I felt like I was watching a horror movie. Paralyzed in fear, I rushed to the door.

There lay Owa on the floor with the EMTs trying to resuscitate her. Keeping everyone away from her, I fought to hold her hand. Praying in the silence of my heart, I asked God to spare her and take anything from my body to prolong her life. I believed it worked, as her heart started beating.

Being rushed to the hospital, she asked for me to stay with her in the ambulance. She whispered in my ear, "It is going to be okay.

Pasquale was smiling; we were holding hands." Tears were falling down her cheeks.

Although trying to stay strong, I burst into a fountain of tears. "Owa, we have come so far together. We need to finish this run to the Super Bowl together. You are the reason I have come this far."

Stabilized and tired, she was clinging to life just as I was holding onto a Super Bowl dream. My dad sat with the doctor and received the diagnosis on her condition. Dad cracked his knuckles, and then walked slowly to the window where he barely opened the blinds. He peered through them trying to clear his head. Borrowed time with severely deteriorated heart valves summed it up. Her heart was failing her and was eventually going to stop.

Sitting next to the hospital bed, I was numb with shock. Although I knew I would lose my grandmother someday, it was not something I was prepared for. Only two years ago she was not only taking the train, but also a bus for the forty-five-minute ride into Boston five days a week to her job in Downtown Crossing. Her Italian glow was taken from her, leaving her skin pale and her body in a fragile state.

Reaching into my gym bag I pulled out my boom box and placed it next to her bed with the station WESX set for the game the next morning. My gym bag also held her little black prayer book as well as the game ball from the Winthrop game. Softly holding back tears, I read her the prayer book that she once read to me. Before I walked out of the room, I placed the football at the foot of her bed so that when she awakened, she would know that I was leaving my strength with her.

I was trying to find inner strength and tranquility, and decided to take a twenty-minute ride up the coast to Gloucester. I felt this would help me deal with the sickness of my grandma. When someone is in search of faith, most people picture a person stepping into a church or temple, but my sanctuary rested at the shoreline. I believed the law of attraction started in water. Walking on the beach, my mind went through my own personal time machine. I went back to the memories

I shared with her. The ocean glistened as the full moon reflected off of it; the stars in the sky shined bright making me realize the greatness of life and how big the world was. I thought about over in Italy where she often visited, if those were the same stars that she once saw as a child. She dreamed about a new world filled with opportunities to live the American Dream. I wanted to capitalize on the opportunities that she laid down the foundation for me to receive. I thought back about the stories she told me as a boy about her upbringing. The landscapes of Italy, the beauty of the Vatican, and the history of my bloodline made me get deeper into my reflection. Looking deep at the stars in the sky, I did not pray to win the Super Bowl, but that God would comfort Owa in her time of need.

Making my way back to my car, I started to visualize myself holding up the gold MIAA State Championship trophy. The wind skidding off the sea whistled through the vents of the car. With mixed emotions, I slowly made my way back home. I had one thought in mind and needed to see Owa one more time before Salem's kickoff.

Eager to start my day, I rose early and popped in the *Why Eagles Soar*, featuring highlights from Doug Flutie while I ate my mom's French toast. With a game ticket in hand, I rushed out of the house on a mission. Ten minutes later I arrived at the hospital and placed the Super Bowl ticket on my grandmother's nightstand. Although she was not able to respond, I talked to her as if we were having a regular conversation back at home. After kissing her goodbye, I was off to the school locker room.

"Super Bowl" was the phrase engraved on a telephone pole in Witchcraft Heights. I used those words as my bullseye, as my motivation to achieve my dream. I threw thousands of balls at that pole throughout the years, imagining myself playing in the Super Bowl and playing like Joe Montana, Phil Simms, and Troy Aikman. Although my dream was becoming reality, it felt surreal.

Stepping onto the Boston University's historic Nickerson field gave me a deeper appreciation for the athletes that came before me. Bedtime stories my father told me were memorized like the lyrics of my favorite Method Man song, "Release Yo' Delf." The original entry gate and right field pavilion from the Boston Braves, who played their home games from 1915 to 1953, remained as portions of the stadium. Standing there, soaking in the moment, I held my head high, looking at the skyscrapers lining the skyline in the horizon. Closing my eyes, I imagined what these sacred grounds were like when the Boston Braves, Boston Patriots, Babe Ruth, 363-game-winner Braves lefty pitcher Warren Spahn, or the hometown legend Harry Agganis graced the field.

My father had been a regular spectator at this field throughout his youth and was part of the Braves' knothole gang. He held onto his great memories and blessed his sons with them. My favorite stories were about Harry Agganis who paved the way for kickers and lefty QBs like me. Agganis was from the neighboring town of Lynn and also was the youngest of his family, although he had six siblings. He was an exceptional athlete on the gridiron and baseball field. During the fall of 1948, 24,000 people would migrate to Manning Bowl every week just to watch "The Golden Greek," Harry Agganis. In his last year of high school he had seventy-five Colleges recruiting him. He chose to stay close to his widowed mother and attend Boston University. After a stellar career at Boston University, he was offered a lucrative deal to play football as the number one draft choice for the 1952 NFL Draft. The Cleveland Browns' coach Paul Brown offered him a $25,000 signing bonus.

As the MLB season came around, the Boston Red Sox tried to control the situation and leverage the power to stay in Boston and play for his hometown team. My father shared his memories of watching Agganis play at Fenway for the first time and seeing him hitting a triple his first at bat.

On June 2, 1955, Agganis was hospitalized for chest pains and a severe fever. He passed away at the age of twenty-six in Cambridge,

Massachusetts, of a pulmonary embolism. Although his life was short, he left a lasting legacy not only in Massachusetts, but throughout the country. In his hometown, there is a series of Agganis All-Star Games which hosts the top high school seniors in Eastern Massachusetts.

An hour before the game, the autumn weather in Boston was mild. Thousands of fans made their way down Commonwealth Ave, and into the stadium. Staleness lingered in the locker room. The white game jerseys symbolized something magical from the last three weeks. The seniors would never wear them again. Whether it was superstition or not, Higley refused to wash his game socks. There were certain rituals each player lived by.

The E-Train took the picture of his late brother out of his locker and placed it in his wristband. It was a different pre-game feeling for The E-Train. A blend of nerves and anxiety released through him. Tweaking his knee on Wednesday on the turf greatly concerned him.

Downes stared into the eyes of a picture that portrayed his late mom with sounds of WuTang "Cream" bringing his adrenaline level skyrocketing. He had been to hell and back. "No softy from Whitman-Hanson going to stop me," Downes declared. "As the world turned, I learned life is hell. Living in the world no different from a cell every day, I escaped from cats getting chased, selling base, and smoking bones in the staircase." Downes stood up on the bench and moved to the beats as he rapped.

Higley left the trainer's table, tearing tape around his wrist, and slowly writing his brother's name. The element of quiet confidence touched down within him. His chin-strap was buckled and motor running; a world of destruction was just moments away.

Mccellon said in a whisper, "We made it. The ring is in reach. I just wish my mom was here. She would be proud of me."

I gripped the Baden ball. Too narrow. *I like the Wilsons*, I thought. I thought about my Owa and dreamed about this day. Trying to bring my body to a state of relaxation, I saw "OWA" on my inner forearm and couldn't stop thinking of her. Internal fire started to run through my veins as I sat in stillness.

On the other side of the stadium, the Whitman-Hanson Panthers started to exit their locker room cage. They were dressed in black shiny helmets, black jerseys with their names on the back, and white pants. Former Syracuse linebacker and current Whitman-Hanson Coach Bob Bancroft passed down the principles of discipline and simplicity that he learned from his former legendary Syracuse coach Ben Schwartzwalder. Like Schwartzwalder, Bancroft developed running backs and won games. Bancroft loved to compete and, thanks to former teammates running back Floyd Little (a three-time All-American), fullback Larry Csonka, and running back Tom Coughlin, he learned to play with great intensity.

He was making his sixth Super Bowl appearance and his teams had won twelve of the last thirteen Atlantic Coast titles. The score 42-7 was programmed in their minds for the past twelve months. It was a vivid memory. They were on a mission to reverse last year's Super Bowl loss to North Attleboro. QB Bill Frazier was starting his twenty-seventh straight game and had won twenty-six of them. Stopping their high-powered four horsemen would be no easy chore for the Salem defense. Fresh legs had facilitated parity to exist all season in their backfield. Bancroft developed more depth as the season went on and it showed. It was clear Salem had not faced this type of versatility all season.

Bancroft had his own concerns with the opponent he was about to face. Bancroft was playing a team battle-hardened by a political war and formidable opponents. The Salem team possessed unity forged by Curtin's accusations against Perrone, urgency stoked by the threats having the team shut-down, talent, luck, and good coaching. Such was a dangerous opponent.

"What was happening in Salem was big news everywhere," said Bancroft. He knew Perrone from the Massachusetts Coaches Association and coaching in the Shriner's game. "The dilemma was incredible for fall coaches to strike, especially that it happened on Halloween where just about every other fall season was over. This put even more pressure on Perrone. The state and national coverage was surreal for the high school level. As a teacher/coach, you want to stand behind the teachers, but at the same time you want to support the seniors, as they only have one senior season which is a very important part of their lives. It would be hard for me to look my kids in the eye and tell them we are not going to have football because I cannot coach you. The coaches really did not have much defense. Unions cannot really defend much for coaches because they're just one-year appointments. Not like the union is going to give you all the protection as a coach. But on the other side of the coin, as a teacher, now you are talking about your colleagues and their livelihoods. It is a nasty thing. I look at unions and appreciate what they do but also see how they can cause problems at times," Bancroft stated.

Whitman-Hanson made their way onto the artificial turf for pre-game warm-ups. Their body movements showed swagger as they progressed through each rep with intensity that brought out a sense of resolve. They were dominated by seniors and veterans in these types of situations. With his hands on his hips, Bancroft watched his team warm up and shifted his eyes to the Salem team. He had scouted us for our last four games. He believed that the strike did not affect our performance. Our magical last second wins impacted the way he prepped his team for this game. He saw us as playing with a purpose, which concerned him.

Shaking his head, Bancroft mumbled, "Adversity. The more they faced, they became a tighter family and a better football team. We had to work harder because we felt everyone who plays high school football is on a mission, but this Salem team was on a mission plus. We understood the situation and that they were trying to win for their coach and what was motivating this team," Bancroft stated.

Stare-downs, yells, and loud claps were being filtered through the stadium. Motors started running and the Panthers were ready to attack. Perrone, Marcoulier, Wilbur, McKenna, and Baldassarri felt as if they were back in time as they stood in the very same room back in 1974 when they were about to play in the school's first Super Bowl. Twenty years of memories accumulated in their hearts. They all realized that anyone who ever buckled the chin-strap and laced up the cleats to play high school football lived for this very moment. The pre-game speeches were prepared well before. Perrone stood closely with me, Sullivan, The E-Train, Mercado, and Freeman.

Marcoulier used the bathroom mirrors to draw up his 44 defense with a stunt and slant used if Whitman-Hanson went to the air. Downes, Whitten, Bouchard, Parsons, Higley, and Daley watched and listened closely as if the Messiah had stood before them. He slowly wrote the names of Frisoli, Wozniak, Burr, and Baldwin on the mirror. "Boys, the equation for a victory is to punish those four running backs, and we win this football game. It will be a feeling you get on your wedding day or when your child is born. Today will be my final game coaching," he paused, "I am going to retire." At this point his glasses started to fog and the hard-nosed coach completely broke down.

Some players could not believe what they were seeing. Downes embraced him with a hug, like a son gives a father. The rest of the defensive unit followed, doing the same. Marcoulier was the only male figure in Downe's life that truly understood and appreciated him. Wilbur had the wide receivers and defensive ends. Baldassarri referred to the Whitman-Hanson defense led by All-Scholastic and Division I-bound linemen Paul Clasby and Chris McEwan, as he touched on areas that the line needed to perfect.

Perrone walked over to every coach, hugging each one. Players clutched each other as a mother to a son before he leaves for war. A touch of unity and faith lived within all of us. Every player in that locker room understood what Ken Perrone and his coaches did for us. A coach's coach does not turn his back on his players.

At a certain time in a person's life, wholeness kicks in, a surge from the inner soul that completes you, almost like creating your own personal euphoria. Seniors Higley, Freeman, Whitten, Downes, Cronin, Jones, Dulong, Russell, Daley, Leopoldo, Mercado, Sullivan, and Sorrento all held hands and took a knee before Perrone. The underclassmen followed their lead. Slowly walking to the whiteboard, Perrone scribbled "Courage" on it.

Perrone stated, "We are one of the best teams in the state. I don't know if I will ever coach another game on the Salem sidelines."

To all of us the world stood still. In retrospect Coach Perrone, like those wrongly accused in Salem 300 years earlier, had a choice: conform to the mandates of the community leaders or lose everything. The accused accepted death instead of confessing to witchcraft and living. Perrone could have sat out the season and retained his job. Those of the 1600s or Coach Perrone would not back down despite the grave consequences. As young as we were, my teammates and I knew that a lifetime of work and dedication would be soon shelved.

My life ambition was to do something really special. Well, I was looking at the most courageous group of players and coaches I had ever been around. David had the courage to stand up to Goliath. Perrone continued, "So what, if they have the four horsemen and have won eleven consecutive conference titles?" Hope was in all our eyes. We had all carried our own crosses through peaks and valleys. "Look around this room, we all have clawed and fought to stay together. That is what molds you. Call this team our own melting pot. Dreams are what this country was built on. Team equals blocking, tackling, running, passing. All of that helps define execution. Big Willie Jones, where are you from? Manny, where are you from? The E-Train, where are you from? Football games are not won on previous wins and championships. You were destined to be football players. This is your time and if you want to steal a piece of time, it starts out on that field." Perrone had their undivided attention. With their equipment on, these young men transformed themselves into a different mental and physical state.

These boys turned into men.

Adrenaline, with a touch of mayhem, started to sweep through the room. The Witches were ready to fly. They were at the point of no return and would not back down.

"The #2 team in the state Peabody is playing after us. We let that game get away from us and are more than capable of beating anyone in the state. Go get that dream," said Perrone. Destiny was on the Witches' side.

I slowly walked into the bathroom. The anxiety had caused me to perspire more than usual before a game. I splashed my face with cold water. Drying my, face I looked at myself in the mirror. "You have trained your body, mind, and soul for this very moment." Bowing my head I began to pray, asking God to bless this team, myself, and bring out all of our ability.

Lifting my head and looking into the mirror, Pep Cornacchio appeared behind me. "You have done some remarkable things to get here. This program has stood strong for 102 years. Greatness is not given to you, it is created." Reaching into his pocket he pulled out the picture of the 1974 team. "I watched you run those stadium steps after that Beverly loss over a year ago and tear this picture out of the program. I took it off the wall Thanksgiving during halftime when the team exited the locker room. It was a clever tactic but it belongs to you. It is part of you. Go win this game for every kid who dreams of making it here. Go win it for every kid who will never get here," said Pep.

Mccellon stood next to Perry in the line getting ready to leave the locker room. Both shared the same memory of sleeping with the light on as kids. At that very moment, a synergy of fear still existed, "Man, I still have that feeling I had before the Swampscott game. I hope they don't turn off the switch and cancel this game,"

Perry said, "I feel you, but that is on the real."

"On dogs that crap could happen," said Mccellon, referring to his word on their bond and friendship.

Making their way onto the faded AstroTurf, the flash of the cameras blinded the kids. All local and major TV and newspaper reporters were covering the game. The Salem team positioned themselves on their sideline with their helmets under their arms.

The Star-Spangled Banner played peacefully throughout the stadium. This was a pure moment where Perrone looked up to the sky and reacquainted himself with his dad, mom, and the rest of his family who had passed on. He would visualize his dad standing alone in the corner of the stadium, smoking a cigarette. In his mind, he could see their faces up in the clouds. They were smiling at him from above. Oh, how proud they would have been of him.

The captains met at midfield for the coin toss. Higley rocked back and forth, staring into the eyes of QB Bill Frazier. He was trying to get in his head. All he was thinking about was them inflicting pain on him and knocking him out of the game. His team was on his mind and his brother was in his heart. Whitman-Hanson won the toss and elected to receive.

Higley glanced briefly at his brother at the side of the field. He exchanged thumbs up with him. Downes took a knee and was alone with his thoughts. I was warming up with Grimes. De Pena's mind was running as he tried to stay calm. The pre-game Wu-tang music did not give him his adrenaline fix. He was scared.

The E-Train buckled his chin strap, but his eyes were not glittering as his face is tense, and Mccellon was back pedaling behind the bench, "It's show time, baby!" he yelled out to one of the reporters. Walking by the bench he smiled at one of the cheerleaders. Looking to his left into the front row of the stands, his brown eyes locked in on his mother. Taken back, he walked closer. She looked good. It was the first game he ever saw her attend. His journey had come full circle. He read her lips, "I am so proud of you." He saw love in her eyes. Making a body gesture that his heart was in his hand, he blew her a kiss. It felt like an eternity, but a connection was finally there. All of this adversity with the football team brought the one person he had searched for to be in his life.

The E-Train got under the ball and kicked it high, and it bounced to the 8-yard line. It got scooped and returned to the 24-yard line.

Ron Plante had helped bring Perrone to Salem twenty-two years ago and would go through any means to keep him there. The former Salem QB of the early 1950s had started a petition in support of the football staff, and his goal was 3,000 signatures to present to Mayor Harrington after the Super Bowl. An established business man, he had one agenda. "Ken Perrone and his staff were placed in a 'no-win' situation because of the recent strike. The coaches have been criticized and penalized because they chose not to let our young athletes down. Perrone and his staff have dedicated themselves to Salem and its youth for twenty-two years. We feel that this is an opportunity to put aside the past by not permitting this controversy to continue. We also believe that enough has been said and done, that now is the time for forgiving and understanding, and not for retribution. The whole purpose of this is to make the mayor aware that there are a lot of Salem citizens who are concerned about what's going on, and we want it to come to a stop," stated Plante.

The petition read:

> We the undersigned are concerned citizens of Salem, parents of students, Salem High football players, cheerleaders, band members, and former students of the Salem High athletic family hereby petition the mayor, school committee, superintendent, principal and athletic director to retain Ken Perrone and his staff.

"This is simply a chance for the city to show Mayor Harrington that there are a lot of people who want this coaching staff to be recognized for what it has done for a long period of time, and that it deserves to be retained," Plante said. (*Salem News*, November 28, 1994)

Plante had twenty-four petitions in circulation at the Super Bowl. From a distance he spotted former Salem mayor and current Judge Sam Zoll, Superintendent Curtin and Recreation Superintendent Larry McIntire. With his game face on, Plante approached Curtin, asking him if he would sign the petition. Curtin did not waste any time informing Plante that he broke the law when he contacted the high school to get names of people in the band to solicit their support.

Plante's response was, "Why don't you arrest me?"

It was clear that Curtin could intimidate his subordinates, but Plante was a tax-paying citizen who had the right to stand up for what he thought was morally right.

Collisions had just started on the field, but tempers were about to explode in front of the stadium. At this point McIntire stepped in and told Plante to cool down. Plante knew he had signatures to get and that is what he went and did.

Salem lined up in a 44 defense with a stunt/slant called. Whitman-Hanson was in a pro-set strong right. Bancroft felt rule block would be more effective than zone blocking and would stick to his philosophy. A wide dive was called and the key blocked down Downes.

Perry always played with instincts, an attribute he developed on the streets of Lawrence. Flying downhill, he drilled their running back, knocking him back. "Not in our house, you soft cat. Welcome to the Northeastern Conference." Any words of intimidation would be part of the witches' brew. Image and attitude were all part of their defensive schemes.

On the fourth play Whitman-Hanson faced a 4th and 3 from their own 33-yard line, and running back Chris Frisoli took the wide dive for a first down. Bancroft was there many times before and knew in his preparation that there was no tomorrow and was ready to gamble. Panther fans chanted, "First down." The chains were moving and Downes punched the ground in celebration.

Downes was edgy. He wanted collisions. With fellow LB Whitten playing at 85 percent, he realized he needed to be all over the field. The tiger was out of the cage.

On the seventh play of the drive Frazier faked the misdirection, rolled left on 3rd and 8 and dumped it to the running back. He slipped through a collision with Perry and Downes for a first down.

The following play they went up top trying to expose Mccellon on a fade ball and he made a diving deflection. His mom cheered with excitement. On the eleventh play of the drive the Panthers faced another 4th down. Lined-up in a double tight where two tight ends were on the line, Bancroft knew this would keep the Salem defense more balanced. A wide dive right moved the chains and their fans again chanted, "First down." Whitten knew the D needed a stop, and that's what he did on the following play on the toss, but was called for a face-mask which moved the ball to Salem's 16-yard line.

Salem was set up in a 44 D. Marcoulier knew his unit had to play perfect. That is how he had shaped them. He had developed them to become an infantry. They bought into his militaristic coaching philosophies and were sculpted into iron witches.

W-H's offensive line was dominating Salem's defensive line. They were executing like a well-oiled machine. It was the fifteenth play of the drive, and Salem audibled out of a 44 to a 53 defense. The play action call could not have been run at a better time. Frazier was disciplined on the fake which froze safety Sullivan and threw a strike for a TD with 3:29 left in the first quarter. The Salem side of the stadium went mute. Licking my lips, I knew the Panthers had showed up to play. The extra point was no good.

The Witches would respond with a drive of their own. The E-Train on the counter picked up a great block from Freeman, churned up 16 yards, Mercado on the dive for 6, Freeman on the toss for 7. Well into Whitman-Hanson territory, Salem faced 4th and 4 and OT Jones got called for a penalty, making it 4th and 14. Salem called a timeout with 1:06 left in the quarter.

Out of the timeout, I scrambled left, multiple receivers drove the safety deep, and De Pena curled up for a reception to the Panthers 15-yard line. Salem fans were on their feet, only to be silenced by yellow flags indicating illegal man downfield. Jones was called for another penalty and just put his hands on his helmet as Salem was forced to punt.

With W-H in possession, Whitten got the audible and Higley shifted to his left. Frazier rolled right trying to toss the ball over a fully-stretched Leopoldo, deflecting it 15 feet in the air. Mccellon exploded off the turf like jumping on a trampoline and intercepted the ball, bringing it to the Panthers' 25-yard line. An exuberant Mccellon got mobbed by the Witches' defensive posse and turned pointing to his mom in the stands. She was touched but at the same time saddened by the amount of time that had passed since she had been part of his life. But the excitement became overwhelming for her. The light was shining on him, and she was determined to play more of a nurturing role in his life.

Whitman-Hanson lined up with nine defenders within 2 yards of the line of scrimmage. Rolling right, I saw Freeman on the corner route. It was six if I could connect. The Panther defensive end avoided the cut block by The E-Train and had a clear shot on me, and I rushed my throw. I overshot Freeman and the ball bounced on the turf. Clapping my hands, I was beyond frustrated. On 4th and 5, The E-Train took the toss picking up the first down. He had one defender to beat and it would have been six, but the ball got stripped with Whitman-Hanson recovering at their own 4-yard line. The E-Train slowly climbed to his feet. He could not believe it. The goal line was in sight. Walking off the field, his head was down as a nightmare was happening before his eyes.

Frazier fumbled the snap and recovered at the inch line. Salem fans called for a safety. It was a game of inches, a game of calls and the Panthers were winning in all areas. The defense was fired-up, playing physical, gang tackling, and making the Panthers fight for every inch. On a quick pass to the flat, Mccellon broke on the ball, leveling the receiver and giving him an earful.

Ryan Daley, who had no business playing defensive tackle, standing 5'6" 165 pounds, shot past All-Scholastic lineman Paul Clasby to tackle one of their four horsemen for a loss. The Panthers were doing something they never did on their second series of the game: punt.

Grimes had a shifty return to their 20-yard line. Mercado moved it to the fifteen. The beat of the drums was coming from the Salem stands. The E-Train dive went nowhere. Sullivan took the keeper to the 11-yard line. The E-Train wanted the ball. He visualized crossing that goal line. Perrone answered his demand calling a toss left. The E-Train saw the hole and juked left, but DE Pat Kelley dived, derailing The E-Train. Pounding the turf, he walked off the field in complete rage.

With 4:23 left in the half W-H faced 4th and 1 from its own 23-yard line. Signaling a timeout, Bancroft did not think twice about going for it. The confidence he had in his players enabled them to feed off these types of game situations, and after Frazier took the QB sneak for a first down, he smiled with pride. Higley was getting blown off the ball, but refused to back down. Getting the blitz signal, he got leverage on the lineman and put Frazier on his back. Salem fans were pleading for an intentional grounding call. The intensity radar in Downes' head flashed as Frazier scrambled toward the Salem sidelines on the next play. Downes unleashed a blow when he was still inbounds that sent their QB airborne, landing five yards out of bounds. It was a pure play on hustle.

But yellow flags shot up in the air like they were shot out of a cannon. A personal foul call moved the ball to the Salem's 17 with just over a minute in the half. Two plays later, the Panthers fumbled and Sullivan recovered it. My interception closed out the half. Salem was trailing by six with the second half remaining. Salem had played its worst half of football but was hanging in the game.

Perrone walked through the locker room at halftime shaking his head. "Eleven plays for 46 yards? Whitman-Hanson was dominating, running 32 plays for 76 yards rushing, 59 yards passing. They had eleven first downs compared to us running only eleven offensive plays," A frustrated Perrone remarked.

Higley strutted around, encouraging every player in that room, challenging them to dig deeper. "Find a way to win this game; it is there for the taking."

The room went into complete silence. The E-Train sat motionless on the bench; his confidence was shot. He knew he was the backbone of the offense and needed to pull it together.

Perrone did not scream, he did not point fingers. Looking every one of his players in the eyes he told them, "Some people say losing is not falling down. I say losing is not getting up. Success is only measured by failure. Penalties and turnovers are defeating us. We are in this football game," his voice began to rise. "Can we play better?"

"Yes, Coach."

"Can we beat this team?"

"Yes, Coach."

Higley screamed out, "Two by two, boys." Making his way up to the front of the line, he turned and addressed the team, "This is our destiny. This is our legacy." Kneeling down by the locker room exit, he had everyone hold hands, "One more time, fellows."

Taking a knee, we prayed together in unison. "God first, my teammates second, and myself third."

Salem received the ball to start the second half. The ball was placed at the 36-yard line. An illegal procedure call on Salem was its 7th penalty of the game. I was doing everything in my power to keep our heads up. That is what The E-Train did on a toss right, picking up 23-yards and moving the ball into the Panther territory. The excitement was there as fire lined the Salem sidelines. One play at a time would put the Witches back on their brooms. The emotion was like our season: powerful and quick.

Two plays later, The E-Train fighting for an extra yard, watched the ball pop from his arm. Like a kid seeing his ice cream cone fall on the pavement, his eyes shut, as he would only listen to the crowd to know the outcome. With the blow horns blaring from Whitman's side of the stands, it was evident more frustration would follow as the ball was turned over again. Confidence was blown and self-pity was taking over. The noise ripped through the stadium like thunder in a storm.

Salem, eagling its linebackers, put them inside the defensive ends to get more protection inside. These adjustments were made but the Panthers would make some of their own. It came on the seventh play of the drive with Whitman facing 4th and 12. Defensive end Leopoldo was taken out on an expected punt. The Panthers coaches had done some homework and Bancroft had complete confidence in his players. They exposed the gaps with a fake punt which got the first down and deflated the Witches.

Methodically, they sliced up Salem's defense and on the sixteenth play of the drive running back Ryan Burr blasted in the end zone for a TD. The point after was good and with 3:09 left in the third, the score was 13-0. Adversity was knocking and we needed to respond.

The Salem side of the stadium was silenced. Perrone stayed upbeat and energized, pumping the kids with confidence. "We have been here before," he spoke out.

Again Salem moved the ball down the field into Panther's territory. I hit The E-Train on a 15-yard out route picking up 28-yards, bringing the ball inside the red zone. My heart went into my stomach as I spotted yellow flags on the ground indicating the play was being brought back. Out of frustration, I roared like a lion. On the next play, lining up in a double wing, Whitman sniffed the play out and blitzed, recovering yet another fumble.

Salem was not ready to lie down. On 4th and 3 for the Panthers, Downes disguised the blitz and drove QB Frazier into the ground to end the third quarter.

Curtin sat smiling in the stands. Giving him the benefit of the doubt, it could have been from the sun glaring in his eyes. Alternatively, Ron Plante shared the same heart when it came to kids and sports. Throughout the game he was seen with his petition in hand, gathering signatures to support Perrone. Late in the fourth quarter, as I completed my third straight pass, Plante's attention shifted to the game. Sweat was pouring off his face and he took out a handkerchief to absorb it. With 4:17 left, he still believed this team had one more miracle, as did I. My mother sat in the stands with her head down and eyes shut. Further down in the stands, Mccellon's mother sat holding her rosary beads, praying. Her son's performance would be bittersweet if they lost. Back in Salem, at Red's Sandwich Shop, The E-Train's mother sat in the back room listening to the game on the radio. Downes could not look at the scoreboard. I called the play Perrone sent in, Jet Left Sprint Pass.

On fourth down, I walked slowly to the line of scrimmage. Seeing De Pena was in single coverage, I gave him a signal. I took the snap and rolled out. Eyeing De Pena, I threw a fade ball to the end zone. The ball hung up in the air, a moment frozen in eternity. De Pena's eyes opened wide, spotting the ball as if his eyes were a telescope, getting in position to out-jump their DB.

Back at the hospital, Owa was in her final moments. Her heart was beating slowly as the sound of the football game over the radio filled the room. The football I left her was next to the radio on the nightstand with her rosary beads draped around it.

At the last split second, the safety knocked the ball down to the turf as I got hit. Lying on my back, there were no shooting stars in the sky. The cheers from the opposing sidelines would not go away, and got louder and louder. Closing my eyes in disbelief, this dream had turned into a nightmare. I envisioned the walls around the field closing in on me. A constant feeling of magic was slowly leaving my body. This was my childhood dream, and I did not want to stop living it. All became clear to me. We were destined for this tragedy just like the accused witches and the crew of the *Pequot*. Curtin's hate of Perrone was no less that Ahab's hat of *Moby Dick*. Curtin's proclamation that Perrone was akin to cult leader was no less than Ahab's breaking of the compass or the acquisition of witchcraft by teenage girls. The evil behind this act poisoned our life experience.

Perrone could only watch as the final seconds ticked off the clock. Heartbreak was felt by his players as the coaches watched in disbelief. Downe's frustration led him to bulldoze their running back as they took a knee. A personal foul was called on his actions. The defense held hands as the final whistle blew. Some fell to their knees, others hugged each other, eye black smeared on faces, blood-stained pants, and un-tucked jerseys. Helmets stayed on to shield their faces. Whitman-Hanson players taunted Salem while a pig pile celebration began.

A fountain of tears streamed down my face, The E-Train's face was stone cold, Downes took a knee at midfield, his cast on his left wrist looked like a boxing glove. In denial, he slowly took off his elbow pads. With his grades, he came to the realization that this was it. The game he thought was his golden ticket could not bring him to the level he desired to get to. Thinking of his mom, with the warmth of the sun on his skin, he looked up to the sky. De Pena was numb. Staring at the scoreboard, he couldn't believe the outcome. This story was not supposed to end this way.

Looking into the stands, he needed clearness. "The poor coaches, they really loved us."

The thought of the champion's parade in the city trolleys, the championship rings were decoded from his thought process like they were never there. All he could do was look back. It would never be the same.

My dad's index finger gently pressed the stop button on his video recorder. The Witches' broom ride was over. At the same moment, his pager went off. Sadness filled his heart and left him empty as he glanced down and saw the hospital's number flash on the tiny screen. Fighting his way through the rowdy crowd, he found a pay phone and made the call he knew he never wanted to make. It was exactly what he feared. His mom had taken a turn for the worse. This was something he knew he had to face, but at the same time, there was part of him that still believed a miracle would happen. He quickly made his way up to the stands to share the sad news with my mom. They quickly decided to make their way down to the boys and quickly leave. Finding only my brother Michael, they left him responsible to bring my brother and I to the hospital.

Perrone, with his captains, slowly made his way to accept the runner-up trophy. Uncertainty and disappointment was felt with every step. For the final time, the team took a knee before Perrone, holding hands in prayer. "Lord you blessed us in so many ways. We learned life lessons and share memories that will last a lifetime. Though the outcome was not what we wanted, you are champions in my eyes."

Some wept, others sat silenced, but they were all together. Higley stared at the ground, feeling empty. He wanted this for his brother who sat at the edge of the turf. Making his way toward his brother, they embraced. No words were shared as their bond grew stronger. Mark took his chain off with his #61 charm dangling and put it around his brother's neck. Wheeling away, the elder brother paused and turning, he softly said, "You are a life champion, my brother."

With the tears filling up his helmet, the boy transformed into a man that very day.

The E-Train sat on the turf with his chin-strap still buckled. It was a real-life horror show for him. Two fumbles. Reporters rallied around him. He had run for 116 yards on 14 carries. He wanted to take the blame on himself, feeling like he was horrible. He said he would never lose it for his team in the Super Bowl, but felt he jinxed himself. Teary-eyed, carrying the defeat on his shoulders, he should have realized he had every right to stand tall on the breakout season that had transpired for him.

Canelo sat in the back and watched his teammate's reactions. Life would go on, but it might not ever be the same. Two years left felt like forever to him.

Perrone, Marcoulier, Wilbur, Baldassarri, Elsaesser, McKenna, and

into Swampscott and beat the Big Blue on their home turf which was no easy task. Even if it was for only three hours, it made seventy kids and an entire community feel good about themselves. You tell me what is wrong with that. That is what Ken Perrone provided for them, and if making someone feel good for a short period of time during a very stressful week, makes him lose his job; shame on the Salem Administration."

I asked how the kids were using this as an opportunity to get out of the system and get a chance to go to college. How important was this to the administration? Lynch responded, "It was not an item to check on a to-do list. Prohibit Ken Perrone. They lost sight; you can make up school but you can't make up a big championship game."

How can a grudge against Perrone last nineteen years? How can Perrone not be in the Salem High School Hall of Fame? Ken Perrone had been voted into the Massachusetts Football Coaches Hall of Fame in 1992, in 2009 the Maine All Sports Hall of Fame, Southern Connecticut Diamond Hall of Fame 2010, John Bapst High School Hall of Fame in Maine 2011, 2011 New Haven Legends Hall of Fame in Connecticut, and a handful of other halls, but not Salem's. Perrone had tied legendary coach Bill Broderick with 151 wins. "The issue is larger than Perrone," Furey said. "The Hall of Fame should be a more public, transparent body, and not the fiefdom of a few."

The Salem High School Hall of Fame, founded in 1990, has five members on the selection board, including former Superintendent Ed Curtin. It takes only one "no" vote to reject a candidate. What qualified Curtin to be on the Hall of Fame committee? He was a former Salem High athlete without distinction. Did he play college ball? Was he an all-star? He never coached at the varsity level in Salem.

Former Salem High Football coach Dave Wilbur stated, "The fact that Perrone is not in the Hall of Fame is a shame to the entire Hall of Fame process. How can you not put the man who has the most career wins in a football town and won championships doing it the right way not in the Hall of Fame? The Hall of Fame is not supposed to be about who you like or do not like. It is supposed to be about achievement and what you did on the athletic field as a coach or player. Looking at the people who are in there and their accomplishments, Ken has equaled or exceeded most people. It is pretty obvious the reason he is not in is because it is personal, and to me it discredits the entire Hall of Fame in Salem."

Neil Harrington thinks time heals all wounds. "I would have no objection to the committee voting Perrone into the Hall of Fame. There is no question he had a tremendous career at Salem High. I think that was then, this is now. I always felt that it was unfortunate that Ken got caught up in the middle. If I was caught up in his situation, I don't know what I would have done, frankly. He was a member of the union, but he was also right in the middle of a historic run for the team. Being a sports crazy as I am, I wished them every success. That is the reason I went to games to cheer the team on and root for my hometown. He did a great job under a very difficult situation in terms of football and preparing the kids. I am sure people were pressuring him one way or another. Everybody has to look in the mirror and decide what the best thing to do is. I have no doubt that Perrone made that decision. Harrington, when asked about this story being written, made the comment, 'It is just not an interesting story. Maybe when you are raised in an upper social class, you really never get to understand how others struggle and fight for survival.'"

Former Superintendent William Cameron drafted a memo on the subject for the school board. "The selection board has no written bylaws and operates by 'informal' rules," Cameron said.

AFTERWORD

On January 3, 1995, the temperature was a frigid 19 degrees. Ken Perrone received the call the day before from the principal's secretary, indicating he had a meeting with acting Principal Gerald Silverman and athletic director Bob Geswell. Perrone slowly approached the office. He hesitated before he went in, thinking about the past few months, all the time knowing what he had given up for his team. The meeting was inevitable, and the time had come to face the consequences. Sitting down in a chair facing Silverman and Geswell was his own death chamber. He blocked out their faces and in his mind. He was back on the sidelines.

As the words came out of Silverman's mouth, it was like fingernails scratching across a chalkboard. "It is a cold day in January," fired out Silverman. Those were the same words Perrone had used in his interview after the Super Bowl when questioned about his future. Perrone said, "They will probably fire me on a cold day in January." Handing Perrone a memo with a gratifying stare, the words slowly began to sink in.

Perrone went on to read: "After a review of everything that has taken place since October 31, 1994, we recommend that the position of head football coach be opened for the 1995 season." Perrone rose to his feet with pride yelling, "You won the battle but not the war."

when Elvin Rodriguez quit the team. Making the most out of his opportunity, he became a defensive starter. He was honored to be voted team captain. Once he recovered from his gunshot wound, which happened the summer going into his senior season when his posse got into a beef down The Point, he healed up and was ready to play. "My cousin got shot in the stomach and almost died." He played out the season after the shooting.

During the games he tried not to look up into the stands. He did not want the feeling of fulfillment to fade. "It affected me that my parents never saw me play. I would always see my friends' dads at the games and their parents videotaping. This really hurt."

"Mazz was for us minorities who were student-athletes. He went as far as helping me write my captain's speech. Most teachers I had just tried to get me by. Mazz tried to have a relationship, giving me hope and confidence. I felt like I was looked upon as dirt by coming from The Point. Mazz kept me motivated."

After graduating Canelo went back to the Dominican Republic to be with his dad, who was dying. The following year after his dad passed, away he was accepted to Bridgton Academy. He was on the football team and maintained a 3.4 GPA. "I felt like I was educated more in one year of prep school than the twelve years I spent in the Salem school system." He made his family proud to be the first one to go to college as he enrolled at Lackawanna in Scranton, Pennsylvania.

After a productive first year, he sustained a 3.0 GPA. In his second year of college after football practice, a fight broke out in the dorm. It was between white and black girls. Marijuana was stolen and all eyes pointed to Canelo. Canelo was called into meet with his coach and the dean of students. They pressured him not to go to court, leave quietly, and they would help him relocate to another college. "Those were all broken promises and the end of my college career. It was disappointing because I had Division I programs reaching out to me."

Times turned tough and he was forced to go back to where he came from. His brother, Alex, got deported. Returning to Salem in 2002, he hit the streets running. Pushing drugs, he became known as the "doctor" on the streets. That lifestyle got the best of him and he was arrested, completing a four year prison sentence on March 1, 2011.

Phil Downes was used to running from things. That is what he did when he saw his mom dead on the sofa. Instead of going back on the streets, he channeled heartache into faith and passion to play the game of football, a game that helped him develop his inner self. His mom passing felt like yesterday to him. "To this day, it haunts me very much." His relationship with his dad did not exist. Downes sometimes thought about what his life would have been like if he had two functional parents. "There are many things that you don't realize that gets factored in with having a mom when you get older. I never had a parent to turn to for advice. It was always like an uncle or friend's father. It would have been good to be able to go to my mom or dad and say this is what is going on in my life, give me some of your life experience with it," said Downes.

During the end of the 1994 season, he started to sense that when college coaches were not speaking to him it was because of his grades. Reality sunk in. Nobody pulled him aside and tried to tailor up a contingency plan. Downes did not know how to move forward, and always felt the college thing was going to come to him.

"We ran that school to a certain degree; if something went down we got a pass," said Downes. He thought that this was how life is going to be: You play sports and the colleges will come.

Reality came hard on Downes after graduation. He exhausted every opportunity to get into prep school, Bridgton Academy, and Maine Central Institute, but nothing panned out. He ended up living with his aunt back in Salem for a year and worked for the city.

His life turned for the best in June 1996 when his daughter Devyn was born. When she was born, his mother-in-law came in the room and held her right away. "That sent me into tears, that my mom is never going to be able to touch my children," said Phil. At that point, his family became his first priority.

Enlisting in the Air Force in 1997 was part of his plan to make a career move. But seven months later he received a medical discharge. Downes always believed in capitalism, which provided him the spirit to start his own business, refinishing hardwood floors and installation. His days were long and parts of his body ached. Today if he tries something new and does not succeed, at least he knows he gave it a shot. Downes will occasionally look in his life's rearview mirror and cannot escape that one regret that stays with him: his athletic career. "I know I could have made it to the next level. A big disappointment for me is not putting in the time and effort like my former teammate, Sean Stellato. I told my son that Sean was probably one of the hardest-working kids that ever came out of Salem. He did not have the most talent, but he outworked the kids who had more ability. Sometimes that is better than having talent. When I was laughing at him working out with the strength shoes, hitting the gym, I was hanging out with chicks, going to the mall, and being counterproductive," said Downes.

Recently an old wooden trunk sat on his living room floor with stories waiting to be told. His children waited patiently as he slowly opened it, revealing his high school football career. His son quickly grabbed his helmet, while his daughter laid out his jersey on the chair, asking about the mom patch. It was like walking down memory lane. "Essentially, when you look back at your life, you want to have shining moments. The 1994 season was a special time for a lot of people. For the ones who did not move on athletically, I think they can look back at that season and absorb a great deal from it. We battled and did something many people did not think we were going to be able to do with all the turmoil."

Downes came from the realization with his upbringing, that family was not valued. "That season we were, in essence, family. Many of us, outside of football, didn't really hang out, but when we were on the field, we were one unit. That is something to be said. No cliques; we played football together and we enjoyed each other when we stepped on the field. Ken Perrone was punished for following his convictions which is a crime in itself."

Downes looked at his family as a blessing and the best thing that has ever happened to him. "That anchored me down." Reflecting on his experiences, he shared, "Outwork the next guy because whether it is school, sports, or business, it will always eventually get you closer to your goals."

Mark Higley received a substantial financial aid package to play lacrosse at Endicott College. He carried his drive and determination to the collegiate level, starting his first three games and scoring eighteen goals. Unfortunately, that was short-lived. Poor study habits and skipping through school at Salem High contributed to his struggle in college. "What was taking kids an hour for homework was taking me four." After failing out of school, he immediately enlisted in the military.

In the Army, he learned how to put acronyms together, which really helped him to be able to focus. After serving two active years in Fort Hill, Oklahoma, he headed back to Salem. Football was constantly on his mind. "Took me a couple of years to really understand why I did not get recruited for football. At first I thought I was getting slighted by our coaches, but then realized the time when college coaches would be coming through to meet with coach, the strike was going on and then he was going through lawsuits when his job was opened up. To give him the benefit of a doubt, his focus was on saving his livelihood," said Higley. He went on to say that, "One of the things I took away from the coaching staff was that academics were not where they should have been, and I should have been pushed harder. Setting standards is an important thing. My kids I coach today, they cannot get anything less than a C-. If they go below that, I make sure they go back for extra help; they need to bring a note back and attend study hall. If Coach Perrone told me to go smash into that guy as fast as I could, I would do that. If

Coach Perrone told me take the dummy pads off school grounds and meet him at Castle Hill Park, I did that. If he told me to get B's and C's, I would have got B's and C's," said Higley.

He got back into the game by coaching freshman football at Salem High in 1996. Coaching was in his blood and he enjoyed being part of it through the 2000 season. In 2004, he went for the Salem head football coaching position and was denied, but was hired as the head lacrosse coach.

"Coach Perrone deserves to be in the Hall of Fame. I have a lot of respect for him. The guy has taught me life lessons that I have taken on. Never quit, be prepared for every endeavor. You see him organized and preparing us for football games, but that is the same approach I take when I go to work in the morning. The night before, I am preparing for the next day. If I am going into a meeting and I have to inform people about their network, I need to be equipped for it. That is the X's and O's for football, taking it to everyday life. He was a very organized, prepared person who was very passionate about what he did," said Higley. "He had the dream team with assistant coaches."

"I think about that season all the time. More than putting the helmet and pads on, I miss the camaraderie with the guys, staying focused, and being professional on the field. A lot of times that season, we were up against the ropes and could have packed it in. We never gave up and believed there is always an option to be successful. God will never give you anything you cannot handle."

Today Higley is a network engineer who builds computer networks. His relationship with his brother is very close. They often go fishing and his parents continue to care for his brother. Higley continues to support the Witches as Salem's greatest fan; he has not missed a game since the first one he attended in 1983. As autumn arrives and the beat of the band drums perform at Bertram Field, a boyish feeling of excitement brings Higley back to 1983 when he would cut through the fence and watch in awe those mighty Witches.

The E-Train set the school record with 1,260 yards but his record was bittersweet. Coach Perrone's firing affected The E-Train and made him decide, late in the summer going into his senior season after his sons first birthday, that he was going to play. Four games into the season, Elvin quit the football team, frustrated and discouraged after hurting his left hamstring against Saugus.

"I don't feel like playing anymore. There are too many problems. It'll never be the same," Rodriguez said. Rodriguez informed an assistant coach as opposed to telling the new coach, Warren Armes, who just ignored him. "I'm also disappointed that as soon as I would leave practice, the coaches would talk junk to the other players about me. If they have something to say, they should say it to my face."

The team led six opponents through three quarters, but got outscored 76-28 in the fourth quarter during the 1995 season. Expectations were high for the 1995 team, since a solid nucleus had returned from the previous year. "The coach, Armes, says we have no talent but that's bull. I think we had enough talent to win," stated Rodriguez.

The E-Train always believed he was going to be a college athlete. Sitting high in the stands, he isolated himself. Walking to the bathroom, he paused as the crowd cheered. It suddenly hit him the feeling of regret and emptiness. "Armes took the love out of the game for me." After leaving the team, he never played a down of football again.

Manuel De Pena, at the end of the 1995 summer decided to return to the football field to play his senior season for the Witches. He was convinced the former coaches got a raw deal, but the kids would be the ones heavily affected. "The new coaches did not understand nor have empathy for what we went through. They treated us like crap. I wanted to quit and was going to when my cousin, Elvin Rodriquez, did." De Pena had a solid senior year, making acrobatic catches and keeping the team in games. "My old coaches helped the best they could, but when they're not your coaches, what can they really do for you? I never even took the SATs."

After two years attending an audio research school in New York City he moved back and lasted one semester at Salem State College. Manuel always tried to keep himself busy so he would not think about it. "I think about my past and I should not have been so quiet. I should have reached out but we were young, vulnerable kids. I had no direction." To this day he still has dreams of going to play for the Florida Gators. He does not try to get involved with football because it hurts so badly. "To be in this moment, living out of my truck and still thinking about the 1994 season and what could have been is very depressing."

Manuel is currently separated from his wife and lives in his truck. Occasionally he will stay with his sister or mom. Everything he owns is in his truck. He has battled alcoholism and depression. "Going to Coach Perrone's and your Hall of Fame Induction was the first time I saw teammates in two decades. It gave me closure. I almost did not show up. But walking in there made me realize that I was part of something special."

Today Manuel works as a kid's counselor. He is quick to give the kids advice. "I think about my life and the people that were there for me. When I speak to them I emphasize to take your time when you make a decision. Put your body and soul into it." He is the proud father of a nine-year-old daughter and six-year-old son.

Jamon Mccellon lay on his grandparent's sofa Christmas night 1994, watching a college football bowl game. He had aspirations of playing at that level someday, three weeks removed from having a career game in the Super Bowl. That instant was a heartbeat. What was supposed to be a breakout senior season transformed into a dreadful failure. "With Coach Perrone gone, football just was not the same anymore," said Mccellon. Instead of being one of the senior leaders on the team, the new coaches viewed Mccellon as an expendable player. "Once the team lost a couple of games, their focus shifted to building for the future and they had no knowledge of me and what I had been going through the past few years and how much football meant to me. It took my mind off of things that were going on at home, things like my mom being missing for weeks at a time and her heavy drug use," said Mccellon. "Football played such a pivotal role in our lives. Many kids did not have many things going on. The administrators turned their backs on us. They were supposed to be educators and doing what was best for their students. Putting us in a situation where we were going to thrive should have been their mission, not for us to crash and burn.

With Perrone gone, Jamon lacked that father figure. That did not come from his biological father whom he never met. He quit football and dropped out of school before the season was over. "It was one of the worst decisions I have ever made. I never really understood how much football meant to me until it was gone," said Jamon.

Shortly after quitting school, he earned his GED and entered the Ecco E-team machinist training program. In 1997, he had his first child, Adelyn. He lived with her until she was seven, but things did not work out with her mother.

Jamon now lives in Tennessee with his wife, Nafeesah, their daughter, Samiyah, and baby son, Raheem. He currently works at Rubbermaid Sharpie and goes to school full-time, studying to be an auto mechanic. His plans are to open his own shop. "Right now things are pretty rough economically, but I believe everything will pay off in the end. During tough times I always reflect on my junior year at Salem High and everything we went through. I will never forget that year, our team, and coaches. Don't give up! Those words I keep close at heart and sum up our journey during that season. My senior season we had one of the best QBs, running backs, and wide receivers in the state, returning with a solid nucleus. I will always wonder what would have happened if Coach Perrone was running the show? So many talented kids' careers were cut way too short," said Jamon.

Today, his relationship with his mom is good, and she does not use drugs. He met his dad for the first time in 2011. "My grandmother is the love of my life," said Mccellon.

The lesson he learned from all this is: "Put your all into every experience and treat every moment like it is your last because you never know how life is going to turn out."

As for myself, I rewrote the record books at Salem for most yards passing and running in a season, most TD passes thrown in a season and career, most completions thrown in a game, and most field goals kicked in a season and career. This was accomplished in less than two full seasons. The 1995 season left a void in my life going 2-6-2 with a win being forfeited because of an ineligible player. This was hard to believe after being the pre-season favorite. The team was winless at home for the first time since 1964. I was in a tough situation. I was a true go-getter who marketed myself to get a full financial package and to do a post-graduate year at The Gunnery School. That year created opportunities that put me in a situation to blossom. The new high school coaches did not help me with colleges at all.

Perrone did make calls and wrote letters. I feel he could have done more, but he moved on. But the new coach showed no loyalty to the seniors. He looked at us as Coach Ken's boys. West Point showed interest, and I took a visit and felt a real connection to the militaristic atmosphere. But I could not make the grade.

I hit the books and kept my dreams at heart of being a dual Division I athlete. The University of Richmond offered me a scholarship, but Marist College came back with a more appealing financial package, and the opportunity to play basketball sealed the deal. I was treated well and was the first collegiate athlete in his family. As a Division I athlete, I had a very demanding schedule. Mentally the schemes were very challenging for me and I was competing against twelve other QBs. I continued to fight and showed glimpses of a bright future.

I made a smooth transition from QB to WR my sophomore season.

It did squash my dream of being the next Doug Flutie, but the glory lived in my heart as I wore #22. Starting for two seasons, I went on to lead the Red Foxes in receiving. The long eight- to ten-hour road trips and taking exams on airplanes and in hotel rooms opened my eyes and made me appreciate the journey even more. But it became even more gratifying that my loved ones did not miss a beat. My dad continued to travel all over the country, videotaping me. Marist College challenged me and transformed my intellectual skills.

I graduated cum laude in January 2002. I always had ambitions to become a professional athlete. It became a reality in February 2002 when I signed a contract to play Arena Football for the Florida Firecats. After a three year stint, I hung up the pads. One of the hardest decisions I ever had to make. The majority of people do not realize that pro sports is strictly business. Not a week goes by and I don't think of the 1994 season. Even after playing at every level, the high of the 1994 season could not be reached again. I still continue to live my life like I am back on the gridiron.

I enjoy inspiring younger athletes to work hard and dream big. I cherish my three daughters and beautiful wife. I maintain a very close relationship with both parents and my two older brothers and Coach Perrone. My faith is my backbone.

Football will forever be in my blood and in August 2005, I officially became licensed through the NFL to become a sports agent. I currently represent a number of NFL players.

On a cool November day, I made my way into the cemetery. Trees outlined the road, leaves sat on the grass, flowers had turned into weeds, but my Owa's memory shined bright from within and would forever live in my heart. A tear fell to the ground, but a sense of relief came to mind that I was able to have a special bond with her. Every level I made it to, I always remembered to leave her a ticket at will-call. It was my way of having a moment with her before I entered a place where all my dreams came true.

I took something from that season and that was a greater sense of self-worth and completion. I now have a deeper appreciation for my coaches and faith. With the sun breaking through the clouds and as the cars passed by on the road outside the cemetery, I realized life goes on. Sometimes conflict opens your eyes to different experiences that mold you, giving lessons that create wisdom.

On June 27, 2013, Coach Ken Perrone and I were inducted into the Salem High Hall of Fame. Perrone did not receive a unanimous vote as board member Ed Curtin did not vote for him. Curtin did not attend the induction.

Several of my former teammates were not mentioned throughout this story but had such an instrumental role in the success of the team. Must give a shout out to the scout team enthusiasts. I will never forget your efforts: Mike Mateo, David Costantino, Justin Kingston, Lee Phommachanh, Eddy Aoude, Tieu Ing, Alex Canelo, Dwyonne Thomas, Kuis Alix, Quinn Hernandez, Ray Jodoin, Chris Feener, Sean Coughlin, Dave Taylor, Nick Semons, Phil Tinkham, Billy Corbett, Dave Hart, Matt Wilkinson, Brian Goolsby, Ben Jones, Jason DeVeau, Dan Krajeski, Luiz Quaresma, Keith Santos, Steve Sorrento, Chris Bresnahan, Zack Billings, Daniel Sheehan, Juan Espinal, Matt Daniels, Tony Dominquez, Mark Viojan, Peter Cicco, Steve Lariviere, Peter Mercier, Frank DeRosa, and Fred Feliz.

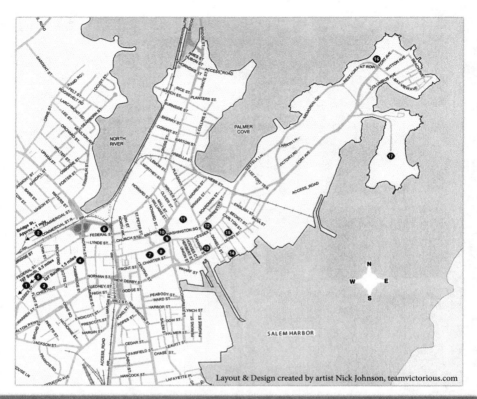

Layout & Design created by artist Nick Johnson, teamvictorious.com

SALEM, MASSACHUSETTS

1

Bertram Field - Home of the Mighty Witches football team
Powderhouse Lane

2

Gallows Hill - Where witches were executed, 1692

3

Phillip's House - Home of a wealthy merchant family
34 Chestnut Street

4

Witch House - One of the oldest dwellings in the U.S., home of a witch trial judge
310 Essex Street

5

Castle Hill Park - Here, Coach Perrone was served his cease and desist letter
Story Road

6  **Essex Superior Court House** - Where Wayne Turner was ordered to bring his toothbrush
34 Federal Street

7  **East India Square Fountain** - Symbolizes the connection between Salem to the Ocean and Far East
Essex Street

8  **Peabody Essex Museum** - World-renowned museum in Salem
161 Essex Street

9  **Hawthorne Hotel** - Historic hotel of Salem, ideal for history lovers
18 Washington Square West

10 **Roger Conant Statue** - Founder of Salem
9 1/2 Washington Square North

11 **Salem Common** - Site of first game, Salem vs Beverly, 1890
Washington Square

12 **Ziggy's Donuts** - Salem's oldest bakery
2 Essex Street

13  **Custom House** - Nathaniel Hawthorne worked as a clerk, sits across from Salem Harbor
176 Derby Street

14  **House of Seven Gables** - America's oldest wooden house
115 Derby Street

15  **Ye Old Candy Shop** - America's oldest candy shop
122 Derby Street, Salem MA 01970

16  **Salem Willows** - Arcade and amusement park, home of the chop suey sandwich
167 Fort Avenue

17  **Winter Island Lighthouse** - 45-acre tract used for search and recovery during WWII
50 Winter Island Road